WORKING DAYS

Robert DeMott is a member of the *Steinbeck Quarterly*'s advisory board, a former director of San Jose State University's Steinbeck Research Center, and a recipient of a Burkhardt Prize for his contributions to Steinbeck scholarship. He has published several books, notably *Steinbeck's Reading*, as well as many shorter pieces in a wide variety of periodicals including *Journal of Modern Literature*, *Modern Fiction Studies*, *American Studies*, *Studies in American Fiction*, *Ohio Review*, and *Windsor Review*. He teaches American Literature at Ohio University, where he has received both graduate and undergraduate teaching awards. He lives in Athens, Ohio.

John Steinbeck

WORKING DAYS

The Journals of
The Grapes of Wrath
1938–1941

Edited by Robert DeMott
Ohio University

PENGUIN BOOKS

Dedicated to Dave Smith: incomparable friend and worker at the impossible

PENGUIN BOOKS
Published by the Penguin Group
Viking Penguin, a division of Penguin Books USA Inc.,
375 Hudson Street, New York, New York 10014, U.S.A.
Penguin Books Ltd, 27 Wrights Lane, London W8 5TZ, England
Penguin Books Australia Ltd, Ringwood, Victoria, Australia
Penguin Books Canada Ltd, 2801 John Street,
Markham, Ontario, Canada L3R 1B4
Penguin Books (N.Z.) Ltd, 182–190 Wairau Road,
Auckland 10, New Zealand

Penguin Books Ltd, Registered Offices:
Harmondsworth, Middlesex, England

First published in the United States of America by
Viking Penguin Inc. 1989
Published in Penguin Books 1990

10 9 8 7 6 5 4

Grateful acknowledgment is made for permission to reprint an excerpt from "Hotel California" by Don Henley, Glenn Frey, and Don Felder. © 1976, 1977 Cass County Music, Red Cloud Music & Fingers Music. All rights reserved. Used by permission.

LIBRARY OF CONGRESS CATALOGING IN PUBLICATION DATA
Steinbeck, John, 1902–1968.
Working days: the journals of The grapes of wrath, 1938–1941/
John Steinbeck; edited by Robert DeMott.
p.   cm.
ISBN 0 14 01.4457 9
1. Steinbeck, John, 1902–1968. Grapes of wrath. 2. Steinbeck,
John, 1902–1968—Diaries. 3. Novelists, American—20th century—
Diaries. I. DeMott, Robert J., 1943–   . II. Title.
PS3537.T3234G858   1990
813'.52—dc20   90–37785

Printed in the United States of America
Set in Bodoni Book
Designed by Francesca Belanger and Michael Kaye
Watercolor portrait of John Steinbeck by Eugene Gregan

CONTENTS

PREFACE

". . . home has ceased to exist except in the mothballs of memory."

—Steinbeck, in *Travels with Charley* (1962)

Judging from both the quality and quantity of his writing from 1936 to 1940, John Steinbeck's residency in the San Jose, California, suburb of Los Gatos ranks as the most professionally satisfying of his entire life. He published a string of best-sellers, including *Of Mice and Men, The Long Valley, Their Blood Is Strong,* and *The Grapes of Wrath;* he witnessed a long-running New York theater production of *Of Mice and Men* and the brilliant Hollywood film versions of that novel and *The Grapes of Wrath;* he conducted the necessary travel and research for the nonfictional prose work *Sea of Cortez;* and he scripted and helped produce a documentary film, *The Forgotten Village.* Honors, awards, and fame were his for the asking, though lasting personal happiness and a thoroughgoing sense of belonging seemed to elude him during his tenure in Los Gatos.

In spite of his unprecedented artistic success, Steinbeck managed to stay resolutely an outsider in Los Gatos, as unassimilated in his day as he is in ours. Unlike Salinas, his birth place, or the Monterey Peninsula, his spiritual home, Steinbeck never established deep roots in Los Gatos, never imbibed its geographical sense of place. Instead he remained a sojourner, always careful to choose home sites that were increasingly isolated from the town's center, as though the omniscient tenor of his writing in the late 1930s might be compromised if he approached too closely to the mainstream of suburban society. Although he wrote repeatedly about Salinas and Monterey during his career as a novelist and essayist, he was unusually silent on the subject of Los Gatos. Of course, there are comments about his Los Gatos homes scattered among his private correspondence and recorded frequently in this journal (these houses were the first residential properties that the Steinbecks could afford to buy, and he was uneasy—often embarrassed—about the implications of ownership), but among the books published in his lifetime there are only a couple of entertaining references to Los Gatos in the autobiographical *Travels with Charley*. Though the notorious effects of success eventually got the better of him, the most significant part of his life during the Los Gatos era was directed inward toward personal and psychological vistas. Steinbeck, it seems, could well have written his greatest novels anywhere at all, so concentrated was his gaze toward the private horizons of his fictional landscape, so intent was he on exposing the enormous cultural contradictions inherent in his fabled native state.

Steinbeck's effacement has been so well maintained that at least one local history of Los Gatos makes no mention of his ever having lived there. Except for occasional items in the Los Gatos and San Jose newspapers (happily, these are more frequent now; until the mid 1980s there had been nothing substantial on Steinbeck in a decade), and reminiscences by long-time residents, Steinbeck's relationship with Los Gatos remains uneasy, somehow "vague and insubstantial," as one old-timer told me. Despite the ample information contained in recent biographical works on Steinbeck, local lore is still limited to a few facts—he lived in two different houses in Los Gatos; he wrote *The Grapes of Wrath* in one of them (erroneously thought to be the Brush Road house at the Summit); he dressed so shabbily he looked like a laborer; he was sometimes seen on Main Street in the company of Charlie Chaplin, Wallace Ford, and Spencer Tracy (usually, and again erroneously, all at the same time); he and his wife, Carol, were both considered to be radical bohemians; and they kept a well-stocked wine cellar for their wild parties. Some vestiges of his outward existence, then, appear to be all that remain in the current atmosphere of Los Gatos; such hearsay supplies little indication of the depth, complexity, and intensity of Steinbeck's inner life during his years of residency there. But perhaps that is not so bad, considering the shameless commercial uses to which Steinbeck's celebrity has been put by some factions of the Salinas and Monterey communities. "Preferably a writer should die at about 28," Steinbeck quipped to British journalist Herbert Kretzmer in 1965. "Then he has a chance of being discovered. If he lives much longer he can only be revalued. I prefer discovery."

Among other reasons, discovering the hidden Steinbeck took me to Los Gatos in early 1984. For nearly two full years, I lived more or less inconspicuously in a transients' apartment complex edging the foothills of the lush Santa Cruz Mountains. The minute I wheeled my Chevy truck, dusty and battered from its journey west over Route 66, onto the main street of that town, I realized the setting was surely one of the most estimable in America, and I sensed the Steinbecks' attraction to the surrounding area (Carol had been born and raised in the Naglee Park section of San Jose). The locale is stunning, the landscape sublime and bounteous, the climate benign and temperate, though as with most things about California, full appreciation of its benefits seemed impossible for a newcomer. Like so many of Steinbeck's characters, falling into Eden, I discovered, was much simpler than getting out, even when I reminded myself that deferred gratifications might prove better than none at all.

Being an outsider does have compensations, however, for it confers a kind of invisibility and promotes observation rather than participation, understanding rather than acquisition. While the residents of that extravagantly expensive and privileged town (it is a cross between Aspen and New Canaan) seemed to go about their usual economic business, I had the advantage of other rewards. My homely dwelling lay roughly equidistant between the two houses John and Carol Steinbeck inhabited during those years, half a century earlier, when they decided to leave the coastal fogs of Monterey for what they hoped would be the clarifying air of western Santa Clara County. From my narrow front balcony I could face eastward toward Monte Sereno to watch the sun break over the vicinity of the Steinbecks' first Los Gatos house, on Greenwood Lane, only a couple of miles away. From my cloistered rear walkway I could turn southward and listen, as they did from their second Los Gatos home, near the Summit, to the Route 17 traffic whizzing between San Jose and Santa Cruz— perhaps carloads of families returning from a day's outing at Sunset Beach, or, in my case, commuters coming back from harried Silicon Valley. Everywhere, the comings and goings of scrub jays, Bullock's orioles, and myriad species of hummingbirds sparked again the lambent air, but never quite loudly or brilliantly enough to efface the incessant whir of automobiles.

Once, headed home from an excursion of my own in Big Basin, above Saratoga, I parked off Highway 9 and hiked into Greenwood Lane. Beneath a dazzling full moon, I stood among oak and manzanita trees and secretly conjured Steinbeck's presence—the ghost of a man whose fiercely concentrated will and driven imagination enriched the literature of his time, and redeemed the tag end of a terrifying decade. For an instant I glimpsed the profound simplicity of his purpose: his willingness to risk everything to write the best he could with what gifts he had, and in doing so to reveal, unblinking, the enduring human spirit among the ruthless shapes of paradise. Like most luminous connections this one has remained essentially valid, even though its edges began to fade as soon as I moved back into traffic and heard the opening chords of The Eagles' song, "Hotel California," blaring from a passing car's stereo.

Still, it seems now, as it seemed then, all I could demand of Steinbeck as a writer, and maybe all any of us can ask of our favorite artists. Sometimes, as though this *Grapes of Wrath* journal weren't occasion enough, in my mind's eye, I see Steinbeck as I envisioned him then—solitary, bent to the task, his pen in motion, gathering light from the air around him to "spread a page with shining." Along with the debts listed below, I think that moment, which is another name for privilege (mine), or maybe for courage (his), is among the best things I experienced in California, and certainly far better than I had any right to expect.

Robert DeMott
Athens, Ohio
June 1988

ACKNOWLEDGMENTS

Like *The Wayward Bus*, which Steinbeck once confessed to an interviewer contained an "indefinite number of echoes" from earlier literary masters, this book, too, is a product of numerous echoes and convergences. There are so many, in fact, that it is difficult to isolate their origins, especially where the enormous amount of information on Steinbeck and his times is concerned. Obviously, I am grateful to everyone who has written on *The Grapes of Wrath*—they have helped this book in ways I cannot fully identify. I am specifically indebted, however, to the following people for facilitating publication of Steinbeck's journal, though responsibility for use of their contributions, and for the selection of its title, *Working Days*, rests solely with me.

Elaine Steinbeck encouraged the project from the start, as did Eugene Winick and Julie Fallowfield of McIntosh and Otis, my superb editor, Gerald Howard of Viking Penguin and his assistant, Renée Klock. Without them, this book would still be a neglected manuscript at the Harry Ransom Humanities Research Center of the University of Texas. Jackson Benson stands tall, both in and out of his *True Adventures of John Steinbeck, Writer;* his knowledge of Steinbeck is matched only by his propensity for sharing it. Ditto for Preston Beyer, John Ditsky, Warren French, Tetsumaro Hayashi, Carlton Sheffield, and Roy Simmonds—their generosity, knowledge, and support have heightened this occasion. Adam Marsh provided a discretionary award from Ohio University's Research Committee at a crucial moment. Without the dedicated help of N. Miki Armstrong at San Jose State University and Donna Spencer at Ohio University I would still be gathering notes. Dr. Susan Shillinglaw, Acting Director of San Jose State's Steinbeck Research Center, cheerfully came to my rescue more times than I can count. I was also aided by Mary Jean S. Gamble of the John Steinbeck Library, Salinas; Joseph Johnson, Reference Librarian, Monterey Public Library; Kathy O'Connor, National Archives, San Francisco branch, San Bruno, California; and Sara Timby and Margaret J. Kimball, Department of Special Collections, Stanford University. Rima O'Connor, Head of Inter-Library Loan, Alden Library, Ohio University, made easier the indispensable microfilm borrowings from the University of Virginia, the University of California, and Columbia University.

I thank Elaine Steinbeck, and McIntosh and Otis, agents for the Steinbeck estate, for permission to quote from Steinbeck's writings. The unpublished Steinbeck manuscripts and correspondence that I draw upon are utilized through the courtesy of the Berg Collection, the New York Public Library; the Bancroft Library, University of California, Berkeley; the Clifton Waller Barrett Library, Special Collections Department, University of Virginia Library, Charlottesville, Virginia; the Department of Special Collections and University Archives, the Stanford University Libraries, Stanford, California; the Harry Ransom Humanities Research Center, University of Texas, Austin, Texas; the John Steinbeck Library, Salinas, California; the Rare Book and Manuscript Library, Butler Library, Columbia University, New York City; the Manuscript Division, Library of Congress, Washington D.C.; and the Steinbeck Research Center, Wahlquist

Library, San Jose State University, San Jose, California. I am grateful to the administrators and staffs of these exceptional Steinbeck archives for their assistance.

Communications with the late Mrs. William Brown (Carol Steinbeck), Gwyn Steinbeck, and Elizabeth Otis, all conducted for my earlier book, *Steinbeck's Reading*, have come into play here as well. And during the several years this project was in the works, I have also benefited from Elizabeth Ainsworth, Bernadine Beutler, Jack Douglas, James Dourgarian, Robert Harmon, Cliff Lewis, Pare Lorentz, Craig Nova, Pauline Pearson, Virginia Scardigli, Thomas Steinbeck, the late Robert Woodward, and Nancy Zane. San Jose State colleagues Hans Guth, Mary Lou Lewandowski, and Nils Peterson repeatedly eased the burden of being a stranger in a strange land. So did Los Gatos neighbors Larry and Adrienne Vilaubi, cronies through thick and thin. Students in my Steinbeck courses at San Jose (especially Greg Moss and friends) and at Ohio (especially Brian Railsback in my graduate seminar), listened attentively to these journal entries and then politely pressed me for helpful annotations. Mark Rollins cajoled me into swapping my typewriter for a word processor, which in turn made creating those annotations considerably easier. My parents, Jim and Helen DeMott, and my daughter, Liz DeMott, were tireless cheerleaders from beginning to end. In them I have been triply blessed.

Best of all, some convergences remain constant—persistent and resonant like familiar music. For me, the ideal audience for this journal of a writer's life is Dave Smith, who lives it. My gratitude to him surpasses everything else.

INTRODUCTION

Boileau said that kings, gods, and heroes only were fit subjects for literature. The writer can only write about what he admires. Present-day kings aren't very inspiring, the gods are on a vacation and about the only heroes left are the scientists and the poor. . . . But the poor are still in the open. When they make a struggle it is an heroic struggle with starvation, death or imprisonment the penalty if they lose. And since our race admires gallantry, the writer will deal with it where he finds it. He finds it in the struggling poor now.

> —Steinbeck, in a self-created interview for
> Joseph Henry Jackson's syndicated NBC
> radio program, April 16, 1939.
> (*Courtesy of Bancroft Library, University of California, Berkeley*)

John Steinbeck's greatest novel, *The Grapes of Wrath* (New York: The Viking Press, 1939), winner of the 1940 Pulitzer Prize, cornerstone of his 1962 Nobel Prize award, and one of the most enduring works of fiction by any American author, was actually written at the same time as another book. The novel itself Steinbeck finally wrote after a couple of unsuccessful attempts in a sustained burst between June and October 1938. Then there is the accompanying journal of its making, which he composed daily during that same stretch, and—a gratifying bonus—which also includes two other sections he wrote in February 1938, and from October 1939 to January 1941. In the past half century the novel has sold more than 14 million copies (it still sells over 100,000 paperback copies a year), has been translated into nearly every language on earth, and has become an accepted masterpiece of world literature. It is one of those novels with its heart in the right place. Like Harriet Beecher Stowe's *Uncle Tom's Cabin* or Mark Twain's *Adventures of Huckleberry Finn*, two other novels that humanize America's downtrodden, *The Grapes of Wrath* has become required reading across our cultural curriculum. And though *The Grapes of Wrath* has attained a legendary reputation, and John Steinbeck's name is recognized worldwide, this three-part journal, containing the personal record of the novel's creation and fevered aftermath, has until now been virtually unknown. *Working Days* ought to enhance our understanding of the novelist's working methods and explain the tangled circumstances from which his greatest writing emerged.

The Grapes of Wrath is a controversial classic because it is at once populist *and* revolutionary. It advances a belief in the essential goodness and forbearance of the "common people," and prophesies a fundamental change to produce equitable social conditions: "There is a crime here that goes beyond denunciation. There is a sorrow here that weeping cannot symbolize. There is a failure here that topples all our success. . . . in the eyes of the hungry there is a growing wrath. In the souls of the people the grapes of wrath are filling and growing heavy, growing heavy for the vintage" (Chapter 25). This novel—part naturalistic epic, part dissenting tract, and part romantic gospel—speaks to a multiplicity of human experiences and is squarely located in our varied national consciousness; nearly every literate person knows, or at least claims familiarity with, its impassioned story of the

Joad family's brutal migration from Oklahoma's dying Dust Bowl to California's corrupt Promised Land. In their ironic exodus from home to homelessness, from individualism to collective awareness, from selfishness to communal love, "from 'I' to 'we' " (Chapter 14), Steinbeck's cast of unsuspecting characters—Ma Joad, Tom Joad, Jim Casy, Rose of Sharon—have become permanently etched in our sensibility and serve constantly to remind us that heroism is as much a matter of choice as it is of being chosen. Similarly, Steinbeck's rendering of the graphic enticements of Route 66—"the path of a people in flight" (Chapter 12)—from Middle America to the West defined the national urge for mobility, motion, and blind striving. The novel's erotically subversive final scene, in which Rose of Sharon, delivered of a stillborn child, gives her milk-laden breast to a dying stranger, then looks up and smiles "mysteriously" (Chapter 30), simply will not fade from view. Wherever human beings dream of a dignified society in which they can harvest the fruits of their own labor, *The Grapes of Wrath*'s radical voice of protest can still be heard. As a tale of dashed illusions, thwarted desires, inhuman suffering, and betrayed promises—all strung on the most fragile thread of hope— *The Grapes of Wrath* not only summed up the Depression era's socially conscious art, but, beyond that, has few peers in American fiction.

Steinbeck's book has been praised by the left as a triumph of proletarian writing, nominated by critics and reviewers as "The Great American Novel," given historical vindication by Senator Robert M. La Follette's inquiries into California's tyrannical farm labor conditions, and defended by Eleanor Roosevelt for its power ("The horrors of the picture . . . made you dread . . . to begin the next chapter, and yet you cannot lay the book down or even skip a page.") But *The Grapes of Wrath* has also been attacked by academic scholars as sentimental, unconvincing, and inartistic, banned repeatedly by school boards and libraries, and denounced by right-wing ministers, corporate farmers, and politicians as immoral, degrading, and untruthful. (Oklahoma Congressman Lyle Boren, typical of the book's early detractors, called it "a lie, a black, infernal creation of a twisted, distorted mind.")[1] In fact, from the moment it was published on April 14, 1939, *The Grapes of Wrath* has been less judged as a novel than as a sociological event, a celebrated political cause, or a factual case study. If the past fifty years have seen little consensus about the exact nature of the novel's achievement, there has been plenty of proof that it elicits widely divergent responses from its audience. Perhaps that is to be expected, considering that Steinbeck intentionally wrote the novel in "five layers," intending to "rip" each reader's nerves "to rags" by making him "participate in the actuality." What each reader "gets" from *The Grapes of Wrath*, he claimed, "will be scaled entirely on his own depth or hollowness."[2] Steinbeck's participatory aesthetic ensured the novel's affective impact on a broad range of readers. By conceiving his novel on simultaneous levels of existence Steinbeck pushed back the accepted boundaries of traditional realistic fiction and redefined the proletarian form. Like most significant American novels, *The Grapes of Wrath* does not offer codified solutions, but instead enacts the process of belief and embodies the shape of faith.

Behind the welter of conflicting opinions and wild imaginings about this most public of novels stands one of the most reclusive of American writers—John Steinbeck (1902–1968). His private story, with its equally impassioned emphasis on the punishing journey toward artistic fulfillment, is recorded in this journal. *Working Days*, too, is a tale of dramatic proportions—false starts, self-doubts, whining complaints, paranoia, ironic intentions, personal reversals, and—woven tenuously throughout—the fragile thread of recovery. And like the novel, the journal has its own cast of characters, all of whom belong, in one way or another, to the moment of Steinbeck's labor. Some lives impress upon his, some overlap, some run parallel, some appear and disappear like chimeras, and some remain unidentified, anonymous, lost forever to the currents of history. Among the people who left their stamp on the novel, two names joined preeminently with Steinbeck's in a kind of spiritual partnership. Without them, the novel might have been far different.

Carol Henning Steinbeck (1906–1983), the novelist's outgoing first wife (they married in 1930), was more politically radical than John, and she actively supported members of the fugitive agricultural labor movement before he did.[3] She too was an energetic, talented person—among other things, a versifier, satirist, prose writer, painter, caricaturist—who agreed to relinquish a possible career in favor of helping to manage his. It seems to have been a partnership based more on reciprocal need and shared affection than on deep romantic love. Their marriage was smoother, more egalitarian, in the struggling years of Steinbeck's career; with the enormous success—and pressures—brought by *Of Mice and Men* (New York: Covici-Friede, 1937), their situation became more tenuous and volatile. Carol, an extremely strong-willed, demonstrative person, was often frustrated, resentful, and sometimes jealous; John, inordinately shy, was frequently beleaguered, confused, and demanding. In the late 1930s, whenever John was writing daily, Carol handled—but didn't always like—most of the routine domestic duties. She also shielded her husband as much as possible from unwarranted disruptions and intrusions, and oversaw some of their financial arrangements (an increasingly large job) between Steinbeck and his literary agents. "Carol does so much," Steinbeck admitted in Entry #45. Once in a while she also served as his cultural envoy and stand-in. Carol, not John, went to New York for the opening of Joseph Kirkland's disastrous play version of *Tortilla Flat*, and during that same visit, in January 1938, she met with documentary filmmaker Pare Lorentz, arranging between them Lorentz's first visit to Los Gatos to discuss a joint Steinbeck/Lorentz movie version of *In Dubious Battle* and a private showing of Lorentz's pioneering documentary films ("APPROVE LORENTZ AFFAIR GREATLY," Steinbeck wired Carol on January 13, 1938).[4]

Most important of all, as she did with all her husband's manuscripts, Carol typed and edited *The Grapes of Wrath*, served in the early stages as a rigorous critical commentator (though by late September 1938, during the book's final stretch, she confessed to having lost "all sense of proportion," and felt unfit "to judge it at all"), and, in a brilliant stroke, chose the novel's title from Julia Ward Howe's "Battle Hymn of the Republic," perhaps inspired by her hearing of Pare Lorentz's radio drama, *Ecce Homo!*, which ends with a martial version of Howe's song. ("Tell Carol she is a whiz at picking titles and she has done it again with the new one," Annie Laurie Williams exulted.) Her role as facilitator is evident throughout this journal and is recorded permanently in one half of the novel's dedication: "To CAROL who willed this book." Eventually, however, in the wayward recesses of Steinbeck's heart, Carol's brittle efficiency, managerial brusqueness, and violent mood swings (she, too, was exhausted by the novel's completion and histrionic reception) seemed to cause more problems than they solved. His involvement with a younger woman, Gwyndolyn Conger, whom he met in mid-1939, and who quickly came to represent everything Steinbeck felt romantically lacking in Carol, signaled the beginning of the end of their marriage.[5] They separated rancorously in 1941, sold their beloved Los Gatos mountain home (which Steinbeck had facetiously taken to calling "Carol's ranch"), and divorced two years later.

The second part of the novel's dedication—"To TOM who lived it"—refers to Thomas Collins (1897?–1961), the novelist's chief source, guide, discussant, and chronicler of accurate migrant information. Collins not only put Steinbeck in touch with the real-life prototypes of the Joads and Jim Casy, but himself served as Steinbeck's real-life prototype for Jim Rawley, the fictional manager of the "Weedpatch" government camp. (That camp became an oasis of relief for the harried Joads, and is featured in Chapters 22 to 26 of *The Grapes of Wrath*.) An intrepid, resourceful, and exceptionally compassionate man, Collins was the manager of a model Farm Security Administration camp, located in Kern County at the southern end of California's Central Valley. The Arvin Sanitary Camp (featured in the fourth installment of Steinbeck's 1936 San Francisco *News* reports, "The Harvest Gypsies," a documentary forerunner of *The Grapes of Wrath*) was one of several proposed demonstration camps intended to provide humane, clean, democratic—but temporary—living conditions for the growing army of migrant workers entering California from the lower Middle West and Dust Bowl region. (More than two dozen camps were planned in 1935 by the Resettlement Administration, the forerunner of the F.S.A.; by 1940, with New Deal budgets slashed by conservatives in Congress, only fifteen were actually completed or under construction.)[6] Collins possessed a genius for camp administration—he had the right mix of fanaticism, vision, and tactfulness—and he and Steinbeck, both Jacksonian democrats, hit it off immediately in late summer 1936, when the novelist went south on the first of several grueling research trips during the next two years to investigate field conditions. (Contrary to popular belief, Steinbeck never traveled with a migrant family all the way from Oklahoma to California.)

Fortunately, Collins was a punctual and voluminous report writer. His lively weekly accounts of the workers' activities, events, diets, entertainments, sayings, beliefs, and observations provided Steinbeck with a compelling documentary supplement to his own researches. In fact, Steinbeck and Collins struck a deal: Collins would guide Steinbeck through the intricacies of the agricultural labor scene, put him in direct contact with migrant families, and supply Steinbeck with valuable information; in return, besides broadcasting news of the workers' plight in his own writings, Steinbeck would edit Collins' reports and pave the way for their publication as a full-length book. Toward that end, at his home in Los Gatos in late 1936, Steinbeck introduced Collins to one of his agents, Annie Laurie Williams, who was in California on a business trip. Williams was immediately impressed with Collins' forthrightness and with the importance of the "social documents" he had compiled. During the ensuing eighteen months she and Mavis McIntosh set about superintending the book's evolution, corresponding with Collins, keeping abreast of additional material, and sending the manuscript around to various publishers for evaluations.

Obviously, the more preoccupied Steinbeck became with his projects, the less he did on Collins' compilation, preferring instead to incorporate some of its "great gobs" of information— always with Collins' permission—into his own writing. ("Letter from Tom. . . . He is so good. I need this stuff. It is exact and just the thing that will be used against me if I am wrong," Steinbeck noted in Entry #24.) By late June 1938, already a month into the final version of *The Grapes of Wrath*, Steinbeck was out of the editorial picture entirely; W. W. Norton Company had hired a writer named Madeleine Ruthven to put Collins' book "in shape for publication."[7] Though he ostensibly "approved" of the Ruthven arrangement, Collins may have been miffed that Steinbeck was unable to maintain his part of their collaboration. That September, after a disagreement with Steinbeck in Los Gatos ("Tom was here. Little trouble Saturday because of liquor and talk," Steinbeck wrote in Entry #69), Collins, increasingly busy with the creation of new camps, simply failed to supply McIntosh and Otis—and hence Norton—with all the material he promised. As a result his documentary book never appeared. In 1940, at Steinbeck's suggestion, Collins worked as a technical advisor to John Ford's striking cinematic production of *The Grapes of Wrath*. And later—probably spurred by the success of both novel and film—Collins himself wrote an autobiographical/fictional memoir, to which Steinbeck, who appears as a character, added a Foreword. This book by "Windsor Drake" (Collins' pseudonym) was accepted by Lymanhouse, a California publisher, though it never reached print because the owner of the publishing company, pleading wartime paper shortage, reneged on the deal.[8] After that, Collins resigned from the F.S.A., and he and Steinbeck passed out of each other's lives.

Besides Carol Steinbeck and Tom Collins, a caravan of other people crisscrossed the novelist's life between 1936 and 1941. George West, chief editorial writer for the progressive San Francisco *News*, instigated Steinbeck's investigations of the migrant labor situation for his paper. Frederick R. Soule, the enlightened Regional Information Advisor at the San Francisco office of the Farm Security Administration, provided statistics and documents for his *News* reports, and otherwise opened official doors for Steinbeck that might have stayed closed. Soule's colleague, Eric Thomsen, Regional Director in Charge of Management at the F.S.A. office in San Francisco, escorted Steinbeck to the Central

Valley, where the writer encountered Collins at the Arvin Camp for the first time. (In a convoluted and unintentional way, the federal government underwrote Steinbeck's research.) A continent away, in New York, Steinbeck's publisher, Pascal Covici, kept up a running dialogue with the novelist. The two men remained loyal to each other through the embarrassing bankruptcy of Covici-Friede in July 1938, and through Covici's relocation as an editor at The Viking Press, a felicitous arrangement which also included the purchase of Steinbeck's contract. Steinbeck had an incredible knack for aligning himself with loyal, generous, and responsible associates. In his literary agents, McIntosh and Otis, he was triply blessed. Mavis McIntosh, Elizabeth Otis, and Annie Laurie Williams not only kept his professional interests uppermost at all times (Otis nearly single-handedly engineered the Viking contract), but did so with the kind of selflessness that made them more like family members than business managers. All three women became trusted confidantes in every conceivable realm of Steinbeck's life. And closer to home, Ed Ricketts, Ritch and Tal Lovejoy, Louis and Mary Paul, Joe and Charlotte Jackson, George and Gail Mors, Martin and Elsie Ray, Charlie Chaplin, Pare Lorentz, Carlton Sheffield, and Webster Street all managed, at various times, to help keep Steinbeck's body and soul together. All these people—and more—left tracks in Steinbeck's journal during the most eventful period of his life.

At the center of this maelstrom Steinbeck remained, if not exactly in control, then at least resolutely committed to his art, to the single vision of his purpose. By nature Steinbeck was not a collaborator. "Unless a writer is capable of solitude he should leave books alone and go into the theatre," he exclaimed years later.[9] Solitude was an increasingly precious commodity in Steinbeck's life in the hectic years from 1934 through 1941, during which everything from the death of his parents to the demise of his marriage conspired to paralyze his will. Despite the constant tumult, he wrote several of his strongest books in stressful situations. "Every book seems the struggle of a whole life," he lamented in Entry #49. A ruminative, grass-growing mood was rarely his, so he managed to do the best he could with the conditions he had. Although it didn't always ensure complete solitude, Steinbeck sequestered himself in the "tiny" work room of the Los Gatos Greenwood Lane house: "Just big enough for a bed and a desk and a gun rack and a little book case. I like to sleep in the room I work in," he told George Albee (Steinbeck and Wallsten, eds., *Steinbeck: A Life in Letters*, p. 133).

By entering his writerly posture, Steinbeck created a disciplined working rhythm and maintained what he called a "unity feeling"—a sense of continuity and habitation with his material. Ideally, for a few hours each day, the world Steinbeck created took precedence over the one in which he lived. Because both worlds can be considered "real," at times during the summer of 1938 Steinbeck didn't know where one began and the other left off; walking back into the domestic world from the world of imagination was not always a smooth shift for him (or for his wife). It was a shift exacerbated by Steinbeck's shrinking sense of humor, his growing popularity, and, of course, by the grim subject matter of *The Grapes of Wrath*. The hard reality of California's contemporary farm labor conditions—the pitiful spectacle of "three hundred thousand" utterly dispossessed migrant workers and their families (Chapter 14)—demanded his attention so fully that he refused to dissipate his energy in extra-literary pursuits: "I won't do any of these public things. Can't. It isn't my nature and I won't be stampeded. And so the stand must be made and I must keep out of politics," he resolved in Entry #92.

Furthermore, Steinbeck, an imposing, but self-confessedly

homely man, literally escaped what he once called his "confused, turgid, ugly, and gross" self when he wrote (quoted in Benson, *True Adventures of John Steinbeck*, p. 291). Where his characters use tools to elevate work to a dignified level, Steinbeck turned to his "comfortable and comforting" pen, an instrument that became an "extension" of the best part of himself: "Work is the only good thing," he claimed on July 6, 1938 (Entry #30). If *The Grapes of Wrath* praises the honorableness of labor it is because the author himself felt it called into being the most committed, the most empathetic, the most resourceful qualities of the human psyche: "Every effort I can bring to bear is and has been at the call of the common working people to the end that they may eat what they raise, wear what they weave, use what they produce, and in every way and in completeness share in the works of their hands and their heads," he reminded San Francisco *News* columnist John D. Barry (Entry #36, Note). The communal vision of *The Grapes of Wrath* begins in the ceremonial sweat of Steinbeck's lonely labor. In fact, Steinbeck believed writing was redemptive work, an act full of transformational possibilities. Ironically, his engagement with the "Matter of the Migrants," from 1936 to 1939, required so much of himself that by the end of the decade he was not only sick of writing fiction, but needed to turn to other arenas for respite and for inspiration.

Before that, however, Steinbeck rarely questioned the risks involved in bringing his whole sensibility to bear on *The Grapes of Wrath*. Like Walt Whitman's *Leaves of Grass*, Steinbeck's novel had a complicated foreground and grew through a similar process of accretion and experimentation. *The Grapes of Wrath* was the product of his increasing immersion in the migrant material, which proved to be a subject of such related intertwining that it required an extended odyssey of his own before he discovered the proper focus and style to do the topic justice. In one way or another, from August 1936, when Steinbeck discovered a subject "like nothing in the world" (Steinbeck and Wallsten, eds., *Steinbeck: A Life in Letters*, p. 129), through October 1939, when he resolved to put behind him "that part of my life that made the *Grapes*" (Entry #101), the migrant issue, which had wounded him deeply, remained a central preoccupation.

Between 1936 and 1938 Steinbeck's commitment to his material evolved through at least four major stages of writing: (1) a seven-part series of newspaper articles, "The Harvest Gypsies"; (2) an unfinished novel, "The Oklahomans"; (3) a completed, but destroyed, satire, "L'Affaire Lettuceberg"; and (4) a final fictional version, *The Grapes of Wrath*. Each stage varied in audience, intention, and tone from the one before it. All the versions overlapped, however, because they shared—with differing highlights and resolutions—a fixed core of elements: on one side, the entrenched power, wealth, authority, and consequent tyranny of California's industrialized agricultural system (symbolized by Associated Farmers, Inc.), which produced flagrant violations of the migrants' civil and human rights and ensured their continuing peonage, their loss of dignity, through threats, reprisals, and violence; on the other side, the powerlessness, poverty, victimization, and fear of the nomadic American migrants whose willingness to work, desire to retain their dignity, and enduring wish to settle land of their own were kept alive by their innate resilience and resourcefulness, and by the democratic benefits of the government sanitary camps. From the moment he entered the fray, Steinbeck had no doubt that the presence of the migrants would change the fabric of California life, though he had little foresight about what his own role in that change would be. His overriding concern was humanitarian: he wanted to be an effective advocate, but he did not want to appear presumptuous. ("I am actively opposed to any man or group who . . . is able to dominate the lives of workers," he announced later to John Barry.)

Not counting a warm-up essay (in the September 12, 1936, issue of *The Nation*), or his editing of Tom Collins' camp reports, Steinbeck's first lengthy excursion into the migrants' problems was published in the San Francisco *News*, a Bay area daily paper. "The Harvest Gypsies" formed the foundation of Steinbeck's concern, raised issues and initiated forces (which reverberate in Part Two of his 1938 journal, and so enter the history of *The Grapes of Wrath*), gave him a working vocabulary with which to understand current events, and furthered his position as a reliable interpreter. This first stage of Steinbeck's commitment actually stemmed from the notoriety caused by his recently published strike novel, *In Dubious Battle* (New York: Covici-Friede, 1936), after which Steinbeck found—often against his will—that he was fast becoming considered a sympathetic spokesman for the contemporary agricultural labor situation. (This was a profound irony, because while *In Dubious Battle* exposed the capitalist dynamics of corporate farming, it took no side for or against labor, preferring instead to see the fruit strike as a symbol of "man's eternal, bitter warfare with himself"; Steinbeck's "unequivocal" partisanship occurred later, in the winter and spring of 1938.)

Thus, at the invitation of George West, Steinbeck produced "The Harvest Gypsies," which, punctuated with Dorothea Lange's graphic photographs of migrants, appeared in the liberal, pro-labor San Francisco *News*, from October 5 to 12, 1936. These hard-hitting, unflinching investigative reports detailed the plan of California's feudal agricultural labor industry. The pieces introduced the antagonists, underscored the anachronistic rift between the Okie agrarian past and the mechanized California present, explained the economic background and insidious effects of the labor issue, examined the deplorable migrant living conditions, and exposed the unconscionable practices of the interlocking conglomerate of corporation farms. Primarily, though, his eye was on the migrants, who were "gypsies by force of circumstance," as Steinbeck announced in his opening piece: "And so they move, frantically, with starvation close behind them. And in this series of articles we shall try to see how they live and what kind of people they are, what their living standard is, what is done for them, and what their problems and needs are. For while California has been successful in its use of migrant labor, it is gradually building a human structure which will certainly change the state, and may, if handled with the inhumanity and stupidity that have characterized the past, destroy the present system of agricultural economics."[10]

Written mostly in a measured, restrained style (the voice is reasonable, the tone is empirical, the ends to be achieved are understanding and intelligent solutions), Steinbeck's *News* articles are full of case studies, chilling factual statistics, and an unsettling catalogue of human woes (illness, incapacitation, persecution, death) observed from close contact with migratory field workers he had met. But in the best tradition of advocacy journalism, Steinbeck concluded his series with a number of prophetic recommendations for alleviating the conflict with federal aid and local support; this in turn would create subsistence farms, establish a migratory labor board, encourage unionization, and punish terrorism. When they were published in 1936 (and again when they were printed in 1938 as *Their Blood Is Strong*), Steinbeck's articles solidified his credibility—both in and out of the migrant camps—as a serious commentator. "The Harvest Gypsies" (and Tom Collins' continuing reports) provided Steinbeck with a basic repository of precise information and folk values. It would still be more than a year before the subjective intensity of his engagement deepened; however, events were already transpiring in his hometown and elsewhere that would eventually change his attitude from methodical reporter to literary activist.

The last of Steinbeck's San Francisco *News* articles ended with a comment that became the basis for the second stage of his writing: "The new migrants to California from the dust bowl are here to stay. They are of the best American stock, intelligent, resourceful, and, if given a chance, socially responsible." Steinbeck understood that the migrants wouldn't vanish from sight, and couldn't be ignored, though official California tried to do just that. Steinbeck built on his *News* experiences and on at least one more month-long field trip, in October and November 1937, with Tom Collins to plan the writing of a "big" book. They started from Gridley, where Collins was managing a new camp, but then roamed California from Stockton to Needles, wherever migrants were gathered to work. By late in the year, after hitting several "snags," he was working on a "rather long novel" called "The Oklahomans," which, he reported a few weeks later, was "still a long way from finished." Steinbeck, generally guarded with interviewers, revealed enough to journalist Louis Walther to indicate that the focus of his novel was on the salutary, irrepressible character of the migrants, who, he believed, would profoundly alter the tenor of life in California. "Their coming here now is going to change things almost as much as did the coming of the first American settlers." Furthermore, "The Californian doesn't know what he does want. The Oklahoman knows just exactly what he wants. He wants a piece of land. And he goes after it and gets it." [11]

Quietly, in late January 1938, Steinbeck stopped work on "The Oklahomans" (the manuscript has never been found and it is doubtful that he had actually written a great deal on it). Judging from his comments to Louis Walther, however, it is reasonable to assume that "The Oklahomans' " uncomplicated duality of conception, the untangled lines of its proposed struggle, and the dispassionate tone of its narrative voice (probably a holdover from "The Harvest Gypsies") struck Steinbeck as belonging increasingly to the reductive world of pulp fiction or wish-fulfillment. The truth was the migrant situation had worsened, and along with it, Steinbeck's capacity for pity and his need for direct involvement had grown. The misery of the migrant condition was heating up in the winter of 1938, especially in Visalia and Nipomo (Entry #1, Note), where thousands of families were marooned by floods. From Los Gatos, Steinbeck wrote Elizabeth Otis in February:

I must go over into the interior valleys. There are about five thousand families starving to death over there, not just hungry but actually starving. The government is trying to feed them and get medical attention to them with the fascist group of utilities and banks and huge growers sabatoging the thing all along the line. . . . In one tent there are twenty people quarantined for smallpox and two of the women are to have babies in that tent this week. I've tied into the thing from the first and I must get down there and see it and see if I can't do something to help knock these murderers on the heads. . . . They think that if these people are allowed to live in camps with proper sanitary facilities, they will organize and that is the bugbear of the large landowner and the corporation farmer. The states and counties will give them nothing because they are outsiders. But the crops of any part of this state could not be harvested without these outsiders. I'm pretty mad about it. No word of this outside because when I have finished my job the jolly old associated farmers will be after my scalp again (Steinbeck and Wallsten, eds., *Steinbeck: A Life in Letters*, p. 158).

Suddenly Steinbeck realized that the issue was not as simple as portraying the "naive directness" of the migrants' desire for land. Indeed, the cauldron of his own soul was beginning to boil with frustration, powerlessness, and anger; "The Oklahomans" could not adequately redress the injustices he had recently contemplated. "When I wrote the *The Grapes of Wrath,*" he declared in a 1952 Voice of America radio interview, "I was filled . . . with certain angers . . . at people who were doing injustices to other people. . . ."

As a novelist, Steinbeck often experienced a delayed reaction to piercing events. He needed time to let them gestate before they rose to the surface of his awareness and began pushing back at him, demanding their transformation to words. From February through May 1938, the third stage of his writing development produced "L'Affaire Lettuceberg." With this abortive—but necessary—venture, Steinbeck's migrant subject matter took its most drastic turn, inspired by an ugly event in Salinas, California, his hometown. Earlier, in September 1936, Steinbeck had encountered the vicious clash between workers and growers in a lettuce strike—"there are riots in Salinas and killings in the streets of that dear little town where I was born," he told George Albee (Steinbeck and Wallsten, eds., *Steinbeck: A Life in Letters,* p. 132). The strike was smashed with terrorism, and recollections of the workers' defeat festered in Steinbeck for more than a year. Then, in early February 1938, galvanized by reports of the worsening conditions in Visalia and Nipomo, Steinbeck felt the urgent need to do something direct in retaliation. "It seems to be necessary to write things down," he said in Entry #1. "Can't stop it." John Steinbeck never became what dyed-in-the-wool activists would consider fully radicalized, but by putting his pen to the service of a political cause, he was stepping as close to being a firebrand as he ever would. He launched into "L'Affaire," a vituperative satire aimed at attacking the leading citizens of Salinas, "the committee of seven," who organize and direct the ignorant army of vigilantes. The cabal of organizers remain aloof, but "work out the methods by which vigilantes are formed and kept steamed up." The vigilantes were assembled from the common populace of Salinas—clerks, service station operators, shopkeepers—all of them "dopes" and "suckers" for creating mayhem.[12]

By all accounts, "L'Affaire Lettuceberg" was the angriest, most thesis-ridden book Steinbeck ever attempted. It presented difficulties from the outset. Carol, his closest critic, did not like its subject (despite her leftist beliefs), its title was concocted and unwieldy, and its approach was a detour from his main concern for the migrant workers, already adumbrated in "The Harvest Gypsies." In fact, "L"Affaire" wasn't really a "literary" work, but a "vulgar" tract. In May 1938 Steinbeck confessed to Annie Laurie Williams: "I'll have the first draft of this book done in about two weeks. It is only a little over seventy thousand words. And it is a vicious book, a mean book. I don't know whether it will be any good at all. It might well be very lousy but it has a lot of poison in it that I have to get out of my system and this is a good way to do it. Then if it is no good we can destroy it. I'll send it on for the opinion of you all though before I destroy it. I feel so ferocious about the thing that I won't have much critical insight. Probably be almost ready to send out by the first of June. But it is going so rapidly there will be a good deal of cleaning up about it."[13]

Within days Steinbeck's critical insight returned. The careful artist triumphed over the ferocious propagandist, and he destroyed "L'Affaire Lettuceberg." Immediately, Steinbeck wrote to Elizabeth Otis, his main literary agent, and to Pascal Covici, who had already announced the publication of "L'Affaire," to inform them that he would not be delivering the manuscript they expected. The following excerpted letter to Otis, written around mid-May 1938, offers a statement of Steinbeck's artistic integrity, because it serves as a covenant with the abiding principles of his art and with the noble qualities of his migrant subject matter, which his blind anger had blurred in the headlong rush for revenge. This letter also sets up a resonant echo with many of the concerns voiced in the main journal section of *Working Days:*

This is going to be a hard letter to write . . . this book is finished and it is a bad book and I must get rid of it. It can't be printed. It is bad because it isn't honest. Oh! these incidents all happened but—I'm not telling as much of the truth about them as I know. In satire you have to restrict the picture and I just can't do satire. . . . I know, you could sell possibly 30,000 copies. I know that a great many people would think they liked the book. I myself have built up a hole-proof argument on how and why I liked it. I can't beat the argument but I don't like the book. And I would be doing Pat a greater injury in letting him print it than I would by destroying it. Not once in the writing of it have I felt the curious warm pleasure that comes when work is going well. My whole work drive has been aimed at making people understand each other and then I deliberately write this book the aim of which is to cause hatred through partial understanding. My father would have called it a smart-alec book. It was full of tricks to make people ridiculous. If I can't do better I have slipped badly. And that I won't admit, yet.

    . . . It is sloppily written because I never cared about it. . . . I had got smart and cocky you see. I had forgotten that I hadn't learned to write books, that I will never learn to write them. A book must be a life that lives all of itself and this one doesn't do that. . . . I beat poverty for a good many years and I'll be damned if I'll go down at the first little whiff of success. . . .

I think this book will be a good lesson for me. I think I got to believing critics—I thought I could write easily and that anything I touched would be good simply because I did it. Well any such idea conscious or unconscious is exploded for some time to come. I'm in little danger now of believing my own publicity. . . .

Again I'm sorry. But I'm not ready to be a hack yet. Maybe later. Carol feels the same way about it.[14]

The fourth and last stage of Steinbeck's writing culminated in *The Grapes of Wrath*. His conscience squared, Steinbeck stood ready to embark on the longest sustained writing job of his life. From late May 1938, when he struck the first words of the new novel to paper ("To the red country and part of the gray country of Oklahoma, the last rains came gently, and they did not cut the scarred earth"), through the winter of 1939, when the last of the corrections and editorial details were settled ("I meant, Pat, to print *all all all* the verses of the Battle Hymn. They're all pertinent and they're all exciting. And the music if you can"), *The Grapes of Wrath* was a task which, as the main section of *Working Days* makes clear, fully commanded his energy. Everything he had written earlier—from his 1936 *Nation* article, "Dubious Battle in California," through "Starvation Under the Orange Trees," an April 1938 essay that functioned as the Epilogue to *Their Blood Is Strong*—became grist for his final attempt. From his numerous field travels with Tom Collins, and from countless hours of talking to migrant people, working beside them, listening to them, and sharing their problems, Steinbeck drew all the concrete details of human form, language, and landscape that ensure artistic verisimilitude, as well as the subtler nuances of dialect, idiosyncratic tics, habits, and gestures, which animate fictional characterization. But the choreography of details alone, the dance of his ear and eye, won't fully account for the metamorphosis from "The Harvest Gypsies" to *The Grapes of Wrath*.

Steinbeck's leap from right-minded competency to inspired vision was the result of one linked experience that hit him so hard it called forth every ounce of his moral indignation, social anger, and pity. In late February and early March Steinbeck witnessed the deplorable conditions at Visalia where thousands of human beings, flooded out of their shelters, were starving to death: "the water is a foot deep in the tents and the children are up on the beds and there is no food and no fire, and the county has taken off all the nurses because 'the problem is so great that we can't do anything about it.' So they do nothing" (Steinbeck and Wallsten, eds., *Steinbeck: A Life in Letters*, p. 161). In the company of Tom Collins, photographer Horace Bristol, and other Farm Security Administration personnel, Steinbeck worked day and night for nearly two weeks (sometimes dropping to sleep in the mud from exhaustion) to help relieve the misery, though of course no aid seemed adequate.[15] What Steinbeck encountered in that sea of mud and debris was so devastating, so "heartbreaking" he told Elizabeth Otis, that he was utterly transfixed by the "staggering" conditions, and by "suffering" so great that objective reporting would only falsify the moment (Steinbeck and Wallsten, eds., *Steinbeck: A Life in Letters*, pp. 159, 161).

What Steinbeck witnessed at Visalia had a profound, if temporarily delayed, impact on his novel. From the outset in creating the Joad family to occupy the narrative chapters of *The Grapes of Wrath*, Steinbeck gave his novel a specific human context, a felt emotional quality, and a dramatic dimension all his earlier versions lacked: "Begin the detailed description of the family I am to live with. Must take time in the description, detail, detail, looks, clothes, gestures. . . . We have to know these people.

Know their looks and their nature," he reminded himself (Entry #17). Steinbeck's symbolic portrayal of this universal human family brought the novel alive for him: "Make the people live. Make them live" (Entry #30). By conceiving the Joads as "an over-essence of people" (Entry #30), Steinbeck elevated the entire history of the migrant struggle into the ceremonial realm of art.

Steinbeck's mythology was one of endings as well as of beginnings. Like Ernest Hemingway, whose physical wounding at Fossalta, Italy, in 1918 became the generative event for a string of stories and novels (especially *A Farewell to Arms*), Steinbeck's internal wounding at Visalia marked him deeply, set him apart from his fellow travelers Tom Collins and Horace Bristol. Indeed, a somewhat mystified Tom Collins recalled a conversation with Steinbeck at Visalia in which the latter claimed: " '. . . something hit me and hit me hard for it hurts inside clear to the back of my head. I got pains all over my head, hard pains. Have never had pains like this before. . . .' " (Collins, "Bringing in the Sheaves," p. 225). Clearly, Steinbeck's experience opened the floodgates of his attention, created *The Grapes of Wrath*'s compelling justification, provided its haunting spiritual urgency, and rooted it in the deepest wellsprings of democratic fellow-feeling. In the same way that the rain floods the novel's concluding chapters, so the memory of Steinbeck's cataclysmic experience, his recollection of futility and impotency at Visalia, pervades the ending of the book and charges its ominous emotional climate, relieved only by Rose of Sharon's gratuitous act of sharing her breast with a starving man.

Steinbeck's deep participation in the events at Visalia also inspired his creation of Tom Joad, the slowly awakening disciple of Jim Casy, whose final acceptance of the preacher's gospel of social action occurs just as the deluge is about to begin: "Wherever they's a fight so hungry people can eat, I'll be there. Wherever they's a cop beatin' up a guy, I'll be there. If Casy knowed, why, I'll be in the way guys yell when they're mad an'—I'll be in the way kids laugh when they're hungry an' they know supper's ready. An' when our folks eat the stuff they raise an' live in the houses they build—why, I'll be there. See? God, I'm talkin' like Casy. Comes of thinkin' about him so much. Seems like I can see him sometimes' " (Chapter 28). When the apocalypse occurs, *everything* becomes a fiction, Steinbeck suggests, and *all* gestures become symbolic. Futhermore, in one of those magical transferences artists are heir to in moments of extreme exhaustion or receptivity, Steinbeck believed that Tom Joad, his fictive alter ego, not only floats above *The Grapes of Wrath*'s "last pages . . . like a spirit" (Entry #87), he imagined that Joad actually entered the novelist's work space, the private chamber of his soul: " 'Tom! Tom! Tom!' I know. It wasn't him. Yes, I think I can go on now. In fact, I feel stronger. Much stronger. Funny where the energy comes from. Now to work, only now it isn't work any more" (Entry #97). With that visitation, that benediction, Steinbeck arrived at the intersection of novel and journal, a luminous point where the life of the writer and the creator of life merge. The terms of his complex investment fulfilled, Steinbeck needed only a few more days to finish his novel.

In matters of form, style, and execution Steinbeck was persuaded or emboldened by another host of haunting voices and visions. Especially in *Grapes'* digressive intercalary chapters, Steinbeck drew on the fluid linguistic style of John Hargrave's novel, *Summer Time Ends* (1935), the daring, elastic form of John Dos Passos's *U S A* trilogy (1937), the narrative tempo of Pare Lorentz's radio drama, *Ecce Homo!*, and the sequential quality of Lorentz's films, *The Plow that Broke the Plains* (1936) and *The River* (1937), the stark visual effects of Dorothea Lange's F.S.A photographs of Dust Bowl Oklahoma and California migrant life, the poetic/photographic counterpoint of Archibald MacLeish's *Land of the Free* (1938), the reverberant rhythms of the King James Bible, the inspired mood of classical music, the poignant refrains of American folk music, the elevated timbre of the Greek epics, and the biological impetus of his own phalanx, or group-man, theory. Steinbeck's conscious and unconscious borrowings, echoes, and reverberations throughout *The Grapes of Wrath* came from a constellation of artistic, social, and intellectual sources so varied no single reckoning can do them justice. All of these elements— and more—entered the crucible of his imagination and allowed Steinbeck to transform the weight of his whole life into the new book. In *The Grapes of Wrath* the multiple streams of subjective experience, ameliorism, graphic realism, and symbolic form gather to create the "truly American book" (Entry #18) Steinbeck had planned.

As a result of shifting political emphases, the enlightened recommendations of the La Follette Committee (that the National Labor Relations Act include farm workers), the effects of loosened labor laws (California's discriminatory "anti-migrant" law, established in 1901, was struck down by the Supreme Court in 1941), the creation of compulsory military service, and the inevitable recruitment of migrant families into defense plant and shipyard jobs caused by the booming economy of World War II (California growers soon complained of an acute shortage of seasonal labor), the particular set of epochal conditions that crystallized Steinbeck's awareness in the first place passed from his view (though not necessarily ours, if we witness the continuing struggles of Mexican-American farm laborers since then). Like other momentous American novels that embody the bitter, often tragic, transition from one way of life to another, *The Grapes of Wrath* possessed, among its other attributes, perfect timing. Its appearance permanently changed the literary landscape of the United States.

The Grapes of Wrath also changed Steinbeck forever. Many "have speculated," his biographer writes, "about what happened to change Steinbeck after *The Grapes of Wrath*. One answer is that what happened was the writing of the novel itself" (Benson, *True Adventures of John Steinbeck*, p. 392). Here, perhaps, is a private tragedy, a cautionary tale, to parallel the tragic aspects of his fiction: an isolated individual writer composed a novel that extolled a social group's capacity for survival in a hostile economic world, but he was himself so nearly unraveled in the process that the unique qualities—the angle of vision, the vital signature, the moral indignation—that made his art exemplary in the first place could never be repeated with the same integrated force. Although he published prolifically after *The Grapes of Wrath*, it would be twelve years before Steinbeck summoned the resources to attempt, in *East of Eden*, another "big" book with a similarly exalted conception and theme. A less hardy writer might have become an anachronism after the success of a celebrated novel like *The Grapes of Wrath*, but Steinbeck showed the capacity to survive through change. His new writing lacked the aggressive bite of his earlier work (he adamantly refused to repeat himself), but it had the virtue of being so different that it generally kept him from becoming a parody of himself. After 1940 much of his important writing centered on explorations of a new topic—the dimensions of individual choice and imaginative consciousness. A prophetic post-modernist, Steinbeck's real subject in *Cannery Row, East of Eden, Sweet Thursday, The Winter of Our Discontent*, and *Journal of a Novel* was the creative process itself.

The mystery of creativity was on his mind during Christmas Week 1950, when Steinbeck was sifting through the memorabilia of his past. His impending marriage to Elaine Scott was about to signal another major turn in his life. He had been married twice before—to Carol Henning (1930–1943), and to Gwyn Conger (1943–1948). The first marriage resulted in some of his most famous books; the second marriage produced two sons and much of the material for *East of Eden*, which he would begin writing a month after his wedding to Elaine. The third, and last, marriage promoted emotional stability, and coincided with the international spread of his fame. One of the items Steinbeck came across in his nostalgic mood was the handwritten journal he had kept when he worked on *The Grapes of Wrath*. He sent it to Pat Covici at The Viking Press, with a letter that read in part: "Very many times I have been tempted to destroy this book. It is an account very personal and in many instances purposely obscure. But recently I reread it and only after all this time did the unconscious pattern emerge. It is true that this book is full of my own weaknesses, of complaints and violence. These are just as apparent as they ever were. What a complainer I am. But in rereading, those became less important and the times and the little histories seemed to be more apparent. . . . I had not realized that so much happened during the short period of the actual writing of *The Grapes of Wrath*—things that happened to me and to you and to the world. But a browsing through will refresh your memory." Steinbeck had two requests: that the journal not be printed in his lifetime; and that it should be made available to his children, Thom (aged 6) and John (aged 4), if they should ever want to "look behind the myth and hearsay and flattery and slander a disappeared man becomes and to know to some extent what manner of man their father was."[16]

Steinbeck's paternalistic concern formed one of the basic impulses for *East of Eden*, which was written in 1951 expressly for his sons. The process of its composition, recorded in the same oversized ledger book with the novel, was published separately, and posthumously, as *Journal of a Novel: The* East of Eden *Letters*. Although the compulsion to write *East of Eden* had been on his mind for several years, its particular ambience was prompted by Steinbeck's rediscovery of his *Grapes of Wrath* journal. Even as he stood poised to enter the longest writing job of his life (*Grapes* took five months of sustained labor, *East of Eden* required nine; both were consummate acts of faith), Steinbeck couldn't quite escape the influence of his earlier life. The passage from California in 1938 to New York in 1950 wasn't as long, or as far, as he imagined, though getting back was another matter.

NOTES

1. The most useful compendium on the controversial background, reception, and reputation of Steinbeck's book is Warren French's *A Companion to* The Grapes of Wrath (New York: The Viking Press, 1963), which includes ample selections of historical, factual, and critical material, all linked with an excellent running commentary. (French's invaluable little book deserves to be updated and reprinted.) The quotes by Eleanor Roosevelt (from her syndicated column, "My Day," June 28, 1939) and Congressman Boren (from *Congressional Record*, 76th Con., 3rd Sess., pt. 13, LXXXVI, 1940) appear on pages 131 and 126, respectively. In April 1940, after inspecting California migrant camps, Mrs. Roosevelt said, "I have never thought *The Grapes of Wrath* was exaggerated." Gratefully, Steinbeck responded, ". . . thank you for your words. I have been called a liar so constantly that . . . I wonder whether I may not have dreamed the things I saw and heard in the period of my research." For current overviews of the novel's public reception, critical evaluation, and place among 1930s art, see Peter Lisca's helpful Viking Critical Edition of *The Grapes of Wrath: Text and Criticism* (New York: The Viking Press, 1972); Ray Lewis White, "*The Grapes of Wrath* and the Critics of 1939," *Resources for American Literary Study*, 13 (Autumn 1983), 134–64; John Ditsky's comprehen-

sive introduction to his edition of *Critical Essays on* The Grapes of Wrath (Boston: G. K. Hall, 1989); Richard H. Pells's perceptive *"Radical Visions and American Dreams: Culture and Social Thought in the Depression Years* (Middletown, CT: Wesleyan University Press, 1973); and David P. Peller's energetic but sometimes cranky *Hope Among Us Yet: Social Criticism and Social Solace in Depression America* (Athens: University of Georgia Press, 1987).

2. John Steinbeck to Pascal Covici, January 16, 1939. In Elaine Steinbeck and Robert Wallsten, eds., *Steinbeck: A Life in Letters* (New York: The Viking Press, 1975), p. 178. Hereafter entered in text of my Introduction. Steinbeck's proprietary attitude toward his recently completed novel, so passionately defended in his January 16 letter to Covici, began to fade with each subsequent writing project. By 1955, invited to respond to a couple of diametrically opposed scholarly essays on *The Grapes of Wrath* which had recently been published in *The Colorado Quarterly*, Steinbeck was content to make only modest claims for his greatest book: "I don't think the *Grapes of Wrath* is obscure in what it tries to say. As to its classification and pickling, I have neither opinion nor interest. It's just a book, interesting I hope, instructive in the same way the writing instructed me. Its structure is very carefully worked out and it is no more intended to be inspected than is the skeletal structure of a pretty girl. Just read it, don't count it!" Steinbeck's complete "A Letter on Criticism" is readily available in E. W. Tedlock and C. V. Wicker, eds., *Steinbeck and His Critics: A Record of Twenty-five Years* (Albuquerque: University of New Mexico Press, 1957), pp. 52–53.

3. Jackson J. Benson had compiled the most useful account of Carol Steinbeck's background, life, and political enthusiasms. See his *The True Adventures of John Steinbeck, Writer* (New York: The Viking Press, 1984), passim. Hereafter entered in the text of my Introduction. Contrary to what most critics have observed—or wished—Steinbeck was not very much interested in doctrinaire political theories at this point of his career. Benson sets the record straight in his *True Adventures of John Steinbeck*, and in his subsequent "Through a Political Glass, Darkly: The Example of John Steinbeck," *Studies in American Fiction*, 12 (Spring 1984), 45–59. Carol, a liberal feminist ahead of her time, was a fascinating person who deserves an accurate biography of her

own. California journalist Gene Detro has made a gossipy beginning, though the tone of his writing is unfairly biased against John. Consult "Carol—The Woman Behind the Man," The Monterey Herald *Weekend Magazine*, June 10, 1984, 3–6, and "The Truth About Steinbeck (Carol and John)," *Creative States Quarterly*, 2 (1985), 12–13, 16.

4. Telegram in the Annie Laurie Williams Papers, Rare Book and Manuscript Library, Columbia University. Pare Lorentz (b. 1905) was another of those forward-looking, enormously gifted men Steinbeck struck up working friendships with in the late 1930s. He had been a movie critic, syndicated political columnist, essayist, short story writer, and documentarian, whose first books, *Censorship: The Private Lives of the Movies* (with Max Ernst), and *The Roosevelt Year: 1933*, appeared in 1930 and 1934, respectively. In two years, working as author, director, and producer on relatively modest budgets from President Franklin D. Roosevelt's New Deal-inspired Resettlement Administration Lorentz had made a couple of pioneering documentary films. Both *The Plow that Broke the Plains* (1936) and *The River* (1937) dealt with human displacement and natural erosion caused by the Dust Bowl and Mississippi Valley floods, themes which were close to Steinbeck's own. Lorentz, one of the most innovative artists of his age, directed the fledgling United States Film Service from mid 1938 through its demise in March 1940. The most detailed account of Lorentz's life and art is in Robert L. Snyder, *Pare Lorentz and the Documentary Film* (Norman: University of Oklahoma Press, 1968). Lorentz met Steinbeck for the first time in Los Gatos in February 1938, when Steinbeck was writing "L'Affaire Lettuceberg," a precursor to *The Grapes of Wrath*. After their initial meeting, the dynamic Lorentz became an increasingly important figure in the novelist's life, providing everything from practical advice on politics and filmmaking (they never made *In Dubious Battle*, but he hired Steinbeck to help with the filming of *The Fight for Life* in Chicago in April 1939) to spirited artistic encouragement, as Steinbeck's numerous references to Lorentz throughout *Working Days* indicate. Although Lorentz would not claim influence on *The Grapes of Wrath* (Pare Lorentz/Robert DeMott, telephone interview, March 22, 1988), Steinbeck thought otherwise, as he told Joseph Henry Jackson, ca. April 1939: "Where I see the likeness now is in the chapter of the route

where the towns are named [Ed.—Chapter 12]. I have little doubt that the Lorentz River is strong in that. But the other [Ed.—interchapters of *The Grapes of Wrath*]—maybe influenced by Dos Passos to some extent. . . . Quoted in Robert DeMott, *Steinbeck's Reading: A Catalogue of Books Owned and Borrowed* (New York: Garland, 1984), p. 142. In "Dorothea Lange: Camera with a Purpose," published in T. J. Maloney, ed., *US Camera 1941, Volume 1: "America"* (New York: Duell, Sloan and Pearce, 1940), Pare Lorentz stated that Lange's photographs and Steinbeck's novel ". . . have done more for these tragic nomads [Ed.—migrant workers] than all the politicians in the country. It again is a triumph of art over politics; or specifically, another proof that good art is good propaganda" (p. 96).

5. Steinbeck's disillusion with his marriage to Carol is graphically revealed in two sources (both so full of venom and convenient lapses that they need to be employed judiciously): a series of confessional letters to his agent Mavis McIntosh, written between May and September 1941, now at the University of Virginia Library; and his second wife's recollections, " 'The Closest Witness': The Autobiographical Reminiscences of Gwyndolyn Conger Steinbeck," a 1979 MA thesis at Stephen F. Austin State University, transcribed and edited by Terry G. Halladay from original audio tapes recorded by Gwyn. (NOTE: In late 1941 or early 1942 Gwendolyn changed the spelling of her name to Gwyndolyn; except for those instances where Steinbeck uses the earlier spelling, all references to her in *Working Days* will be spelled with a *y*, as she preferred.) See also Benson, *True Adventures of John Steinbeck* (p. 460), who writes that Steinbeck ". . . perceived Carol as the cause of his malaise and Gwyn as the one person who could give him peace."

6. For background on the Depression, the migrant labor issue and its historical evolvement, the Farm Security Administration programs and/or Tom Collins's pivotal role as a camp manager, the following are recommended: Carey McWilliams, *Factories in the Field: The Story of Migratory Farm Labor in California* (Boston: Little, Brown, 1939), still the most telling testimony and companion to the veracity of *The Grapes of Wrath* (Chapters XVI and XVII of McWilliams's sociological study cover ground plowed by Steinbeck's novel, including Collins's reports, and the disaster at Nipomo); Sidney Baldwin's detailed but long-winded

*Poverty and Politics: The Rise and Decline of the Farm Security Admin-
istration* (Chapel Hill: University of North Carolina Press, 1968); Walter
J. Stein's eminently readable *California and the Dust Bowl Migration*
(Westport, CT: Greenwood Press, 1973); and Dick Meister and Anne
Loftis's excellent *A Long Time Coming: The Struggle to Unionize America's Farm Workers* (New York: Macmillan, 1977), to which I am indebted at the end of my Introduction for information about the "resolution"
of the Dust Bowl Refugees' plight. Although he has updated it twice
(once for *True Adventures of John Steinbeck,* and once for inclusion in
Ditsky's anthology on *The Grapes of Wrath*), the most informative, best-
illustrated study ever done on Collins is still Jackson J. Benson's original
version: " 'To Tom, Who Lived It': John Steinbeck and the Man from
Weedpatch," *Journal of Modern Literature,* 5 (April 1976), 151–210.
In unpublished correspondence, written ca. January 20, 1939, Steinbeck told Annie Laurie Williams: "Letter from Tom. He's sneaking a
new camp into the pea picking district and has to do it at night. . . . When
he gets a fence and a flag up they don't dare bother him because he's
on government land then—so he gets his fence and his flag up at night.
It's very melodramatic but the only way. The Associated Farmers would
kill him if they could." (Annie Laurie Williams Papers, Rare Book and
Manuscript Library, Columbia University.)

7. Annie Laurie Williams to John Steinbeck, Letter, July 2, 1938.
Benson gives no indication that an edition of Collins's reports went
beyond the stage of being rejected by Covici-Friede, who thought the
reports too sectional for wide interest (an odd decision for such a socially
minded house). In breaking news of Pat Covici's decision, Steinbeck
wrote Collins in the spring (?) of 1937 (not, I suggest, as Benson dates
it, in 1938): "The only thing left to do that I can think of is to utilize
the material in other forms. You know of course my plans for the long
novel dealing with the migrant [Ed.—probably "The Oklahomans"]. I
can use the great gobs of information. But the thing that hurts me is
that I had hoped that from this piece of work which I still think is the
finest social study I have ever seen, you could make a little money to
carry on with. . . ." Quoted in Benson, " 'To Tom, Who Lived It' " (p.
205), and in more truncated form in *True Adventures of John Steinbeck*
(p. 376). In constructing my version of events I have also relied on

unpublished letters by Annie Laurie Williams to Steinbeck on January 4, 1937, and November 18, 1937. The latter concludes: ". . . Tom's new material is fine. Mavis has it out with a publisher now. I just had a nice letter from Tom and am answering it right away. I sure do like that man and think it is a privilege to have him for a friend. Know you must have enjoyed your days with him." (Annie Laurie Williams Papers, Rare Book and Manuscript Library, Columbia University.)

8. For the background of Collins's memoir, variously called "They Die to Live," and "Bringing in the Sheaves," consult Benson's 1976 *Journal of Modern Literature* essay, " 'To Tom, Who Lived It' " (pp. 206–10). Benson's piece concludes with an appendix which reproduces Steinbeck's "Foreword," and prints those sections of "Bringing in the Sheaves" in which Steinbeck appears (pp. 211–32). Hereafter entered in the text of my Introduction.

9. John Steinbeck, interview with Herbert Kretzmer, London *Daily Express*, January 15, 1965. "What some people find in religion a writer may find in his craft . . . a kind of breaking through to glory," Steinbeck added.

10. John Steinbeck, "California's Harvest Gypsies," Chapter 1, San Francisco *News*, October 5, 1936, p. 3. Uniformly referred to as "The Harvest Gypsies," Steinbeck's series, with minor alterations in the text, and with the addition of a piece that appeared first on April 15, 1938, in The Monterey *Trader*, was reprinted as a pamphlet, *Their Blood Is Strong* (San Francisco: Simon J. Lubin Society, 1938). The text of this booklet is available in French, ed., *A Companion to* The Grapes of Wrath (pp. 53–92). The whitewashed answer to "shiftless Okies" of *Their Blood Is Strong* and *The Grapes of Wrath* appeared from Frank J. Taylor in *Forum*, CII (November 1939), reprinted in Peter Lisca's convenient The Grapes of Wrath: *Text and Criticism* (pp. 643–56). It was one of many unsuccessful knee-jerk attempts to discredit the accuracy of Steinbeck's charges. Benson, *True Adventures of John Steinbeck* (pp. 418–25), is especially informative about various responses to Steinbeck's portrait of California migrant conditions.

11. Louis Walther, "Oklahomans Steinbeck's Theme," San Jose *Mercury Herald*, January 8, 1938, p. 12. Obviously in *The Grapes of Wrath* Steinbeck did not abandon the land-hunger theme or his belief that the

migrants represented a specific phalanx group within the large mass movement the nation was experiencing in the 1930s. They would change California, Steinbeck later said in a self-created interview, because ". . . they are brave, because although the technique of their life is difficult and complicated, they meet it with increasing strength, because they are kind, humorous and wise, because their speech has the metaphor and flavor and imagery of poetry, because they can resist and fight back and because I believe that out of those qualities will grow a new system and a new life which will be better than anything we have had before." Quoted in Lisca, ed., The Grapes of Wrath: *Text and Criticism* (p. 862).

12. John Steinbeck to Elizabeth Otis, May 1938. In Florian J. Shasky and Susan F. Riggs, eds., *Letters to Elizabeth: A Selection of Letters from John Steinbeck to Elizabeth Otis* (San Francisco: Book Club of California, 1978), p. 7. Steinbeck was "treasonable enough" to believe that California subverted human liberty with its own brand of fascism. For a long time after the lettuce strike, he feared that vigilantism in Salinas would continue to suppress workers' democratic rights. In this statement, written in November 1937, and published in May 1938, he established a telling connection between tyranny at home and abroad: "Just returned from a little tour in the agricultural fields of California. We have our own fascist groups out here. They haven't bombed open towns yet but in Salinas last year tear gas was thrown in a Union Hall and through the windows of workingmen's houses. That's rather close, isn't it? Your question as to whether I am for Franco is rather insulting. Have you seen anyone not actuated by greed who was for Franco? No, I'm not for Franco and his Moors and Italians and Germans. But some Americans are. Some Americans were for the Hessians England sent against our own revolutionary army. They were for Hessians because they were selling things to them. The descendants of some of these Americans are still very rich and still touchy concerning the American Way, and our 'ancient liberties.' I am treasonable enough not to believe in the liberty of a man or a group to exploit, torment, or slaughter other men or groups. I believe in the despotism of human life and happiness against the liberty of money and possessions." In *Writers Take Sides: Letters about the war in Spain from 418 American authors* (New York: The League of American Writers, 1938), pp. 56–57.

13. Letter in the Annie Laurie Williams Papers, Rare Book and Manuscript Library, Columbia University.

14. An uncut version of Steinbeck's letter can be found in Lewis Gannett, "Steinbeck's Way of Writing," which served as his Introduction to Pascal Covici's enlarged second edition of *The Portable Steinbeck* (New York: The Viking Press, 1946), pp. xxi–xxiii, and in Tedlock and Wicker, eds., *Steinbeck and His Critics: A Record of Twenty-five Years* (pp. 32–34). Until now little has been known about New York's response. On May 24, 1938, Annie Laurie Williams replied: "I admire you for having the courage of your convictions and know you would feel better if you could have heard what Elizabeth and Pat both said when they read your letter . . . [W]e all admire you more than ever for sticking by your instincts about your work." (Annie Laurie Williams Papers, Rare Book and Manuscript Library, Columbia University.)

15. Years later, Steinbeck told a British interviewer that, following his experiences at Visalia, he had written *The Grapes of Wrath* "protesting at what I had seen . . . during the migration of thousands of dispossessed families. I saw people starve to death. That's not just a resounding phrase. They starved to death. They dropped dead." Quoted in "The wrath *hasn't* left Steinbeck," London *Daily Mail*, September 18, 1961, p. 8. Furthermore, Steinbeck had apparently agreed to collaborate with Horace Bristol, not simply on a piece for *Life* magazine, which has commonly been supposed (in his letters to Elizabeth Otis, Steinbeck talked only of invited assignments for *Life*, which he agreed to, and for *Fortune*, which he rejected as being the wrong audience for his efforts), but on an entire book devoted to the Okies' travail. The book would incorporate Steinbeck's text and Bristol's photographs, in the manner of Margaret Bourke-White and Erskine Caldwell's 1937 book, *You Have Seen Their Faces* (Horace Bristol/Robert DeMott, letter, April 26, 1988). After his traumatic encounter at Visalia, however, Steinbeck knew he had witnessed the stuff of tragedy, and he decided once again to terminate a proposed collaboration. Some of his sentences from *The Grapes of Wrath* were later chosen to accompany Bristol's photographs of Visalia, published in *Life*, June 5, 1939 (pp. 66–67). Bristol's photographs appeared a second time in *Life*, on February 19, 1940 (pp. 10–11), in order to prove the authenticity of John Ford's movie version: "These photographs, here republished, were taken by

Life Photographer Horace Bristol in March 1938, when he and Author John Steinbeck toured the Okie camps in search of material for a picture book and a story for *Life*. The picture book was dropped to make way for the best-selling novel called *The Grapes of Wrath*. Never before had the facts behind a great work of fiction been so carefully researched by the newscamera." Although Bristol and Steinbeck participated in the same devastating events at Visalia, they "saw" things far differently (despite *Life*'s contentions), and ultimately used their experiences in wholly opposite ways. Bristol's photographs speak for themselves; Steinbeck's visual realism became a means to a symbolic end. Bristol's brilliant photograph of a young mother nursing her child was obviously the prototype for maternal Rose of Sharon, but Steinbeck's "use" of that image, by having her give her breast to a total stranger, represented a leap beyond facticity, a leap Bristol himself admitted he did not fully understand: "So far as I know, this event was a figment of Steinbeck's imagination. I won't say it didn't happen—just that it didn't happen in my presence. I still look with compassion at the print of the young mother who was Rose of Sharon's prototype, her breasts swollen with milk, but nursing a young infant instead of an old man. My impression was that Steinbeck wrote this episode to shock and titillate his readers. . . ." See "Faces of 'The Grapes of Wrath,' " Photographs and story by Horace Bristol, photo captions by John Steinbeck, *This World* (San Francisco *Examiner* Magazine), October 25, 1987, p. 14, and a glossier portfolio in his "Documenting *The Grapes of Wrath*," *The Californians*, January/February 1988, pp. 40–47. Also consult Carol Shloss, *In Visible Light, Photography and the American Writer: 1840–1940* (New York: Oxford University Press, 1987), pp. 201–29, for an intriguing look at Steinbeck's relatedness to documentary photography, especially Dorothea Lange's.

16. Letter, December 1950, in the Pascal Covici Archive at Harry Ransom Humanities Research Center, University of Texas, Austin. A stenographer at The Viking Press transcribed Steinbeck's handwritten journal manuscript, but then destroyed or lost the original holograph version (all efforts to locate it have failed). Although Steinbeck might have reviewed—perhaps even reread—the typed version, he apparently did not make any corrections in it. This present edition (with Steinbeck's entry numbers normalized) provides an unexcised readable text of the

typed journal. Annotations and explanatory notes (indicated by asterisks in the text) appear at the end of the book where they will not impede the narrative flow of Steinbeck's entries. Grammatical/spelling regularizations have been kept to a silent minimum, a pleasurable result of having a substantially clear and intelligible typescript to work with in the first place.

" 'You can check out any time you like, but you can never leave.' "

The Eagles,
"Hotel California"

PART I:

Prelude

(February 1938)

For the moment now the financial burdens have been re-moved. But it is not permanent. I was not made for success. I find myself now with a growing reputation. In many ways it is a terrible thing. . . . Among other things I feel that I have put something over. That this little success of mine is cheating.

—Steinbeck, in a 1936 entry in his
Long Valley/Of Mice and Men ledger book.
(Courtesy of Steinbeck Research Center, San Jose State University)

Commentary

Steinbeck composed his first journal entry on or about February 7, 1938, shortly after the death of his brother-in-law, and just prior to at least two separate field trips (in February, and again in early March) to observe the horrid conditions at Visalia. He had recently abandoned "The Oklahomans" and in its place had begun "L'Affaire Lettuceberg," an incendiary tract that occupied his attention until May 1938, when—in disgust at having compromised his own ability—he destroyed the 70,000-word manuscript.

The winter of 1938 was a period of intense activity and vexation for Steinbeck. In January and February California was being inundated by torrential rains ("This is the 19th day of rain," Steinbeck wrote Elizabeth Otis, his literary agent and confidante, on February 14); the deluge provided a symbolic backdrop for Steinbeck's pessimism. He would be thirty-six years old on February 27, but he hardly felt like celebrating. His growing sense of anger about the plight of Visalia's starving migrants colored nearly everything in his life, including, temporarily, his will to write. "Funny how mean and little books become in the face of such tragedies," he confessed to his agent. As if that weren't enough to undercut his emotional equilibrium, several other personal disturbances occurred in February, including a trumped-up paternity charge (which was eventually dropped), and the dissolution of an intimate friendship with George Albee, a fellow novelist who had become jealous of Steinbeck's artistic achievements. "I've needed help and trust and the benefit of the doubt," Steinbeck told Albee in his characteristically frank way, "because I've tried to beat the system which destroys every writer, and from you have come only wounds and kicks in the face" (Steinbeck and Wallsten, eds., *Steinbeck: A Life in Letters*, p. 157).

Privately, Steinbeck was contending with the ironic fruits of his public success. Deeper yet, he struggled with the paralyzing fear that his talent was inadequate for the writing task at hand. His success had been honorably earned, but Steinbeck, ever his own harshest critic, remained unconvinced. In fact, self-denunciation became a repeated theme throughout the entire journal. His brilliant novella, *Of Mice and Men*, published by Covici-Friede a year earlier, had sold well over 120,000 copies, thanks in part to its being a Book-of-the-Month Club selection. More immediately, the play version (directed by George S. Kaufman, and starring Wallace Ford, Broderick Crawford, and Clare Luce), which had opened at New York's Music Box Theatre on November 23, 1937, was still packing the house three months later. It eventually ran for 207 performances and won, that April, the prestigious New York Drama Circle Critics' Award. In addition, Pare Lorentz, whom Steinbeck had been expecting in Los Gatos since January (he finally showed up around February 13), wanted to discuss filming *In Dubious Battle*. And later in the month both *Fortune* and *Life* magazines wanted Steinbeck to write essays on migrant conditions. His name had suddenly become a hot property, with all the attendant traps, seductions, and demands that accompany rapid fame. (As bad as things seemed in the winter of 1938, they were only a minor rehearsal for the turbulent drama to come during the next few years.) A month or so before his opening journal entry, Steinbeck complained to Joseph and Charlotte Jackson:

> I get sadder and sadder. The requests and demands for money pour in. It is perfectly awful. WPA worker in pencil from Illinois—"you have got luck and I got no luck. My boy needs a hundderd dollar operation. Please send a hundderd dollars. I will pay it back." That sort of thing. Getting worse every day. . . . Someone told a Salinas ladies' club that I had made three hundred thousand dollars this year. That's the sort of thing. It is driving me crazy. "If you will just send me a railroad ticket to Boise I can come to California and get rid of my rheumatism." They're nightmarish. Some may be phonys but so damned many of them aren't. . . . The damned things haunt me. There's no way of getting over the truth . . . that we have very little money. . . . Its nibbling me to death (Steinbeck and Wallsten, eds., *Steinbeck: A Life in Letters*, p. 153).

Depressed by requests for money, tainted by the public aspects of fame, and shocked by the workers' plight, Steinbeck felt so tired he wished he were dead. Instead, he threw himself into the writing of "L'Affaire Lettuceberg" as a way of exorcising his frustrating anger and reclaiming his discipline.

Entry #1
February [7?] 1938—[Monday]

It seems to be necessary to write things down. Can't stop it. February now and raining steadily. The play M & M [Ed.—*Of Mice and Men*] went on and is a success. And with its success, I know there is never to be any ease, any pleasure for me. People I liked have changed. Thinking there is money, they want it. And even if they don't want anything, they watch me and they aren't natural any more. Gene* died two weeks ago; it could so easily have been me and I wish so much it had been. I'm tired of living completely tired. I'm tired of the struggle against all the forces that this miserable success has brought against me. I don't know whether I could write a decent book now. That is the greatest fear of all. I'm working at it but I can't tell. Something is poisoned in me. You pages—ten of you—you are the dribble cup—you are the cloth to wipe up the vomit. Maybe I can get these fears and disgusts on you and then burn you up. Then maybe I won't be so haunted. Have to pretend it's that way anyhow. There's Lorentz who should be here by now and there are the starving people of Visalia and Nipomo.* I really don't care about the moving picture. Really don't—but those people who are starving—what can be done? And the people with panaceas of all kinds. Will you lend your name to this and to this? What do I care about my name? It is battered and completely out of shape anyway. It hasn't any meaning and I haven't any meaning. "Seen about your luck." I got no luck. "Send one hundred dollars." Luck! He thinks it is luck. He is poor and he thinks I am rich. And he seen about my luck. In the cheap welter, he seen about my luck. He seen about my destruction only he couldn't understand that. The Greeks seem to have known about this dark relationship between luck and destruction. It is so hard to know anything. So impossible to trust oneself. Even to know what there is to trust. My will is low. I must build my will again. And I can do it even as I have done before. The time passes. The thoughts race.

PART II:

The Diary of a Book
(May–October 1938)

But the sureness of touch, the characters that move about, the speech that sounds like speaking, the fact that it happens, that one is never conscious of how a thing is said but only of what is said. I know the why and how of that. It's the millions of words written, all the short stories, even the ones that weren't any good. Without the millions of words written it is impossible to write a book like this. And by the same token—those millions of words are a guarantee that the last half will not falter for a moment.

—Steinbeck, on reading the manuscript
of Louis Paul's novel, *The Wrong World* (1938).
(Courtesy of University of Virginia Library)

Commentary

The following ninety-nine entries, which cover the summer and fall of 1938, constitute the truest story of the making of *The Grapes of Wrath*. They comprise Steinbeck's attempt, with a kind of scientific preciseness, "to map the actual working days and hours" of his novel, and they provide an unparalleled record of the shapings and seizings, the naked slidings, of his creative psyche. No other account matches this one for personal intensity, dedication, investment, and drama.

Unlike the sprawling, digressive entries on symbolism, characterization, and philosophy that mark Steinbeck's daily log for his 1952 novel *East of Eden* (the entries were published posthumously in 1969 as *Journal of a Novel: The East of Eden Letters*), here Steinbeck is working in a different mode—more focused and sharper, less self-reflexive and expansive, but of course no less revealing about his habitual writerly concerns. Readers accustomed to the tone of familiarity and camaraderie of *Journal of a Novel* (the entries were daily letters to Pascal Covici) will find this "diary of a book" limited in intention and scope, and hermetic—even claustrophobic—in tone and attitude. Brief, direct, staccato, these daily notes took the place of his normally voluminous "warm-up" correspondence. They helped regulate his discipline in the face of an inordinate number of interruptions—

some worthwhile, most merely bothersome—that his growing public fame had brought him. (A cheeky agent for Selznick International Pictures set the tone of the summer by requesting an "advanced reading" of the unwritten novel "to review its motion picture possibilities"; exasperated, Steinbeck directed his agents to reply that "the book will not be for sale!")

Despite the "leisurely" pace he hoped to establish for his novel, most of these entries have a breathless quality, as though they were written impatiently in shorthand. Steinbeck, it seems, could hardly wait to address the day's fictive project before his concentration and inspiration waned. Morever, the entries attest to Steinbeck's covenant with the written word. His subject was incendiary and as contemporaneous as the day's newspaper headlines, but his compact with the fiction-making process took precedence over sociological or political demands. He was writing a novel, not a journalistic tract. If this section reveals comparatively few new secrets about Steinbeck's novel, it says plenty about the tumultuous conditions of his life, and his mode of working, during the stretch that produced his finest novel. Like most great books, *The Grapes of Wrath* was certainly not created in a vacuum.

Understandably, maintaining his intensity was paramount. Without looking back, Steinbeck overcame the disappointing "L'Affaire Lettuceberg," which he had destroyed in mid-May; within a week, or perhaps ten days at the most, he started headlong on the new, unnamed manuscript, which wasn't actually titled *The Grapes of Wrath* until early September. However, his work on "L'Affaire" wasn't wasted, and certainly cannot be underestimated, because it cleared the way for *The Grapes* by purging his deep personal depression, and by exorcising his base instincts, including unchecked anger and the desire for his own brand of artistic vengeance. Naturally, his partisanship for the migrants and his sense of indignation at California's labor situation carried over to the new book, but they were given a more articulate, and therefore believable, shape. The whole process of passing through a "bad" book proved beneficial. Without stopping to analyze its effects, he told Elizabeth Otis on June 1, ". . . it is a nice thing to be working and believing in my work again. I hope I can keep the drive all fall. I like it. I only feel whole and well when it is this way. I don't yet understand what happened or why the bad book should have cleared the air so completely for this one. I am simply glad that it is so" (Steinbeck and Wallsten, eds., *Steinbeck: A Life in Letters*, p. 167).

The epic scale and engaged purpose of *Grapes* had been building for some time, but apparently crystallized between May 15 and May 25, 1938. During that time—perhaps the most fertile germinative moment in Steinbeck's writing life—the organizational plan of the novel, with its alternating chapters of exposition and narrative, leaped to life in his mind. Judged against his contemporary, William Faulkner, Steinbeck was not a sophisticated literary practitioner, and while he wrote nothing to rival the architectural virtuosity of *Absalom, Absalom!* (1936), he did achieve in *The Grapes of Wrath* a compelling combination of individual style, visual realism, and rambunctious symphonic form that was at once accessible and experimental. Furthermore, as these entries suggest, he actually envisioned the novel whole, all the way down to the subversive last scene "ready for so long" (Rose of Sharon giving her breast to a starving man), which became both the propelling image of the book and the imaginative climax toward which the entire novel moved.

Indeed, except for a few particulars, *The Grapes of Wrath* was written with remarkably preordained motion and directed passion. Steinbeck apparently did not work from a formal outline (nothing of the kind has ever turned up); rather, he sketched out the novel in his head—in aggregate first, then followed by a brief planning session each day. He had plenty of questions about his ability to execute the plan, but few about the plan itself; from the outset he knew the direction his book and his characters would take. Unlike his other "big" novel, *East of Eden,* which discovered its form (and sometimes its content) in the act of composition, *The Grapes of Wrath* was an intuited whole. This journal records the sweaty process through which Steinbeck liberated his materials, gave them direction, shape, and form nearly commensurate with his primary vision. *The Grapes of Wrath* embodies the form of his devotion: in the entire 200,000-word handwritten manuscript the number of deletions and emendations is proportionately so few and infrequent as to be nearly nonexistent. (The textual changes—mostly minor—occurred in Carol's typescript and on Viking Press's galley sheets.) Ironically, though Steinbeck severely doubted his own artistic ability, in writing *The Grapes of Wrath* he was creating with the full potency of his imaginative powers. His ability to execute a work of its magnitude so flawlessly places him among the premier creative talents of his age. From the vantage point of history, the venture stands as one of those happy occasions when a writer simply wrote better than he thought he could.

Undeterred by the failure of his vigilante novel, Steinbeck set out immediately to establish a unified work rhythm, a "single track mind" that would allow him to complete the enormous task in one hundred days, or approximately five months. Though he had written steadily throughout the 1930s (he published eleven books and/or limited editions in the first eight years of the decade), the work never seemed to get easier. Averaging 2,000 words a day (some days as few as 800, some days, when the juices were flowing, as many as 2,200), Steinbeck began the novel unhurriedly to keep its "tempo" under control, hoping at the same time to keep alive the large rhythmic structure of the novel. This he accomplished by listening to Tchaikovsky's ballet *Swan Lake*, and Igor Stravinsky's "very fine" *Symphony of Psalms*. Music inspired him by setting a mood conducive to writing and by establishing a rhythm for the day's work. Even more important, classical music provided Steinbeck with formal, harmonic, and lyric analogies for his fiction. In writing *The Grapes*, he said, "I have worked in a musical technique . . . and have tried to use the forms and the mathematics of music rather than those of prose. . . . In composition, in movement, in tone and in scope it is symphonic" (John Steinbeck/Merle Armitage, letter, February 17, 1939; courtesy of University of Virginia Library). The contrapuntal form of the novel, with its alternating chapters, its consonant combination of major chords, is deeply rooted in the attentiveness, the tonal acuity, of Steinbeck's ear. (But not to put too fine a construction on this, when Steinbeck didn't have his music, he listened to the washing machine—its metronomic beat was soothing, at least for a while).

As Steinbeck's anxiety escalated during the late summer, his pace became increasingly frenetic, his attention splintered, and his work became a chore. "Was ever a book written under greater difficulty?" he asked himself on September 1. That he completed the novel within the time he had allotted testifies to his discipline, resilience, willpower, and singleness of purpose. This story of the composition of his novel is a dramatic testimony to triumph over intrusions, obstacles, and self-inflicted doubts. Nearly each day brought unsolicited requests for his name and new demands on his time, including unscheduled visitors, unanticipated disruptions and reversals. Domestic relations with Carol were frequently strained, even hostile (Steinbeck apparently subscribed to the theory that sexual intercourse dissipated the creative drive). Throughout the summer a procession of house guests trooped to Los Gatos, including family members and longtime friends Carlton

Sheffield, Ed Ricketts, and the Lovejoys, plus new acquaintances, such as Wallace and Martha Ford, Broderick Crawford, Charlie Chaplin, and Pare Lorentz.

As if that weren't enough to erode the novelist's intitial composure and solitude, the Steinbecks' tiny house on Greenwood Lane was besieged with the noise of neighborhood building, which nearly drove them to distraction. "This place is getting built up and we have to move. Houses all around us now and so we will get back farther in the country. . . . I can hear the neighbors' stomachs rumbling," he complained to Elizabeth Otis on July 22 (Steinbeck and Wallsten, eds., *Steinbeck: A Life in Letters*, p. 169). By midsummer, hoping for permanent sanctuary, they began looking at secluded real estate, finally settling on the Biddle ranch, a forty-seven-acre spread in the Santa Cruz Mountains above Los Gatos. Even though it was the most stunning location they had ever seen, its original homestead was in utter disrepair, so besides buying the land the Steinbecks would also have to build a new house, and that too became the source of additional frustrations and distractions. They didn't move there until November 1938—the month after the novel was finished (all final corrections of the typescript and galley proofs took place at the Biddle ranch)—but preparations for its purchase took up a great deal of Steinbeck's time and energy from mid-July onward.

Although Steinbeck insisted on effacing his own presence in *The Grapes of Wrath,* the fact is that it was a very personal book, invested with biographical import. In a general way, the "plodding" pace of Steinbeck's writing schedule informed the slow, "crawling" movement of the Joads' journey, while the harried beat of his own life gave the proper "feel" and tone to the beleagured Joads. Specifically, aspects of Steinbeck's life bore directly on manuscript decisions. For instance, on July 12, confused by increasing distractions and lured by the possibility of owning the Biddle ranch, Steinbeck did not know which "general" chapter he would use next. During the planning session of Wednesday morning, July 13, he settled on what would become Chapter 14, one of the most important theoretical chapters in the novel, and perhaps the most significant summation of organismal philosophy Steinbeck had yet written. The first half of the chapter augurs changes in the Western states' socioeconomic basis, and includes a paean to the universal human capacity for creation: "For man, unlike any other thing organic or inorganic in the universe, grows beyond his work, walks up the stairs of his concepts, emerges ahead of his accomplishments." The second half of the chapter expresses the central core of Steinbeck's mature phalanx theory, the creation of an aggregate, dynamic "we" from distinct, myriad selves. The summary quality of this chapter suggests that Steinbeck intended to use it later in the novel as a kind of climactic crescendo. Instead he inserted it at the midpoint of the novel for several reasons: its dithyrambic tone and heightened language reawakened his flagging attention; its optimistic, theoretical values restored focus and clarity to the narrative line; its extolment of creativity, based on humanity's willingness to "suffer and die for a concept," provided an immediate reminder that his own compositional process could be endured for the sake of the cause he espoused; and its concern for families who had lost their land may have partly assuaged his guilt, if not his sense of irony, as he was about to make the biggest property purchase of his life.

Emerging ahead of his accomplishments seemed insurmountable at times that summer, because major interruptions kept occurring, any one of which might have sidetracked a lesser writer. August proved the most embattled time of all. Early in the month Steinbeck noted in his journal: "There are now four things or five rather to write through—throat, bankruptcy, Pare, ranch, and the book" (Entry #46). His litany of woes included

Carol's painful tonsil operation, which temporarily incapacitated her; the bankruptcy of Steinbeck's publisher, Covici-Friede, which threatened the end of steady royalty payments and an uncertain publishing future for the novel he was writing; Pare Lorentz's interest in making a film version of *In Dubious Battle:* the purchase of the Biddle ranch, which Carol wanted badly and Steinbeck felt compelled to buy for her (they argued over the pressure this caused); and the book itself, still untitled (and therefore still without "being"), which now seemed more recalcitrant than ever. "My work has been slowed by many people coming and beside I think I am a little tired," he confessed to his agent. "We still haven't a name for this book. I've reached a point of weariness where it seems lousy to me. . . . Lord I hope this book is some good. Right now, it doesn't seem so" (John Steinbeck/Elizabeth Otis, letter, August 1938; courtesy of Stanford University Library). And to a fellow novelist, Steinbeck apologized for the "tangle" that prevented their usual visits. "I'm getting frantic about this work. Have to work through and around a dozen things. . . . Getting pushed around pretty much from a number of directions" (John Steinbeck/Louis Paul, postcard, August 3, 1938; courtesy of University of Virginia Library).

By mid-August, roughly halfway through the novel, Steinbeck took stock of his situation: The Viking Press had just bought his contract, hired Pat Covici as part of the deal, and planned a first edition of 15,000 copies for *The Long Valley:* a string of famous houseguests had either just departed or were scheduled to arrive; and he and Carol had closed on the purchase of the Biddle ranch. "Demoralization complete and seemingly unbeatable. So many things happening that I can't not be interested. . . . All this is more excitement than our whole lives put together. All crowded into a month. . . . My many weaknesses are beginning to show their heads. I simply must get this thing out of my system. I'm not a writer. I've been fooling myself and other people. I wish I were. This success will ruin me as sure as hell. It probably won't last, and that will be all right. I'll try to go on with work now. Just a stint every day does it. I keep forgetting" (Entry #52).

On the weekend of August 20 the elusive, peripatetic Pare Lorentz arrived (Steinbeck had not seen him since spring). As the newly appointed director of the United States Film Service, Lorentz was supervising filming of the Grand Coulee Dam construction scenes for his *Ecce Homo!* (the cinematic version was never finished). Lorentz was one of the few major artists in America working in the same arena of the "Common Man" as Steinbeck, so it should come as no surprise that the novelist considered the filmmaker a spiritual ally. "You know what I think of Pare. I'll back him and work with him to the limit. And he's about the *only* man I would do a picture with" (John Steinbeck/Elizabeth Otis, letter [August 4 and 5, 1938]; courtesy of Stanford University Library). Together they discussed further a full-length dramatic film of *In Dubious Battle*. Their plans had been in the works for several months, and between his other time-consuming duties Lorentz had already begun shopping around Hollywood for the properly liberal studio and producer (Lorentz was to direct; Steinbeck was to write the script; filming, they insisted, was to be done on location). But more importantly, Lorentz, a man of "terrific" vision and shared sympathies, made Steinbeck feel less depressed about the "temper" of the country at large, and about the novelist's own accomplishments, praising sections of Steinbeck's new book as "monumental" (Annie Laurie Williams/John Steinbeck, letter, September 9, 1938; courtesy of Rare Book and Manuscript Library, Columbia University). Temporarily buoyed up by Lorentz's prediction that the novel would be "among the greatest novels of the age," Steinbeck managed his daily stint through the "interminable details and minor crises" of August and September (Carol Steinbeck/Elizabeth Otis, letter [mid-October 1938]; courtesy of Rare Book and Manuscript Library, Columbia University).

In early October, rebuked often enough by his wife's example and by her words (Ma Joad's indomitableness owes much to Carol's spirit), Steinbeck roused himself from "self-indulgence" and "laziness" to mount the final drive. Blessedly, the last five chapters of the novel came to him so abundantly that he had more material than he could use. Some time around noon on Wednesday, October 26, he completed the last 775 words of the novel; at the bottom of the concluding manuscript page, Steinbeck, whose writing was normally minuscule, scrawled in letters an inch-and-a-half high, *END#*. It should have been cause for joyous celebration, but between bouts of bone-weary tiredness and nervous exhaustion, he felt only numbness, and maybe a little of the mysterious satisfaction that comes from giving his all. He certainly had no grasp of the book's effectiveness or its potential popularity, and he even warned The Viking Press against a large first printing. Following a four-day recuperation in San Francisco, the Steinbecks moved to their new home (still under construction), where Carol finished typing the 751-page typescript, and together they made "routine" final corrections. The only "clean" copy of the book was sent to his New York agents, McIntosh and Otis, on December 7, 1938, roughly six months after he sat down to write the novel. Elizabeth Otis's visit to Los Gatos in late December 1938, to smooth out some of Steinbeck's "rough" language, its enthusiastic reception at Viking (marred briefly by the wrangling which ensued over the novel's controversial ending) all struck the novelist as anticlimactic. (He was by then suffering from severely painful sciatica, undoubtedly caused by a herniated spinal disk, one of the ironic results of his sedentary existence.)

Right after the novel appreared in April, Steinbeck took off for the Middle West to work as an "Assistant Cameraman" for Lorentz, who was planning to film Paul de Kruif's *The Fight for Life* at Chicago's Maternity Hospital. Steinbeck appreciated the anonymity that came from long hours of hard work in a strange city, and the challenge of learning the nuts and bolts of a new artistic vehicle, but there was still an element of "pure escapism" in his trip (Pare Lorentz/Robert DeMott, telephone interview, March 22, 1988). It was a pattern Steinbeck would repeat several times over the next few years. Though he wasn't aware of it then, he had closed the door on an entire chapter of his life. The frenzied public clamor and vicious personal attacks over *The Grapes of Wrath* confirmed his worst fears about the fruits of success and pushed the tensions between the Steinbecks to the breaking point. "Something has to be worked out or I am finished writing," he told Otis on June 22, 1939. "I went south to work and I came back to find Carol just about hysterical. She had just been pushed beyond endurance" (Steinbeck and Wallsten, eds., *Steinbeck: A Life in Letters*, p. 183). Steinbeck did not quit writing, but by the early 1940s, no longer content to be the chronicler of Depression-era subjects, he went afield to find new roots, new sources. He would never be the same writer again.

Entry #2
[May 31, 1938—Tuesday]

Here is the diary of a book and it will be interesting to see how it works out. I have tried to keep diaries before but they don't work out because of the necessity to be honest. In matters where there is no definite truth, I gravitate toward the opposite. Sometimes where there is a definite truth, I am revolted by its smugness and do the same. In this however, I shall try simply to keep a record of working days and the amount done in each and the success (as far as I can know it) of the day. Just now the work goes well.* It is nearly the first of June. That means I have seven months to do this book and I should like to take them but I imagine five will be the limit. I have never taken long actually to do the writing. I want this one to be leisurely though. That is one of the reasons for the diary.

Entry #3
June 1, 1938—Wednesday

To work at 10:30. Minimum of two pages. Duke* expected today making it not so good. Yesterday turtle episode which satisfies me in a number of ways. Today's project—Joad's walk down the road and meeting with the minister [Ed.—opening section of Chapter 4]. Dinner tonight at Pauls'* with Rays* along. Day is over. Finished my two pages. I think pretty well. Casy the preacher must be strongly developed as a thoughtful, well-rounded character. Must show quickly the developing of a questing mind and a developing leadership. Duke not here yet. Tomorrow must begin relationship between these men [Ed.—Tom Joad and Jim Casy].

Entry #4
June 2 [1938]—10:30—Thursday

Drive continues. Today the argument against sin and the means of losing it—the quest for the true spirit [Ed.—middle section of Chapter 4]. This should be a good sharp section. Duke did not arrive. Probably today. Dinner at Louis's very interesting. He read two sections and there is a very fine tone to them. Conversation re hay fever, a curious rationalization. Locked her [Ed.—Steinbeck's Airedale terrier] in my bathroom last night. She was good. Weather is superb—hot but not too hot. Letter from Paul Jordan Smith* who wants to come up end of the month. One hundred days of writing will finish this book, I think. That is four months. Means I should get first draft done in October and that is allowing lots of lee way for last. Must leave room every day for further comment. Turtle sequence stands up [Ed.—Chapter 3].

Entry #5
June 3 [1938]—[Friday]

Duke arrived yesterday. Left this morning. Sue and Bob showed up this morning. Had to kick them out. Simply can't have people around on working days. Carol spending the day down on the [Ed.—Monterey] peninsula. Telephone ringing pretty badly. Suggested *The Long Valley** as title for shorts. Irritated today. People want to come to see me next Monday. Can't be. Just want to sit. Day not propitious. Have a loose feeling that makes me nervous. Will get to work and try to forget all the bothers. I get nuts if not protected from all the outside stuff. Dinner tonight at Tolertons'.* I like them very much. Must make note of work progress at the end of this day. I want to finish my stint if I possibly can. Impulses to do other things. Wind blowing over me, etc. But must continue today for sake of discipline. Well, the stint is done but I think I'll try to finish out the chapter tomorrow [Ed.—Chapter 4]. Be about one more page. Lionel Smith came over. Bob C.* and Margery Bailey* coming down tomorrow night. Glad I got done. I hate to break the discipline.

Entry #6
June 4 [1938]—2:40—Saturday

Going to do a little work today—perhaps a page to finish the chapter of Casy and Joad. If it doesn't get done, it doesn't matter. But since the next chapter [Ed.—Chapter 5] tells of the coming of the tractors and must have a symphonic overtone, and, moreover, may not be more than four or five pages long, it would be just as well to limit the day's work to this chapter. Hence this attempt. Finished Chapter II [Ed.—Chapter 4]. Now must make music again. But on Monday and that will be

Entry #7
June 6 [1938]—11:30—[Monday]

Have really only one page to do to keep up with schedule but I want to do this short over-chapter complete in one day and so I will work at it until it is done. I had wanted to hear some music first but the washing machine is going and I'll have a fairly hard time. I would do it tonight but must go to the dentist and my jaws will be battered. My whole nervous system is battered. Don't know why. I hope I am not headed for a nervous breakdown. Lack of solitude* is doing it I think. But I don't know. I am very happy in this work, I do know that. It satisfies me so far. But I wish I could have the music. I really need the music.* Too many things happening. It would be interrupted and that would be worse than not playing it at all. Well—to work and if it doesn't go well, I'll wait until the washing machine stops and then do it. Try now though. Now the two pages are done and I think well done. But there is one more day of work on the inter-chapter 3 [Ed.—

Chapter 5]. Have to make the sound of the tractors and the dust of the tractors. I'll have to have music before that, and the date will be

Entry #8
June 7 [1938]—11:00 [Tuesday]

Now it is a fairly early start. Today's work is the overtone of the tractors, the men who run them, the men they displace, the sound of them, the smell of them. I've got to get this over. Got to because this one's tone is very important—this is the eviction sound and the tonal reason for the movement. Must do it well. I am one page ahead so that if I should go no farther I should still have caught up. And so to do it. I am not frightened of this any more. Too much a part of it finally. Letter from Rodman* this morning. My traffic fine was $2.50. Thought it might be twenty-five. But now to work. Well that is finished and I hope it is good [Ed.—second half of Chapter 5]. I think it is. Now back to the particular [Ed.—the Joad narrative] again. And the date will be

Entry #9
June 8 [1938]—10:45 [Wednesday]

This is the longest diary I ever kept. Not a diary of course but an attempt to map the actual working days and hours of a novel. If a day is skipped it will show glaringly on this record and there will be some reason given for the slip. Yesterday the general and now back to the particular. I find I am not very satisfied with the numbering of these chapters. It may be that they will simply be numbered with large numerals for the general and small for the particular. The reason is that I want the reader to be able to keep them separate in his mind. Today Joad and Casy come home and find the house deserted. They meet Muley Graves and he tells them where Joad's parents are. They sleep in Muley's deserted house. Background for the moving comes in here. This is followed by the general [Ed.—Chapter 7] of the old cars, of the equipment, of the moving technique, and then the Joad family enters and the book really gets moving. Well, that's done but only a little into this chapter. I think maybe two or three more days on this chapter [Ed.—Chapter 6] I think. And tomorrow will be

Entry #10
June 9 [1938]—11:45 [Thursday]

Late start today. Last night two boys down from Stanford. They tied me in knots as nicely as I could do it to anyone when I was in Stanford. Nice kids and bright and alert ones. I like to see them and hear them. They cross examined me on the universe and man. I found difficulty in getting out of this book long enough to be anything but dull. This single track mind seems to be a narrow gauge as well. Now to the day's work and now Muley comes in and the reason for the desertion becomes apparent. Also the night comes with sleeping in the darkening plain and stars [Ed.—Chapter 6]. And after that I think a small inter chapter or maybe a large one dealing with the equipment of migration. Well here goes for Muley. Well that is done. I like Muley. He is a fine hater. Must write a few letters now.

Entry #11
June 10 [1938]—11:30 [Friday]

Friday around again. And a little mail. Wire from Crawford, letter from Ford.* Says he is going on the road with the show for which I am glad indeed for I think he is fine. I hope it has a good run. With luck I should be finished with this first draft in October sometime and then God knows what I'll do. I'll surely be ready for a rest. Sometimes now I get a little bit tired just with the multitude of this story but the movement is so fascinating that I don't stay tired. And the leisurely pace is good too. This must be a good book. It simply must. I haven't any choice. It must be far and away the best thing I have ever attempted—slow but sure, piling detail on detail until a picture and an experience emerge. Until the whole throbbing thing emerges. And I can do it. I feel very strong to do it. Today for instance into the picture is the evening and the cooking of the rabbits and the discussion of prison and punishment. And the owls and the cat catches a mouse and they sit on the sloping porch [Ed.—Chapter 6]. And tomorrow the beginning of the used car yard if I am finished with this scene. Better make this scene three pages instead of two. Because there can never be too much of background. Well to work on the characters. Friday's work is done and I think pretty good work.* Tomorrow is Saturday.

Entry #12
June 11 [1938]—10:30—Saturday

(Optional)

The placing of an optional page on Saturday is to try to maintain a certain writing speed. Then if for any reason I miss a day (and I probably shall), there will be days piled up. Two days a month in fact, to draw on. Two weeks gone now out of 20. 18 weeks to go. I figure about 200,000 words and I have 10,000 words a week as a minimum. Today I will have one spare day in case anything happens. I hope it won't, but if it does. Today Tommy Joad tells about prison and I don't know whether the chapter will finish or not. That's not the problem. Bob and Mary write they want to come down. They can't. I am well into this now and nothing is going to be allowed to interfere. When I am all done I shall relax but not until then. My life isn't very long and I must get *one* good book written before it ends. The others have been make shifts, experiments, practices. For the first time I am working on a real book that is not limited and that will take every bit of experience and thought and feeling that I have. And so to work. The page is done now but not the chapter. This is a very long chapter [Ed.—Chapter 6]. And now I have an afternoon and a day to rest but I won't rest. I know that anyway tomorrow is Sunday, a no work and no work day number.

Entry #13
June 13 [1938]—11:40—Monday

Now a new week starts and unpropitiously for me. Last night up to Rays' and drank a great deal of champagne.* I pulled my punches pretty well but I am not in the dead sober state I could wish. However, I will try to go to work. Don't have to because I have a day caught up. All sorts of things might happen in the course of this book but I must not be weak. This must be done. The failure of will even for one day has a devastating effect on the whole, far more important than just the loss of time and wordage. The whole physical basis of the novel is discipline of the writer, of his material, of the language. And sadly enough, if any of the discipline is gone, all of it suffers. And this slight fuzziness of mine may be a break in the discipline. I don't know yet. But right now I intend to find out.

Entry #14
June 14 [1938]—11:30 [Tuesday]

Yesterday was a bust. I could have forced the work out but I'd lost the flow of the book and it would have been a weak spot. Luckily I had the day to lose, but now I haven't and so, until I have piled up another reserve day, I can't lose anymore. Maybe Saturday I will try to do two pages. But right now, my job is to get my daily work done and so to it. Well, I got it done. Thank god. Stomach still not so good. Tomorrow used car yard. Must be good—and that will be—

Entry #15
June 15 [1938]—11:15 [Wednesday]

Not an early start today but it doesn't matter at all because the unity feeling is back. That is the fine thing. That makes it easy and fun to work. It is hot today. Not too hot but enough so that I am working in the lightest bathrobe and may have a shower soon. Letter from Beth* this morning about the move to Bass Lake. Letter from Fred S. about Dick's job.* Hope he gets it. Wrote to Pare asking him to bear down on it. Don't know whether he can. I would be glad if Dick got in and it would help me too. Now, concerning work. Today used cars, people and methods of selling, and hustle, profits, trades [Ed.—Chapter 7]. I think I can make it. Must be good, general and fierce. It will be just one day's work. A short chapter. Must get the sense of the yard in it. Must get the sense of cheating in it. Cars, trucks, trailers. Well here goes. Got her done and I think it's all right. Feel good about it anyway.

Entry #16
June 16 [1938]—11:15 [Thursday]

Comes now the—fifteenth day. Charley Cushman's mother killed in an accident. Letter today. Last night Carol, reading *Tristram Shandy*,* suddenly got an impulse to make her will. Copied mine for form. Can't see the connection—T.S. and wills. Just a business proposition and a wise thing to do but nevertheless it got into my dreams which have been deep and clear lately and I dreamed a confused mess made up of Dad and his failures and me and my failures. Some way connected with the store. Poor Dad couldn't run a store, he didn't know how. And I used to eat pies at noon hour and was ashamed of selling things. No mercantile ability in either of us and the store failed and left a terrible mark on Dad.* That was all in the dream and Gene's death. It was a dark mess and I have trouble throwing it off. And the news now is so stupid, insane. The race in its leaders any way hardly deserves to survive. And now I am ready to go to work and I am glad to get into other lives and escape from mine for a while. Yesterday the used car lot and today Tom and Casy go home to the family, if they get there [Ed.—beginning of Chapter 8]. Must go slowly and introduce these people fully and carefully for I will be with them a long time. After spending nearly seven thousand dollars to be alone and quiet, the neighbors run their radio all day and I get the benefit of it. Carol can hear them reading their letters to each other. We may have to move from this beautiful place. This is a day when I could readily lose myself in irrelevant reflection and recrimination and so I must go to work now and stop such a possibility. This book can't stop any more and this chapter must get under way. Well she's done. Slow but I think good. I wanted this part slow. Tomorrow there is difficulty.

Entry #17
June 17 [1938]—11:15 [Friday]

This is getting to be almost a standard time for starting work. Last night the itching, burning jitters and no sleep until 3:00. Maybe coffee. Hope my nerves aren't weak because they have a long haul ahead. Doc Bolin* here yesterday. Fine people. He is going on a collecting trip to the south seas and is very excited about it. Will see him in Honolulu in February. I'd like to go but won't or can't or something. Now some reference to the work today. Begin the detailed description of the family I am to live with for four months. Must take time in the description, detail, detail, looks, clothes, gestures. Ma very important. Uncle John important. Pa very. In fact all of them are important. Got to take it slowly. I don't care how long it is [Ed.—Chapter 8]. We have to know these people. Know their looks and their nature. Must. And now to work. Rest of the line for after work comment. Finished her. I don't know how well. Tomorrow I'll have to fight my willpower.

Entry #18
June 18 [1938]—9:45 [Saturday]

Now it is Saturday and we got up early and I am to work early. I don't see any reason for not doing a full day's work [Ed.—2,000 words]. This is a huge job. Mustn't think of its largeness but only of the little picture while I am working. Leave the large picture for planning time. If only I could do this book properly it would be one of the really fine books and a truly American book. But I am assailed with my own ignorance and inability. I'll just have to work from a background of these. Honesty. If I can keep an honesty it is all I can expect of my poor brain—never temper a word to a reader's prejudice, but bend it like putty for his understanding. If I can do that it will be all my lack of genius can produce. For no one else knows my lack of ability the way I do. I am pushing against it all the time. Sometimes, I seem to do a good little piece of work, but when it is done it slides into mediocrity. Well the day—Ma, Pretty Boy Floyd, Grampa and Granma and maybe Noah. Can't tell whether I will get to Noah. To work now. Well, that's done and I've caught up for my hangover—one day ahead [Ed.—Chapter 8]. Try to get another next Saturday. Watch the old people. Might get out of hand but I want them mean and funny. And Monday will be

Entry #19
June 19 [1938]—(Sunday, no work)

Mrs. Gragg and Julia and [indecipherable] came. And I had the insistent sad feeling that I should never see Mrs. Gragg again. She told the best story in the world—the tripes of Josh Billings.* I must write this some time.

Entry #20
June 20 [1938]—11:15 [Monday]

Now a new week. Must slow down and take it easier. Saturday had a feeling of exhaustion near to collapse. I guess I'd been working too hard. It's not the amount of work but the almost physical drive that goes into it that seems to make the difference. I should take it a little easier or I won't be finishing. I have just a page or so over 100 typescript pages done out of 600. I have five times as much work left to do as I have done already, so I must conserve strength because I do want to do this novel and finish it this time. Must get no fatal feelings about it. Change from Shawnee to Sallisaw [Ed.—Oklahoma]. Make earth red, not grey—and above all I must take my time. That is the most important of all. Take it easy. I don't mean to write less or less forcefully but to keep the frantic quality out of my approach. Well it is time for work now. Now the day's work is done. The prayer and Al comes home [Ed.—finish of Chapter 8]. Tomorrow the sorting of things to go and this should be a well done thing. I think I'll play *The Swan** before because there too is the loss of a loved thing of the past. I think I'll do that. Beth is coming tomorrow and she has done just that. Just that. Sorted over the trappings of her dead life. And so the book moves on steadily, forcefully, slowly, and it must continue to move slowly. How I love it. Dinner with Louis and Mary tonight. Now on to thought. Tomorrow must be poetry.

Entry #21
June 21 [1938]—9:30 [Tuesday]

Out late last night and Carol mad at me for staying. The house above with its radio blasting has spoiled this place for us completely. Have to fight noise worse than in P.G. [Ed.—Pacific Grove]. That poor little letter in the *Record** seems to be causing a fuss. Now I'll be deluged with requests for letters by other magazines. And I can't do anything about it. Well forget it. That's best. And some time before too long, forget every thing for always. Feeling low today but not tired or workless. I'll be early at work. Beth is coming tonight. I'll get my work done slowly and if she comes before, she won't mind if I go right on. I don't know about starting now. I'd just stop for coffee. However, I should start now. Then I can get some time off. And if I had started at 5:30 when I first awakened, I should be through now. Why not maybe a page now. Good idea. 11:15 actual work starts. Wire from Pare. Must see it. Says job for Dick practically assured as far as Washington is concerned. Now back to work. (Actually only half a second page today but the chapter only went that far anyway and there's nothing I can do about that.) [Ed.—Chapter 9.] I can't go on. I hope this general is good. It has to be. Read it to Louis. He says it is good. Only half a page though. But that didn't matter at all.

Entry #22
June 22 [1938]—11:45 [Wednesday]

Beth came last night. Looks much better than she did and her interests are awakening again. By the end of the summer I think she will be in good shape. She needs not to think too much about anything. But now to work. Little sleep last night. Couldn't get to sleep. And other things. And today I'll have to buck into it. Beginning of a particular chapter [Ed.—Chapter 10] and that isn't so bad. I'll try to go through with it but for some reason I'm slightly skittish. That does not always mean anything. I'll just take a running dive at it and set down what happens. Start with Tom and his mother. And works to the return of the men and begins the conference of the men. And the reports and circulars and ads for labor. (Got her done. And I'm afraid she's a little dull.) Think. Think tonight and tomorrow work harder but get sleep tonight. Need sleep.

Entry #23
June 23 [1938]—11:00 [Thursday]

This seems to be the approximate usual time. Good sleep last night and I feel fine and relaxed. I'm not going to work on Saturday this week so that I will get fresh and rested. Something has been hard on me. I don't know whether the intensity of the work or what. John Street* is in the hospital. We'll go up to see him tonight. Don't know what to take him. Cigars maybe. We'll eat on the way. I go to the dentist at four. After which digression, get back to work. And I feel relaxed about it too. Yesterday was a nervous drive. I notice my handwriting shows that. Beginning at any rate of the conference [Ed.—Chapter 10]. Enter all the rest of my actors. John, Rose of Sharon, Connie, and the two little kids [Ed.—Ruthie and Winfield]. The circle of squatting men and the plans, the order of authority, and the texture of the family. I only expect to crack the surface of this conference today for it is important and should be dealt with at some length. Carol got new dresses today. Glad to see the cracking of the poverty complex. But she does feel a little sinful. Should lose that. It isn't good. Wrote to Pare today and to Le Roy.* The last about Louis and a trick just to see if it would work. And now I should go to work. And will with a note to follow. (Well, there she is— just the truck coming home with the new people entering, and tomorrow the conference.) And that will be

Entry #24
June 24 [1938]—10:45 [Friday]

Now another day and one to take easy and to finish. I am going to take the Saturday off this week and so I think I will get thoroughly rested. Carol trying out vacuum cleaner this morning. Letter from Tom [Ed.—Collins] with vital information to be used later. He is so good. I need this stuff. It is exact and just the thing that will be used against me if I am wrong. Well today work is to indicate the curious democracy of the larger group. I think the whole day's work will deal with this conference and maybe spill over into the next day. I must get this down convincingly. The squatting men, the standing women and children. Well anyway the time has come for it. (Done. And I think if no interference I'll do a page tomorrow.)

Entry #25
June 27 [1938]—12:00 [Monday]

Now it is Monday. And I took two days off and have a little trouble getting into the swing. For one thing Pat* can't meet royalty payment and is paying one third, with notes for another two thousand. This is all right if it doesn't indicate that he is in difficulty. That worries me a little but not much. Ed came for the weekend. Good Ed.* We ran down to [Ed.—Pacific] Grove Saturday night to inject 300 hagfish—ugly, slimy brutes, and much better looking full of formaldehyde. That knocked the slime. Ritch and Tal* drove back. They are all coming next Saturday night for the week end of the Fourth. Short story volume [Ed.—*The Long Valley*] comes out in early Sept. It will collapse of course but I'll be glad to have it out. May sell three or four thousand copies. People looking at the next lot. We really must get out of here. I would love so much to go over to the Aptos country [Ed.— south of Santa Cruz]. Hear the ocean that I love. But must let Carol decide since she lives so much in her environment. Got a mild muscle [Ed.—spasm] in my chest and was dizzy this morning. I don't know why. This place is getting as noisy as a city lot. There is a lot of talk in the diary this morning—reason is to relieve the tension and get even with myself. Doesn't matter since I can work later this afternoon. Now for a discussion. Moment I stopped work the drive became sexual. Now the work will take that up. Now today's work is the pig killing and salting and the loading of the truck and the departure and the capture of Grampa

[Ed.—last sections of Chapter 10]. That is at least two days or maybe three, and then the next general is the empty house. Take out the last paragraph of the last general for the next. I'm a little sick today. I don't know why. I guess that's why I'm so talkative this week—it is time to go to work and that is all there is to it.

Entry #26
June 28 [1938]—9:20 [Tuesday]

For all that burst and bally hoo yesterday, I got only a half day's work done. Must catch it up little by little this week. Didn't tell Carol. Stomach went to pieces, dizziness, and blind nausea. Dick G.* called and I had to take him to the house from Saratoga. Stayed all night. Result—today's work not planned out as it usually is. Result—have to work longer hours today. Stomach very sore and me feeling very ill. And that's the way it is. Dick is still here. He or any one must not come again in the week. Might as well try going to work now and see whether I can't do a little over the two pages today to start picking up the lost page. I'll give this day a number depending on how much I make up. Well I caught up half a page and only half more to make it; and four days this week yet to do it so it will be all right I guess. Tomorrow I'll have [indecipherable] and also the empty houses and the empty land and that will be the end of Book One.

Entry #27
June 29 [1938]—11:30 [Wednesday]

Late start today and for no reason at all. Grey day and wind. Carol going to S.J. [Ed.—San Jose] for hair wave. Going to see John [Ed.—Street] in hospital tonight. Bill Richardson wants to come down to discuss new S.F. [Ed.—San Francisco] *Chronicle* magazine. Wants to see Louis. Louis dedicating his new book to us.* Very flattered. It is a good book. Will see him tonight. Went yesterday to see some land. Beautiful but impossible. Too remote and too many difficulties. What a view though! Lots of things happened. Now to the work. Book One is coming to a close— one more day—today of particulars and one of general and it is closed. I'm tired and a little fed up. I think the new line will ease me out of it. Lots of sleep last night. Afraid of repetitiousness. Must watch that. And I really am doing a great number of words a day. Well, it is time to get to it. Time passes. But I have plenty of time. My system is collapsing towards the end of Book One. Just finished chap [Ed.—Chapter 10]. No more. Tomorrow the general. Then the first book will be done in a little over a month.

Entry #28
June 30 [1938]—11:15 [Thursday]
End of Book One

My system of time has indeed collapsed. Today—the last day of June and I have finished in one month Book One, the background of this novel. One general chapter today and it will be a short one, too. The empty and deserted houses [Ed.—Chapter 11]. Yesterday the work was short and I went over the whole of the book in my head—fixed on the last scene, huge and symbolic, toward which the whole story moves. And that was a good thing, for it was a reunderstanding of the dignity of the effort and the mightyness of the theme. I felt very small and inadequate and incapable but I grew again to love the story which is so much greater than I am. To love and admire the people who are so much stronger and purer and braver than I am. This morning a letter from Barry saying his group was non partisan,* and I wrote back to place myself on record as partisan to the common people.

There can be left no doubt of that. And now the sun is shining and the birds, 50 different kinds, are singing in the trees outside my window, and the woods are green and beautiful. It is a good day in which to finish the first book. I have all of my people in whom I shall use, some of them well described. I hope all of them alive because they must live. Carol is washing now. I thought I would move but I can't. There is more noise in the house than out here, even with the washing machine going. So I'll stay out here [Ed.—porch deck] and work through it if I can. It isn't very long after all. My head aches today I don't know why. But I'll finish and I hope I'll have the new part ready by tomorrow. It would be good to have a few days off. I think I'll take them. Carol is right. Why should I rush? October and November and December will be enough to get it finished. Maybe I'll take the time off. I'll see. It would be good for me. And now to finish Book One. It occurs to me that I'll finish Book Two by the end of July and then two months for Book Three. And now Book One is done— rhyme, rhyme. And I am going to take Friday, Saturday, Sunday, and Monday off. I feel a little daring doing this but I think it will be better if I do. I'm getting a tenseness and a weariness. I must get fresh. This will be the last until the 5th.

Entry #29
July 5 [1938]—11:30 [Tuesday]

Now time has caught up with me. I've been four days off work, am all rested but by the same token I've got to get back the rhythm. I think I can for I jolly well must. There are no two ways about it. Beginning the second book today and it must have the rolling sound of wheels and the clutter of cars and the panting across the country. The first general [Ed.—Chapter 12] and it must have the meat of the whole second volume in it. For a moment I was afraid to start but this diary is a good idea for it gives me the opening use of words every day. Long weekend. Ritch and Tal and Ed here. Danced Sunday night, went completely mad dancing. Never did such dancing—every one for himself and Ed tippy-toeing around like a bear. All of us more drunk with high spirits than with anything else. Read Ed some little parts of this book and he finds them moving for which I am glad. They went home last night. This morning lots of quail. Play goes on the road with original cast.* Moore wants information for a critique* of some kind. Norwegian translation* coming, etc. Exciting but I can't allow excitement. Leave that for this winter. I want this done before the show comes out here. It is getting warm after all this time. Now back to the work. I feel fine about it. But during the four days off I have thought of the whole book. And it is rather like the prison term. Must not think too much of the end but of the immediate story—instant and immediate. It is a long haul but what do I care[?] It will be done all of the rest of my life—whatever is left of it. And that is not moody. When this book is finished a goodly part of my life will be finished with it. A part I will never get back to. But now the time is here to get to work and so I go. All done* but I don't know. I'm afraid of that chapter. Two [Ed.—Chapter 13] is of the family again on the road. Must get down to business now and work hard and tomorrow is

Entry #30
July 6 [1938]—11:05 [Wednesday]

Now the land work starts again. Now the crossing and I must get into it the feeling of movement and of life. Review of my work* in a magazine this morning. All wrong. But the writer was dishonest. Still some of his criticism was valuable. Make the people live. Make them live. But my people must be more than people. They must be an over-essence of people. Critics understand very little. They have to be taught the long hard way. But I am in the suck hole of work again. Immersed in it. And this chapter [Ed.—Chapter 13] will be a long one. It is the first day and night. And it has in it the first communication with other migrants. This is important, very important. Letter from George Hedley at work in school, wants us to go up there. Wish I could but I can't. Got to stay here and work. Must do that. I simply must get this book done before anything else. No matter what other things are going on. And I can't leave. I must get back to the Joad family on their movement to the west. And now the time has come to go to work. Well that is done. And the story grows again. Work is the only good thing. Tomorrow is

Entry #31
July 7 [1938]—11:00 [Thursday]

Now it's Thursday. Strange how I'm fighting this book now. I think it is about to change now though because I am feeling more and more like work. The despair came on me for a while but although still nervous from it I think I am recovering. Today will be a kind of test case I guess. As Carol says, stay with the detail. Let the damn book go three hundred thousand words if it wants to. This is my life. Why should I want to finish my own life? The confidence is on me again. I can feel it. It's stopping work that does the damage. Today I finish another section of this big book, a page section that is. I wish this [Ed.—ledger] book were all full. This daily work diary is really working this time and it is a good thing. Today word from Barry,* who wants to print my statement. Also from teacher's association asking for a speech, and *Who's Who** for correction of proof. That's all the mail.

Swedish translation* of T.F. arrived today, and the Norwegian is on the way. Getting quite a collection of translations. It will be a nice thing to have. Today I feel finally relaxed after the Fourth of July holiday. That seemed to wear me down rather than rest me. The work itself has rested me. Now the time is here to go to work. And I must go to work. And I'm anxious today. Report later. Finished and I have a good feeling about today's work. I think it is better. More easy and moving.

Entry #32
July 8 [1938]—10:30 [Friday]

Fairly early start today. And a beautiful day. Carol goes to look at real estate today. Wilkus came out with a word about a ranch in the mountains—360 acres for $12,000. Could sell off what we didn't want. We'll look at it anyway. It might be fine. No mail of any consequence today. French translation of M & M and IN. D.B. are in progress.* They get about. I wonder how this book will be. I wonder. Yesterday it seemed to me that the people were coming to life. I hope so. These people must be intensely alive the whole time. I was worried about Rose of Sharon. She has to emerge if only as a silly pregnant girl now. She has to be a person. Noah I think I'll lose for the time being and Uncle John and maybe for a while Casy. But I want to keep Tom and Ma together. Lots of people walking along the roads in this season. I can hear their voices. Louis has finished his book, first draft.* He must be glad, I guess. Well, it's time for me to go to work. Time to go and today I must get them camped. And the tent effect built. And the new people. And maybe a part of the history of this new couple [Ed.—the Wilsons]. Well, that's done. The death of Grampa [Ed.—Chapter 13].

Entry #33
July 11 [1938]—10:30 [Monday]

Monday again. The weeks swing by but they don't seem to get me much nearer to completion. They do, of course, only they don't seem to. Sunday Julia B [Ed.—Breinig, from Monterey] and two others. Today after four Bill Richardson. I don't know what he wants. Louis will be down though. Nothing much else to report. We made plans to go to the Rodeo* next Saturday and night and then back to Santa Cruz. Ought to be fun. I just hope I don't get into any trouble—I mean with publicity. Salinas would exploit anything—anything, even me, whom it hates. Well, there it is—the daily life. Now back to work. Always on week ends I have the feeling of wasted time. And I am terrified that through illness or something the work may stop. Once the first draft is done, it will be all right because someone could read it even if I passed out of the picture. But I simply must get the draft done. Must avoid every side influence. Must get to be tough about so many things now. Once it is finished of course—then I'll take time off I hope. But I haven't really done much work the last two years—for me, I mean. In wordage, more than most, but not for me. But once this book is done I won't care how soon I die, because my major work will be over. Today comes the funeral in the night of Grampa. That will be the whole day's work. And it closes one whole part of the book. It must be good and full of fullness and completions. And that feeling must go into it. Must. I seem to use the word must more than any other. It's a good word though; I've nothing against it. The force of folk ceremonial. Well there she is and Grampa is only half-buried. Tomorrow is

Entry #34
July 12 [1938]—10:30 [Tuesday]

This is a beautiful day, hot and clean. Last night Richardson of the *Chronicle* down. Spoke about a new literature section. I have nothing for it and the price is too low for Louis. Well, there you have it. This morning a request from CIO* to head a committee for organization of farm workers. Can't do it until this book is done. Mail was sparse today. This is a hell of a time to be writing a book. Everything in the world is happening and I must sit here and write. Well if I ever finish, it will be some kind of triumph. This good pen holds up beautifully. I guess it will last out the entire book. The more I think of it, the better I like this work diary idea. Always I've set things down to loosen up a creaking mind but never have I done so consecutively. This sort of keeps it all corralled in one place. Soule phoned* that he wanted me to talk to the President, but I don't know what about or why. I'll do it if I can do any good but I'll be damned if I'll be another shirt front in a curious mob. I can't go on this way forever. My hand today will steady down I think because I am calm. And it is time now.

Chapter end. It was Book Two, chapter two [Ed.—Chapter 13]. General tomorrow. I don't know which one.

Entry #35
July 13 [1938]—11:00 [Wednesday]

I don't know why, but everything seems to be happening now. We are looking at ranches today, too. And yesterday we saw the most beautiful I have ever seen. I want that ranch.* We'll try to get it. Carol wants it too. And it is reported that [Ed.—Wally]

Ford is coming and all the time I go on working but I wonder whether my work isn't getting a shot-full-of-holes feeling. No word from Soule so I guess I won't have to meet the President. I would have but I didn't like it. Most brilliant weather now. Lovely. And time slips through my fingers. But so far the work has slipped through too so that in fifteen days I shall be half through this book. Probably the first of August no less. I don't know whether I can do the whole thing in one jump without a rest. We will see. May take a few days off when Book Two is done. Took four days when Book One was done. Tried to get some music but couldn't. Routine of the house more important. Will have to get on without it. Having to work through and around a thousand things anyway. Wish I could run away from everything to do my book. God, how I wish I could! It will be full of jitter at this rate. No other way, I guess. Well, to work—or to try.

I did it but it may not be good. I don't know. But it is in, the I to We [Ed.—Chapter 14].

Entry #36
July 14 [1938]—12:15 [Thursday]
Book II   Chap. 4

Today much to my disgust the time has slipped away and it is the latest since I started this book. Not that it matters a great deal. Just work later. I'll get it done but it scares me to be late. We're hipped on this ranch. Can think of little else. But I must. Carol is mad over the place and so am I. Well I don't have to meet the President for which I am thankful. My lazy tendency is setting in now and I'll have to combat it. This book must be ready by the first of the year. Simply must. And that means solid work, completely solid. So this tendency must be put out of the way. Little mail this morning for which I'm glad. Rusty sent sixty bottles of the fine red wine. Nice people. Too many things are happening. No word from the east [Ed.—from Pat Covici, or from McIntosh and Otis]. *News* printed my letters* and I imagine the reaction will be immediate. Now to work god damn it and different work. Must get to it.

Finished it [Ed.—beginning of Chapter 15]. By God and for a while I didn't think I was going to. But I got the full day's work done.

Entry #37
July 15 [1938]—11:15 [Friday]

Today I have a leisurely feeling getting into the work whereas yesterday it was one of frantic rush. Today it will be 68 pages [Ed.—of handwritten manuscript]. According to the thousand words to the page gauge, that would be about 70,000 words, but it is more I think. And it is the 35th day. In other words, in 16 more days I'll be half through. And I must get my people to California before then. By the first of August they should be there, come what may. I think all of today will be in the hamburger stand [Ed.—Chapter 15]. That is an important place. Carol going to San Jose today. That ranch sinks back now. Won't have to think of it for awhile. It would be fine to finish the book before thinking of it. Then I could think of it all I want. But today I can take my time and what difference if I don't finish until late? I don't care. Must be sure not to drink too much and little but beer or short ones in Salinas. Poison on town. I'm going there in the same way that some people go to a slaughter house or a morgue. Anyway, I'm going. This day is good. Letter from Ed and all his teeth are out now. And now to work. On with the hamburger stand. Carol just left with Elsie [Ed.—Ray] and my time has come. No more nonsense. Well, I got her and the eating joint is through and I think pretty well. Now a week end.

Entry #38
July 18 [1938]—11:15 [Monday]
Book II   Chap. 4

Only a quarter page. Rodeo blues and weakness.

Now another week begins. Went to Salinas for the rodeo. Drank lots of whiskey and had a fair time. Empty feeling, empty show. Same enthusiasm circus had whips up. Taken to task by Arline. Sorry. That was the only example of their hatred. I make enemies and friends. And now home with a little stomach ache that doesn't come from the stomach. Terrible feeling of lostness and loneliness. I don't know. No word about the ranch. Nice letter from Pat. How nice he is. Trying to reassure me. I don't need it. Now to the work. The families move on today. I'm in no hurry, so let them move slowly. Got this god damned nasty rodeo to get out of my system. Problems pile up so that this book moves like a Tide Pool snail with a shell and barnacles on its back. Well, I've got to get to it. The Joads and Wilsons move on [Ed.—beginning of Chapter 16]. Think I'll take them quite a way this time before I stop them. Get my map* going.

Entry #39
July 19 [1938]—11:05 [Tuesday]

Yesterday was a bust and I'm sorry but I think today will be all right. I just can't go on these week ends. Confusion lasts too long. Got to stay home and keep my nose down low to my story. Agreed to head a committee to gather funds for field workers' organization. If it takes time or effort away from this work, I'll resign. Warned them of that. I'll have to turn back pages pretty soon to a new set for this diary. I'll finish another section this week and that will be good. Cut it out and start a new one. That will be very good. I feel the book again today and I think it will go on now.

Done at last and it was a chore for some reason. Be glad to get them there.

Entry #40
July 20 [1938]—11:15 [Wednesday]

Well last night a wire that Pat is in trouble. I've been expecting it. I'm so sorry for him. Our two thousand dollars, our year's royalties, are pretty important to us but we're eating and working and that's more than we have any right to expect. Being broke won't kill us but it will wipe Pat out. And he is such a nice fellow. The irritations are increasing. I wonder whether I will ever finish this book. And of course I'll finish it. Just work a certain length of time and it will get done *poco a poco*. Just do the day's work. Some days I think I am getting sour but I don't know. Then comes a good day and I am lifted up again. And I can't tell from the opening. Often in writing these beginning lines I think it is going to be all right and then it isn't. Just have to see. I hope it is all right today. It is hot today, but by powdering my arm and hand it seems to be all right. I hope the whole rest of the summer isn't boiling, but if it is, it is, and that's all there is to it. The work must go on day after day until one day it will be finished. In ten days I will be half done. 50 days of work. I hope we get to California by then because I would like half the time out here. That is the important part—out here. Today I must get the family split—perhaps Tom and Casy to Santa Rosa, or

Tom at least for the part [Ed.—Chapter 16]. I think it may be all right. I hope so and I am going to sign this off now and try at it.

Finished, but at 7 PM.

Entry #41
July 21 [1938]—10:15 [Thursday]

Yesterday was a terrible day. Telegrams and phones and auspices. Pat is really in trouble. Today his creditors meet and if they force him into bankruptcy our whole year's royalties go up the flue. I wish it worried me more but it doesn't. Morrow [Ed.—William Morrow Publishing Company] wired and phoned. By three o'clock we should know how the meeting of the creditors comes out. That is one of the reasons for going to work a little earlier. Gets me done before hell breaks out. I don't want to work until 7 tonight. Director of L.A. Federal Theatre came over last night. Nice fellow. I liked him. When I am through I must do some work for the theatre if I have it in me. I don't know. I think, now that I'm tied down, that I will do lots of things, but I wonder if I will. We'll see anyway. Now to the work. Note to be added concerning Pat when word comes through, if it does. Finished early and I'm glad.

Entry #42
July 22 [1938]—10:20 [Friday]

This is Friday and the last day of a short week. I am ashamed of the short week but it must be put down to accident. Actually I am just about up to schedule on wordage. And I have to take a small loss. So far it is very small. Pat did not have the creditors' meeting yesterday. I have a feeling he will pull out of this. He has an advance sale list of 8000 on the short stories a month before publication, which is phenomenal. I hope to goodness he can pull out. He is a plugger though. Letter from Burns Mantle for a reprint of M & M.* I hope everything will blow over and let me go on with this work. Only 8 days to finish half. And today I cut out another section. Record from Ford today. Jokes and very good. Startling effect hearing yourself addressed from the phonograph. No word from Pare. Have been expecting him. I won't mind a rest after today. I'm taking my time now but the wordage continues. That's the way it should be, too. Now I should be getting back to work. To the Rays' tonight for dinner and I suppose I'll get tight and I don't much care. In a way it is good and in a way bad. But if I am to drink anything Friday night is the best night for it. I'm a bit addled but I can do it all right. If my self discipline will let me go on working while hell pops around my ears, I'll be all right. I'll know I am all right. I just hope the work isn't suffering. And now to it. Must build some on this one-eyed man [Ed.—the junkyard scene in Chapter 16].

And now that's done and I can rest and the Dodge is fixed and Monday the scene shifts to the first migrant camp [Ed.—final section of Chapter 16].

Entry #43
July 25 [1938]—10:20 [Monday]

Lots of excitement. Carol went with Nellie [Ed.—her mother, who was vacationing in Santa Cruz] last night. Good for her, the change. Restless night for me on account of eating melon and strange and scary to be alone. Must write about this some time. It is a curious thing. Wind blew terribly. This morning lots of mail. Elizabeth writes everything that has been happening. I think Pat will get clear some way—letters from John [Ed.—Barry], from Henning,* and from the O'Brien guy.* Pleasant weekend but a little exhausting. Cerf* wired some plan whereby he carries Pat. I don't know. Wired Elizabeth. Mustn't interfere with her in any way. They're a fine bunch of people. I like Random House. Of course, I don't know anything about them financially, but I like the books they print. And I like Cerf. Well, anyway I haven't lost a minute of work on account of this difficulty. That's good. That's the fine discipline. If I can only keep that up this book will be finished in due course. Now I have all day to work and there is no need of hurrying. I can piddle out the two thousand words. Working in the main house because of telephone—so I won't have to run in, I mean. It is a curious windy day with the weather changing and fallish and leaves falling. Probably be an early and mean winter. It is time for me to get to work. Got to. Even if I have plenty of time. I get assailed with old times. Last night particularly. The flies are in this house on my arms. Here I could have had only half a page of work done [Ed.—still on Chapter 16]. This diary is really valuable to me though. Keeps me from writing letters. And now to work. This pen writes thinner if it is steeper. This has been a good pen to me so far. Never had such a good one. To work now.

The following three days were lost.* Lost completely. Carol went to the hospital for her tonsils. This morning my neck is stiff.

Entry #44
August 1 [1938]—12:00 [Monday]

Now I didn't work then or all week. Carol had her tonsils out and has been so sick and miserable that I just can't concentrate. Weakness maybe but can't cut her pain out of my mind. Pat's trouble piddles on and that interferes some. Just have to drop last week. It was out. Brod Crawford* came for the weekend. Nice fellow, but what a time to come. My nerves are very bad, awful in fact. I lust to get back into it. Maybe I was silly to think I could write so long a book without stopping. I can't. Or rather I couldn't. I'll try to go on now. Hope to lose some of the frantic quality in my mind now. It's just like slipping behind at Stanford.* Panic sets in. Can't organize. And everybody is taking a crack at me. Want time, want to use me. In aggregate it is terrible. And I don't know where to run. Ought to go into the wild some- where but I am needed here. Got to calm down. Simply must. I'm jumpy. And it is hot. Good for fog. Don't know who will publish my book. Don't know at all. No reason to let it slide though. Must keep at it. Necessary. Carol says I'm pampering myself. I guess I am. Wish I could control the jumping jitters though. Time to make the break and another try now. Time for it. I made it [Ed.—Chapter 16].

Entry #45
August 2 [1938]—11:15 [Tuesday]

So many things are going on I'm nearly crazy.* I simply must keep my head. Pare is at last making headway and I wish to God I could jump in but this book comes first. I wonder if I am dramatizing myself. I wouldn't be surprised. Let's get down to earth. This book I'm working on is just a book like any other. Let's work on it and not get wild. If it flops it flops, and that is that. I think I want it to be fine mainly because Carol does so much. But no reason to go nuts about it. Still no clarification of Pat's business. It should clear up in the next little while. It has to. There must be some way but they'll work that out. Now at last I am growing calm. This diary is a marvelous method of calming me down every day. Pretty soon I'll have to turn back pages to continue it. I really should have word today how Pat comes out. Carol's throat is better today. I'm going in and kiss her now. And then I'll feel better. And then I can go to work. And this day is the real restoration of the technique of stogyness. Which is what I am. And now to work.

Entry #46
August 3 [1938]—11:00 [Wednesday]

Well still we're hung up in the matter of the east [Ed.—Covici's situation]. No word today at all and this is Wednesday. Carol is improving in the throat now. She dreamed about the Biddle ranch last night. She wants it terribly. I must make every effort to get it for her. It is the most beautiful place I have ever seen. No doubt of that at all. There are now four things or five rather to write through—throat, bankruptcy, Pare, ranch, and the book. If I get this book done it will be remarkable. Well, two pages a day will do it in time. And the time slips by. Just a matter of doing the daily stint. Feel pretty good but am impatient about all the things hanging over me. Can't help it. But I'll get it done. I just hope it is some good. With this split attention I don't know. I really don't. Today I'll finish this general chapter [Ed.—Chapter 17] of the change on the roads and the enemies, though maybe the enemies should wait until California. I think so. The end seems ages away and it is too ages away. It is hot now but not sufferingly so. Now the time has come to go to work and I only hope that I am worthy to work. Here goes.

Made her, by God.

Entry #47
August 4 [1938]—11:00 [Thursday]

Today is the last day before I turn back some pages of this diary. I had no idea I would keep at it or that I would write so much in it every day. But it is so, and it is good. Letter from E.O. My affairs are still mixed up. I wrote the threat to the printers.* It may never be used. Don't know but I want Elizabeth to have it. And that was all. No other mail of any note. Ranch business tied up yet, too. Can't tell. Carol wants it terribly. Must get it for her. But how if we're never [Ed.—financially] clear? Have moved my table to the shady side of the room. I hope to God this book isn't suffering from all the inroads of other things. Now today I must move my family fast. I think I want to get them through the desert in this chapter [Ed.—Chapter 18] and to Bakersfield. Ten pages to this chapter will be 92 [Ed.—manuscript pages] and that isn't far off my plan. Will be 108,000 words. So if the chapter is a little shorter it will still be well over a hundred. I'm 96,000 now. In [Ed.—typed] pages I am not far from 400 now. I think it will be about 800 or slightly under. Anyway, I am well along. And I don't care much about anything. Gail and George* just came by and took Carol to the city for the day. It will probably be good for her. But I've got to go on and think of nothing but this book. I'm behind now and I want not to lose any more time, and so I simply must go on. It's good to work even if the absolute drive isn't in you. Here goes.

Entry #48
August 8 [1938]—11:00 [Monday]

Well the work has pretty much gone to hell. Might just as well take it in stride. The pressure broke down the strict discipline and Friday went to S.F. with Ed. I was tired. Then the difficulty and that didn't help, and the trouble in the east is still going on. Should break out of this this week I think. Then a letter from Muni* about T.F. Which I would like to do. If I could get Louis to work with me it would be good. I'll try when the time comes but meanwhile the pressure increases with little way out nor hope of ease. And so I simply must establish the discipline again and maintain it for a while. A slightly less frantic outlook would make some difference. The dog [Ed.—female in heat] has been completely frantic lately and it must stop. Carol is entirely well now and able to take over the phone, etc. Not entirely well, but on the road if there are no complications. I should be able to go ahead. I am so lazy and the thing ahead is so very difficult. I think it is laziness that is getting me. How easily we can transpose our laziness into something else. But I've done books before and what I have left to do now is one ordinary length novel. About the length of I.D.B. or a little longer and that will be the end. And now it is time to go to work.

Finished.

Entry #49
August 9 [1938]—11:00 [Tuesday]

Now a new era. Don't know how it will work. Now cleared in N.Y. Viking Press* bought contract. New one made. I hope it is a good one. Will hear in a day or so. Wellman Farley* coming down today. Hope G.S.K. [Ed.—George S. Kaufman] has called him but I don't know. Probably late today. The washing machine slows me down. But I can't complain. It's so good mostly. And if I'm a little late, what of it? I am removing the time dead line on this book. I think that a good idea. It will freshen the manuscript. Too many things. I'll do it as I can. But I do want to get it out. The other things—T.F. and I.D.B [Ed.—movie versions]—are good to think about but this book is my work. When it is done I can do what I want, but until then—this is the stuff. I feel pretty good. If we could get this ranch I'd feel better. Certainly it is the most beautiful place I ever saw. Must remember the trouble I had in M & M.* Thought I'd never get it done or make it work. I don't know. Every book seems the struggle of a whole life. And then, when it is done—pouf. Never happened. Best thing is to get the words down every day. And it is time to start now.

Entry #50
August 10 [1938]—11:20 [Wednesday]

Although I got up early this morning I'm late getting to work and I don't in the least know why. No word from the east today. Be a letter tomorrow and all the trouble will be done. For a while at least. No more word from Muni. My stipulations were tough and perhaps turned them away. Now this work is getting very hard. Wellman down yesterday and apparently G.S.K. doesn't intend to give him a chance. Well I've done all I could there. I'm getting worried about this book. I wish it were done. I'm afraid I'm botching it. I think it would be a good thing to stop and think about it but I hate to lose the time. But I want it to be good and I'm afraid it is slipping. But I must remember that it always seems that way when it is well along. I think I'll plug them into California today. Letter from Tom [Ed.—Collins]—worried about this committee. So am I sometimes. But the trip isn't so bad. Whatever that means. I have no reason except laziness, but I simply must get these people across the desert and into the field. Must do that and soon. Now to work at least into thought of work. So long!

Got it done, by God, and still they aren't across the desert. Just starting. Tomorrow the desert and the valley and Granma and the agricultural station [Ed.—Chapter 18].

Entry #51
August 11 [1938]—11:00 [Thursday]

Again to work. And lots of things have happened. Pare called from L.A. Will be here next week end. I'll be glad to see him. And perhaps many things will be clear. No word from Muni. I don't know how that stands. And no word from the ranch. I don't know how that stands either. Either they are bluffing or they are arguing it out. I don't know which, or maybe they have lost interest in us. Can't tell. Just have to wait, I guess. Now I think that covers what has happened. Did ever a book get written under such excitement? Well, two got written while mother and dad were ill* and if that could happen—anything could. The Viking contract went through I guess. And so the time approaches to get to work and I wonder whether I can. Well I've got to and there's no end to that.

Bad Lazy Time

Entry #52
August 16 [1938]—10:45 [Tuesday]

Demoralization complete and seemingly unbeatable. So many things happening that I can't not be interested. Viking bought the contract and every one is happy about it. Pat and all. I wonder if I will ever have a manuscript to turn in on it. Last week end a big one. Joe and Charlotte* Friday and Saturday—Wally Ford and Martha Saturday [and] Sunday. Good time but Jesus how the work suffers. Wednesday—Dan James and Chaplin are due, Friday—Pare, Saturday—Gail and George. And me supposed to be working. We closed on the Biddle ranch Sunday, $10,000 net. Bought 10,000 feet of lumber for $75.00. Lawrence is going up to look over the place today and we'll get on with it as soon as possible. I almost feel that it would be a good thing to go up there to write but I won't I guess. All this is more excitement than our whole lives put together. All crowded into a month. First edition of *Long Valley* is 15,000. Too much. Too much. I should really not try to write books in the summer. It is just too much. Too much. I feel like letting everything go. But I won't. I'll go and I'll finish this book. I have to. My whole damned life is tied up. Most people would like it tied up. And maybe I do. My many weaknesses are beginning to show their heads. I simply must get this thing out of my system. I'm not a writer. I've been fooling myself and other people. I wish I were. This success will ruin me as sure as hell. It probably won't last, and that will be all right. I'll try to go on with work now. Just a stint every day does it. I keep forgetting.

Entry #53
August 17 [1938]—10:20 [Wednesday]

Early to work this morning and this is a general chapter [Ed.—Chapter 19], which—although they are highly charged—are nevertheless the repository of all the external information and material. In a way they are easier to write and in a way harder. But yesterday I got into the swing of doing my daily stint again. The hammering next door nearly drives me nuts, but no way out of that, I guess. Just have to work through it. Take all the time I need. Mustn't think of the hammering. Dan James and Chaplin coming up this afternoon. I'll be done early though. The hammering got me and I came into my room which is now the quietest in the house. And it seems pleasant to me. Looking forward to seeing Pare very much. Such a nice guy. Such fun if he isn't too tired. Want him to see the ranch, too. I'm dawdling today. The hammering is terrific even in here. I don't care if I do dawdle some. The lady who is doing the thesis* writes fearfully. The ranch is still the most beautiful place in the world. I love that place. We will enjoy it. I've sneaking fears that it is too good and too beautiful for me. Beth will love it, too. In fact, every one we like will love it. It is so beautiful. But I can't go on this way for I must get my slow day's work done. And now is a good time to start on it. What a wonderful pen this is. It has and is giving me perfect service—never stops flowing for a second and never overflows and blots a word. But I'm stalling now to keep from going to work. To work.

Finished.

Entry #54
August 18 [1938] [Thursday]

Another day and out in my study again. The pounding isn't so loud or the wind is in the other direction or something. I don't know. This has been the most crowded week so far in our lives and it will carry through. For Pare comes tomorrow and Chaplin* was here last night. Lots of fun, good fun. Dan James looks as young as ever. Gail and George Saturday. Big week end all in all. Today the wind is blowing hard and it makes Carol miserable. She did such a good dinner last night and so beautifully. All this entertaining falls heavily on her shoulders. Now away from the daily life and into the book. I read a couple of chapters to company last night and could see the whole thing clearly. Also it doesn't sound bad. Today is going to take a long time. I have to get on the line of my family again. The outline of today will carry over some days. Must get it straight, must get it clear and straight. The summer is passing. I don't think I'll be finished before the end of October. Sorry, but I'm losing time and so much company and excitement. So much. But I'll just piddle along my two thousand a day. Going to take a long stretch today. Must see Tom's letter re crops before I start.

Entry #55
August 19 [1938]—10:20—Friday

Today Pare arrives. Yesterday was too much for me. I fought it really hard until I realized that the fight was obscuring the picture. I have some force but not enough for that apparently. Today I feel better I hope. Anyway I try to go on today. I'm afraid for this book, really afraid. Part of the difficulty lies in all the shooting at me, but the other half lies within myself. That's why it is going to be good to see Pare. Maybe it will be easier when I see him. My dream of early finish goes glummering. Plodding is all right until a day comes when I can't even plod anymore. I feel limited, too. M.B. [Ed.—Margery Bailey] hunting. C.A.S [Ed.—Carlton Allyn Sheffield] hunting and sniping. No help for that. The book is to do. I've fallen in these holes before even in the little Mice book. I had great trouble.* None are east and they aren't even going to grow east. Good luck is even worse for work than bad luck. I have been too fortunate lately. Of course it balances with the long years on the other side. Can't tell. Can't tell. Just have to plod for 90,000 words. Plod as the people are plodding. They aren't rushing. And now to work and the first life in Hooverville [Ed.—Chapter 20].

Entry #56
August 23 [1938]—11:15 [Tuesday]

This is Tuesday. Pare came over the week end. Big time. Carol sprained her ankle. Went down to the peninsula with Pare and spent night at Chaplin's place [Ed.—Pebble Beach]. Talked all night. Of course, I lost a day of work. I am afraid that Pare doesn't need me on this job and I think he knows it but hasn't admitted it yet. I'll work if I am needed. But I wish I could be left alone until Christmas. I am getting tired—very tired. I have at least 6 weeks yet of work by any measuring, and I must re-establish the discipline. Must get tough. So many attractive things are happening that it is difficult. And the ranch on top of everything else. But I must get this done. After all, I've always worked under some kind of pressure: T.F. while mother was ill, I.D.B while Dad was ill, M & M while this house was going up. Always something. Just more this time. I can do it and I will do it, by

God. It is just the discipline that is all. I'm wasting time today and I don't care much. Everything goes in circles and I must think WORK. Such strangeness, such strangeness. I've re d parts to people and they like the parts or say they do, but I wonder whether the whole thing will bear up. I wonder. I don't want to get cocky about it. I really shouldn't have told anyone. I get the benefit of the doubt now when before I didn't. The hammering on the next door house is awful. Everything is curious. Pare made me feel better about the country at large. But I am very confused. French rights to I.D.B. are sold now. So many things are happening. This is probably the high point of my life if I only knew it. I will spend today getting straightened out and on a level again—thinking. I am fresh again and that is good. My brain is clear for details. I can almost finish in one piece I should think. I want to. I shouldn't be thinking about getting done. Should be thinking only of the story and, by God, I will. I can't let future interfere with the hardest, most complete work of my life. I simply can't. Always I have been weak. Vacillating and miserable. I wish I wouldn't. I wish I weren't. I'm so lazy, so damned lazy. This year though I have made up for last year's lay off. I really have batted out a lot of words. I would go through until winter if I could. But if I don't lay off it will be done, and if I do lay off I'll lose the thread. I am simply incapable of working any way but hard and fast. That is the only way I can make it. This is too bad. It is almost impossible in fact but I must get calm and quieted before I can go on. I mean that streak yesterday was curiously indecent. I don't know why but it was. So many things. How impossible it is for me to think. Just writing words, but the thing is starting in my brain. I must get the tempo.

Entry #57
August 24 [1938]—11:00 [Wednesday]

My nerves are going fast. Getting into confusion of many par-
ticles—each one beatable, but in company pretty formidable.
And I get a little crazy with all of them. Too bad. Just too many
things. Must beat them off. I wish I could go to a furnished room
some place where I knew no one and just disappear for a while.
I wish that. But I guess it is impossible. I guess it is. I must get
back into the stride and sweep. It isn't just noise and bustle, it's
all the shots in my direction. The wants, the demands, the dis-
satisfactions. They're breaking me down, and every now and then
my head goes spinning and that frightens me. Some time it might
not stop spinning. Nowhere to turn. Nowhere. Can't think of these
things any more. Where has my discipline gone? Have I lost
control? Quite coldly we'll see today. See whether life comes into
the lives and the people move and talk. We'll see.

Got her, by God.

Entry #58
August 26 [1938]—11:00 [Friday]

Yesterday we bought the Biddle ranch. And there were very
cautious inquiries into water rights. Very cautious. And now it
is ours. That doesn't mean anything. There is a great weight on
my heart. I guess it comes from having property. More and more.
It is such a beautiful place. I hope we can sell everything else
and just have that one thing. My work is no good, I think—I'm
desperately upset about it. Have no discipline any more. I must
get back. An ordinary novel would be finished now, but not this
one. This one must be good. Very good. And I'm afraid it is not.

Carol is going to try to pick up and start putting it in type. I hope she can. It would help. I so want this to be a good book. So much. I don't know what to do. I'm slipping. I've been slipping all my life. Shouldn't think of that. Is this all laziness, I wonder? I must try to get ahead. Must try that. The week has been shot to hell. Just shot to hell. I've always had these travails. Never get used to them. Never. This place has become an absolute mad house—voice culture on one side, linemen shrieking on another. I don't know what to do. I wish—Jesus!

Entry #59
August 29 [1938]—10:30 [Monday]

Now I have lost a great deal of time. I have been remiss and lazy, my concentration I have permitted to go under the line of effort. If this had been the first time I should be very sad. But I am always this way. I can concentrate and under some circumstances I can work. My job is to get down to it and now. For all the pressures, there is only one person to blame and I must force him into it. The point is that I am over half through with this book. What remains is in length an average novel. I can do it and must. Nothing must interfere from this time on. We had rest and change and relaxation and now there is no excuse. Every day now—every day. It is just like starting all over, the reluctance and everything. Today is Monday. This is the start into the final [Ed.—stretch]. I've been interested in other things. Can't be anymore. Nothing but the Joads. Must get to it. That is getting to be the forerunning statement in a failure. Expectation. I don't know what I expect or what is expected of me. Nor care. This family must live. I have the laziness and the reluctance that is always present in the beginning. The ranch is bought and there's nothing to do about that. Business is set. Nothing in the world to interfere. And there is this frightful fear that I won't be able to do it, that it is too much for me. And there are dates that mustn't be kept, and arrangements that must not be made. And the time has come. I must get down to the work although my stomach is water about it.

I made it!

Entry #60
August 30 [1938]—10:45 [Tuesday]

I'm nearly nuts again. Too many things are happening. Steve arriving tomorrow. Abramson* wants to send 75 books. Must stop this right now. And I'm having a hell of a time concentrating with so many things going on. Mabel Ferry and Frank Fenton want to come down. And I would like to see them very much. If they come down in the evening. Just everything. Carol is typing manuscript and I'm losing my thread. Got to keep it. I hope this book is some good, but I have less and less hope of it. It has been shot to pieces too much. I hoped that Carol's working on draft would help but I don't know that it does. No time today for comment. I've got bugs under my skin. To work now.

Entry #61
September 1 [1938]—11:30 [Thursday]

Was ever a book written under greater difficulty? Now it's the house. We listed it for sale and we're swamped. People [who] want to buy it want to look at it. We'll be living in a gold fish globe until it is sold I guess. No mail but bills. And the weather is beautiful. Yesterday John Collier* and Jerry [indecipherable]. Went up to the ranch and fooled around and lost time. I can't help it. I'll get finished by Christmas, and that's all I can hope for. Pare's plan I am pretty sure has no place for me and I'm glad of it. Now it is time to go to work and to lose all of the nonsense about selling and buying and moving. Now is the time to go to work. And I wonder about it.

Entry #62
September 2 [1938]—10:20 [Friday]

The time goes on and the manuscript crawls on. And after a long time it will be done. I am not sad. In fact, I am pretty glad now. Time is going. The noise of pounding* next door is simply terrific. There are days when they pound their heads off. Today they seem to be just hammering as loudly as they can. There is proof today how bad a merchant I would be. Our house is for sale and a quasi-customer is coming out. I am full of resentment— not that I don't want to sell it, but that I don't like the position of seller. The new ranch is so lovely. And we're in no hurry to sell. But it is listed and I guess we'll have to show it. Hope there isn't a train of people looking. Now for today in the work. I'll finish a chapter today and be ready for a general on Monday. I think this last chapter has been weak in detail. Must get it back. Got to get them out of Hooverville and into a federal camp for they must learn something of democratic procedure. But today it is just a matter of getting them out of camp [Ed.—end of Chapter 20]. Casy is in jail. Uncle John is drunk. Tom will go to the grocery and trail Uncle John. God, this pounding is terrible today. I have to ignore it as much as I can. They're laying floors, Christ! What a place, and we came here looking for quiet. No mail today except requests. That's about all my mail is any more. People who want things. What more can I expect? I've really asked for it in a way. There doesn't seem to be any other way. Here they come to look at the house. I wish I didn't feel so much resentment about being a seller instead of a buyer. Seem to be a lot of women. Let Carol take care of them. I'll stick out here and do my own work. Finish out this page. I feel really very good today. The flow of story is coming back to me. The feel of the people. And the feel of speech and the flow of action. So it must go and if it takes until Christmas, then that is the way it must be. I can't be rushed. I must have enough time. I do hope that Pare won't need me, much as I'd like to work with him. I must do my own work and I have a feeling that he is this picture not me. Now to work.

Entry #63
September 3 [1938]—11:00 [Saturday]

Today is Saturday and half a day's work will finish the chapter.* So I'll do it. The end of the Hooverville chapter. Carol is typing now and the book is beginning to seem real to me. Also Carol got the title last night "The Grapes of Wrath." I think that is a wonderful title. Must query Elizabeth, but will use it any way until I am forbidden. The looks of it—marvelous title.* The book has being at last. I think really that a good month will finish it. Middle of October anyway, which is six weeks. No mail again but requests. Young man wants to talk, wants to be a writer. What could I tell him? Not a writer myself yet. But the story is having a reality finally. I said that before but I am stunned with the fact. I think I never really believe I will finish a book until it is finished. And Carol's draft is going to be the final. Let them [Ed.—The Viking Press] pay for retyping if they want. We'll put it in shape so it is readable with ease. I just hope it is good. Now to work. Finished the chapter, by God. Now a general and I don't quite know which one it will be.

Entry #64
Sept[ember] 5 [1938]—9:40—Labor Day [Monday]

Beginning Chapter 9 general [Ed.—Chapter 21]. This one will be of the locals and their fight to preserve themselves. It should be a decent one. First, our house is sold.* Just one more thing. We hadn't intended to sell it so soon but the first people who looked at it wanted it. Well—the last four books have been written in a mess. This one might as well be. There hasn't been a moment of peace since I started. And it gets worse. The Stones are still on the ranch. Must see whether we can get them off. We have to have some place to lay our heads. And I need some place to work. How I wish my book were done. But I feel very good about it now. It is really moving and I can finish it if I am only given time. I say six weeks more. It may take more or less. But I want to take plenty and yet not too much. The title is still good. I like it very much. Today I have an early start and except for a little stomach ache from too much excitement, I feel fine. And now even the stomach ache is gone. And I am about ready to start Chapter 9. I hope it is good. Time to go and if I have a good day, I'll be finished by noon. Go!

Entry #65
Sept[ember] 6 [1938]—11:00 [Tuesday]

111-112*

Late start today. We have sixty days to go in this house, so I can finish my book here. Yesterday we put out the stakes for the new house* up at the ranch. It is going to be a beauty. Letter from Tom [Ed.—Collins] this morning. He has been on the road. Will be here this week end. I'll be glad to see him. Carol crossed the first hundredth page this morning. That is a curious kind of milestone. No other until the end, or maybe the five hundredth. I've never gone to five hundred, but this time I will. About six hundred all told, or six fifty I think. Middle of October I'll finish I think. No mail this morning. Thought there would be a lot. Lot tomorrow maybe. Europe still tense. Hitler waiting for heaven to speak. Maybe war, but I don't think so. He waited too long. I think he is about through any way. Hope so. Germans are such nice people. This state about to blow up. This winter is going to be a mean one. Hope I can help a little bit. I'm late getting started today. But I don't care. I'm so glad for these sixty days that I don't care. Just plug along. And now comes the time. Not so fast as yesterday.

Finished.

Entry #66
Sept[ember] 7 [1938]—10:30 [Wednesday]

[113-114]

So many things to drive me nuts. Fred Soule phoned yesterday to ask me to go on the radio concerning migrants. Trying to get out of it because it would be deadly to my life. I'll try to dodge it. Would start a million fights. I feel very sick today. Dreamy sleep and coughing from too much smoking and confused by too many things happening and pretty worn out from too long work on manuscript. Have to cut down smoking or something. I'm afraid this book is going to pieces. If it does, I do too. I've wanted so badly for it to be good. If it isn't, I'm afraid I'm through in more ways than one. Carol is working too hard now, too. And I've been with this book so long now that I don't know much about it, I'm afraid. Well—have to take that chance. After all, if only I wouldn't take this book so seriously. It is just a book after all, and a book is very dead in a very short time. And I'll be dead in a very short time too. So the hell with it. Let's slow down, not in pace or wordage but in nerves. I wish I could do that. I wish I would write only one page a day but I can't. Got to go on at this rate or suffer for it. It must go on. I can't stop. But oh! if I only had lots of time. I need to settle down some. Burned my pen finger with a match the other day and the blister comes right where the pen fits. And it hurts like hell and my handwriting reaches new heights of badness because of it. Taylor [Ed.—next-door neighbor] just rakes his yard and putters. But he would probably do a better job of this than I am doing. More ship-shape. I wish I were he sometimes. Just rake the yard and mix a little cement. How did I ever get started on this writing business anyway? To work.

Entry #67
Sept[ember] 8 [1938]—11:00 [Thursday]

115-116
Now—just slow down. Have been working and thinking at top speed. Must go slow. Soule really wants me to do that radio work. If he insists I know I can't refuse, but it is hard to accept right at this time. Letters from Putnam, who has something he wants; from Louis, who doesn't like my title; from Eric, who has been travelling. Alice Cohee is coming tomorrow. All in all, it is a tough time with so many things, so many demands, that if I am not careful, I'll crash. I feel the weariness creeping up on me again as it did that day when I was really in danger of collapse. But I can't now. Must finish this book. Simply must. And I don't know how near it is to finished. I just can't tell. It ought to be long. Carol has 150 pages typed now and she is racing ahead. She'll turn two hundred this week. This is really a God send, getting it all in type so quickly. But I wonder whether it will be any good. I've got to slow down. My nervousness will get into it

if I don't. The trouble is that I'm getting a <u>finish</u> feeling into it, and I shouldn't. Can't get that for a long time yet. Must go slow. I have plenty of time. It's this god damn moving that makes it hard. When Carol finishes what I have finished it will be easier because then she will be able to take care of the outside business again. Now we just have to let things go and it is that letting go that bothers me so much. Our house sold so quickly that it made our heads swim. One partial visit was all and now the money has gone in and we don't own our house any more. God damn dog is barking now and it is time to get to work anyway. Well that is the end of another big section all finished [Ed.—Chapter 22]. Pare wired that he advised against my going on the air right now.

Entry #68
Sept[ember] 9 [1938]—10:00 [Friday]

117-118

Admission day.* Lucky this state had some pressure from without put on it. Our royalists really think they own the world. Wire from Pare with advice not to go on the air. Much relief to me. Long letter from Martha Ford. Apparently everyone wants a cut of M & M on the road and there is nothing left. I don't know and I don't care whether it goes on the road or not. Alice arrives today. We are looking forward to her. Letter from Ritch and Tal.* I wish they would come up. We're so darned busy that any time would do. Wouldn't matter. We'll just be a little crazier than we are and we haven't far to go. The amazing thing is that the work goes on. And one day it will be through. It is hot today. Working without clothes. All out of sheets. I may do a washing when I get through. I'm getting a fairly early start and the work is fairly well worked out. I should get done fairly early. And I could do all of the sheets easily. Will try to do it. But I won't think of it until I get through. The noise at the next house is abating. I always put down the time that I start on this work diary. Should be the time actually on the manuscript. But it doesn't matter. Today, I'm going to deal to a large extent with Ma [Ed.—Chapter 22]. She hasn't had an exclusive [Ed.—section] for a long time if ever. And I want to build her up as much as possible. Her possibility as a member of an organized society. I want to show how valuable Ma* is to society—what a waste there is. And now is the time to get to work. Glad to be in the book once again. I hope I don't rip out the sections [Ed.—of the ledger book] until I am through after this. There's a kind of safety in keeping in the book that I like. Tomorrow I must find Noah and send him down the Colorado River. And now to work.

Entry #69
Sept[ember] 12 [1938]—10:50 [Monday]

119-120

Things get no more peaceful. Today Hitler* is to make his war or peace speech. That may toss the world into a mess. Apparently the whole world is jittery about it. All armies mobilized. It might be a shambles by tomorrow. And it might recede for a while. Can't tell. And personally there are so many things. New books are here [Ed.—*The Long Valley*]. Haven't seen them yet. Go for them later. Tom was here. Little trouble Saturday because of liquor and talk. Alice Cohee due today. I hope after our work is done. Stones will get off the ranch on Friday they say. Lawrence is starting work on the new house tomorrow. How I wish we would be in on it. But we can't. I want Carol to catch up with me. Then she can quit and work at the house. She should catch up in two weeks. I must untighten my jaw. Too many things are happening. Must be calm and not disgusted. But it is hard because I have

Richard Allman, La Crescenta, California

of Wrath. [Steinbeck made the stake fence and the sign himself.]

BELOW: Contemporary view of the Santa Cruz Mountains from the front of the house the Steinbecks built at the Biddle Ranch, near the Summit, Los Gatos. Its breathtaking view and secluded site inspired Steinbeck to call it "the most beautiful place I have ever seen." (See Entry 46.)

TOP AND INSET: The Steinbecks' first Los Gatos house, Arroyo del Ajo (Garlic Gulch), where they lived from 1936 through 1938, and where the novelist wrote all of *The Grapes*

Robert DeMott

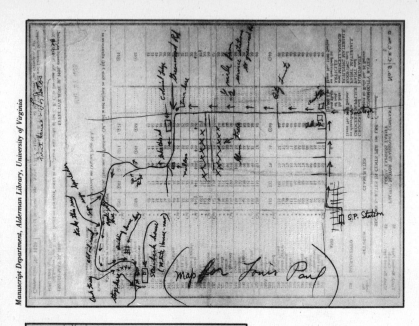

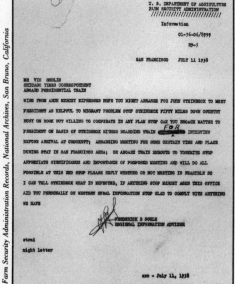

area is now Monte Sereno).

LEFT: Frederick R. Soule's letter concerning plans for Steinbeck to meet President Roosevelt. (See Entries 34 and 35.)

OPPOSITE TOP AND INSET: Photographs of Thomas Collins ("To TOM who lived it") by Dorothea Lange, circa 1936, at Weedpatch, Kern County Migrant Camp, Arvin, California. Besides providing Steinbeck with guidance, information, and documents, Collins also served as the model for Jim Rawley, manager of the government camp in *The Grapes of Wrath*.

TOP: Steinbeck's hand-drawn map for Louis and Mary Paul, showing directions to the Steinbecks' house, Los Gatos (this

Jackson J. Benson, La Mesa, California; and the Library of Congress

BELOW: Carol Steinbeck ("To CAROL who willed this book"), photographed in 1941 near the swimming pool behind the Steinbecks' Summit home, Los Gatos.

John Steinbeck Library, Salinas, California

New Start
Big Writing
I.

To the red country and part of the grey country of Oklahoma, the last rains came gently and they did not cut the scarred earth. The plows crossed and recrossed the rivulet marks. The last rains lifted the corn quickly and scattered weed colonies and grass along the sides of the roads so that the grey country and the dark red country began to disappear under a green cover. In the last part of May the sky grew pale and the clouds that had hung in high puffs for so long in the spring were dissipated. The sun flared down on the growing corn day after day until a line of brown spread along the edge of each green bayonet. The clouds appeared and went away and in a while they did not try any more. The weeds grew darker green to protect themselves and they did not spread any more. The surface of the earth crusted, a thin hard crust, and as the sky became pale so the earth became pale, pink in the red country and white in the grey country. In the water cut gullies, the earth dusted down in dry little streams. Gophers and ant lions started small avalanches. And as the sharp sun struck day after day the leaves of the young corn became less stiff and erect; they bent in a curve at first and then as the central ribs of strength grew weak, each leaf tilted down ward. Then it was June and the sun shone more fiercely. The brown lines on the corn leaves widened and moved in on the central ribs. The weeds frayed and moved back toward their roots. The air was thin and the sky more pale and every day the earth paled. In the roads where the teams moved, where the wheels milled the ground and the hooves of the horses beat the ground, the dirt crust broke and the dust formed. Every moving thing lifted the dust into the air; a walking man lifted a cloud as high as his waist, and a wagon lifted the dust as high as the fence tops; and an automobile boiled a cloud behind it. The dust was long in settling back again. When June was half gone, the big clouds moved up out of Texas and the gulf, high heavy clouds, rain-heads. The men in the fields looked up at the clouds and sniffed at them and held wet fingers up to sense the wind. And the horses were nervous while the clouds were up. The rain heads dropped a little spattering rain and hurried on to some other country. Behind them the sky was pale again and the sun flared. In the dust there were drop and in the dust there were clean splashes on the followed the rain clouds the drying corn

Migratory Farm Workers!

For your protection, follow these instructions before accepting employment from any LABOR CONTRACTOR:

1. Demand to see his LICENSE or his BOND receipt. The state law compels a labor contractor to have a bond and a license. Be sure the license or bond is dated 1938.

2. DO NOT accept his verbal offer, or his say so, of a job some place else. DEMAND that he write you an ORDER to go to the other job, and DEMAND that he include in the ORDER a statement that he WILL PUT YOU TO WORK on your arrival there. DEMAND that he sign his name to the order with ink or pencil. His name stamped with a rubber stamp, or printed or typewritten or mimeographed, does not make the order any good. He MUST sign it.

3. If you do not receive your wages when due, report at once to the nearest office of the State Labor Commissioner. He will collect your wages free of charge. You do not need a lawyer. All wages MUST be paid in cash or its equal.

4. If you follow these instructions you can protect yourself because you can obtain redress from the LAW, because you can go to the LAW in case you do not get the job after you arrive where the labor contractor told you to go. SAVE YOUR GAS AND OIL FOR FOOD AND CLOTHING FOR YOUR FAMILY.

EDUCATIONAL BULLETIN NO. 1   D. F. No. 65

1 ⟨⟩ 2

OPPOSITE: The opening page of the holograph manuscript of *The Grapes of Wrath*. ". . . I feel that this is Carol's book so I gave her the manuscript," Steinbeck told Pascal Covici in 1939 (Steinbeck and Wallsten, eds., *Steinbeck: A Life in Letters*, p. 180). Carol sold the manuscript fifteen years later through the San Francisco rare-book dealer Warren R. Howell. It was purchased by Clifton Waller Barrett and is now housed at the University of Virginia.

OPPOSITE INSET: Inside front cover of first edition of *The Grapes of Wrath*, showing placement of Julia Ward Howe's "Battle Hymn of the Republic" (1862). It was the source for the novel's title, discovered by Carol on September 2, 1938. ". . . Carol got the title last night '*The Grapes of Wrath*.' I think that is a wonderful title. . . . The book has being at last." (See Entry 63.)

ABOVE: *Educational Bulletin No. 1*, distributed to migratory workers in California. Steinbeck drew on the first two points for the scene in Chapter 20 of *The Grapes of Wrath* where Floyd Knowles challenges the unlicensed work contractor.

ABOVE: Steinbeck worked on Chapter 20 (Chapter 8 in the manuscript) of *The Grapes of Wrath* from August 18 through September 3, 1938. The chapter covered fourteen pages in his 18-by-12-inch lined ledger book. At the bottom of manuscript page 109, he added, "long son of a bitch too."

"On'y way you gonna get me to go is whup me," She moved the
jack handle gently again. "An' I'll shame you, Pa. I won't
take no whuppin', cryin' an' a-beggin'. I'll light into you.
An' you ain't so sure you can whup me anyways. An' if ya do
git me, I swear to God I'll wait till you got your back turned,
or you're settin' down, an' I'll knock you belly-up with a
bucket. I swear to Holy Jesus' sake I will."

Pa looked helplessly about the group. "She's sassy,"
he said. "I never seen her so sassy." Ruthie giggled shrilly.

The jack handle flicked hungrily back and forth
in Ma's hand. "Come on," said Ma. "You made up your mind.
Come on an' whup me. Jes' try it. But I ain't a goin'; or

Printer:
Pick up type
from dummy

To the red country and part of the grey country of
Oklahoma, the last rains came gently, and they did not cut the
scarred earth. The plows crossed and recrossed the rivulet
marks. The last rains lifted the corn quickly and scattered
weed colonies and grass along the sides of the roads so that the
grey country and the dark red country began to disappear under
a green cover. In the last part of May the sky grew pale and
the clouds that had hung in high puffs for so long in the spring
were dissipated. The sun flared down on the growing corn day
after day until a line of brown spread along the edge of each
green bayonet. The clouds appeared, and went away, and in a
while they did not try any more. The weeds grew darker green to
protect themselves, and they did not spread any more. The
surface of the earth crusted, a thin hard crust, and as the sky
became pale, so the earth became pale, pink in the red country
and white in the grey country.

In the water-cut gulleys the earth dusted down in dry
little streams. Gophers and ant lions started small avalanches.
And as the sharp sun struck day after day the leaves of the
young corn became less stiff and erect; they bent in a curve at

To my darling dancing partner John, Here's hoping you to your way to the tops! XO & kisses Bette Grable Conger

PREVIOUS PAGE: Sample pages from the typescript of *The Grapes of Wrath*, submitted directly to McIntosh and Otis, and then to The Viking Press. Carol Steinbeck's typescript (which was the second, and final, draft of the novel) was so clear that a third draft was not needed: ". . . there is to be no final draft, thank goodness," Steinbeck wrote. (See Entry 98.)

ABOVE: Publicity photograph of Gwyn Conger, circa 1939, inscribed playfully to John Steinbeck—"To my darling dancing partner John, here's hoping you tap your way to the tops"—from "Bette Grable Conger." Gwyn and Steinbeck met in Hollywood in 1939, and were married in New Orleans in 1943, shortly after Steinbeck obtained his divorce from Carol.

been working too long on this book, longer than on anything in my life. If this book is bad, I'm going to be terribly disappointed. Today Ma meets the ladies committee [Ed.—Chapter 22] and it must have some charm. It must. It can't flop because here is the great contrast. Here is the tremendous contrast. It must be charming. And I am late getting started today. Jaw is too tight.

Entry #70
Sept[ember] 13 [1938]—11:00 [Tuesday]

121-122
Very short note today. Beth is here and will stay the night. Books arrived and they are very good looking. Good advance sale which is tremendous for shorts. Must get to the ranch today and find out what that old fart [Ed.—Lawrence] is up to. He is messing around. The work today will include the great toilet paper scandal.* And it is very funny. I hope I can make it funny. And now it will be a good idea to get to work.

Entry #71
Sept[ember] 14—Out [Wednesday]

Ed came up and we took the day off. And needed it too. I think the rest did both of us good.

Entry #72
Sept[ember] 15 [1938]—11:00 [Thursday]

123–124
Late this morning and a little ashamed of it. The war has not broken yet. Chamberlain has gone to see Hitler. Double cross by England seems inevitable. Can't tell yet. England is making every

effort to avoid war. And tension increases. Can't tell yet. Last night to Pauls' for dinner. Ed looks fine in his new teeth. Gaining weight and looks pretty happy. This week end to Jacksons' to meet Adamic.* Should be fun. Went to the ranch yesterday. Ed quite crazy about it. Stones still on it. Supposed to go on Monday or Tuesday, I hope. We must get our work started there. Today my work is not so well mapped out. Just have to work along. And the end is not in sight. Have that time trouble.* Don't know yet how I am going to get over it. Maybe I'll figure it out later. Seems an awful problem now. But I'll get it worked out, I guess. It might strain the whole structure if I am not very careful. And I can't go on through it. I suppose it would be best to be very direct about it. That is usually the best. Today I think the general and I don't quite know which one it is. Can't very well do two more on camp life, or can I? I can to a certain extent. And then tomorrow do a general on music possibly, or on joy possibly. But today I should close up the first camp chapter [Ed.—Chapter 22] because the next is the dance chapter. Just have to figure it out. Time to work.

Entry #73
Sept[ember] 16 [1938]—11:00—Friday

125-126
Comes now the end of the week and a new general chapter. And this one is all the amusements of the people [Ed.—Chapter 23]. The things they do for pleasure. It is a short general. Not over four thousand words. I want all of the things they do. I want this to precede the long chapter of the dance [Ed.—Chapter 24]. Beginning a review of *Long Valley*—lyrical and without much meaning. However the book hasn't much meaning. Another wire

from Pat this morning saying that he still likes the new title *T.G.O.W.* I am pleased. I like it better all the time. I think it is the best title so far. Louis's dislike disturbed me but I am sure it is the right title. Tomorrow to S.F. and Berkeley. Tonight to dinner at Ben and Sally's. Seems to be a busy week end. Next week the ranch will be vacant. Shower last night. The first of the season. Laid the dust and this morning felt like Mexico. Nostalgic air. Full of curious whispers. Carol will get to page 270 today. How she is working! She'll be caught up in two more weeks. And then she can lay off for the duration and that will be good. I should be through in another month if I last. 25 days. Fifty thousand more words will finish it I am sure. Now to work.

Entry #74
Sept[ember] 19 [1938]—11:00 [Monday]

127 the departure of Noah

This seems to be the usual time of getting to work. War seems closer than ever. France and England are either selling out or being very clever. If the Czechs fight they won't be able to stay out. I think that there is probably skullduggery but I can't tell. To Jacksons' for the week end. Met a number of people—Adamic, and Covarrubias.* Nice people. Tiring though to meet so many of them. I feel pretty good today. Must go back and send Noah down the river.* May take something off today's work, but it's necessary. And still I don't know how soon I'll be through. Can't tell. I won't put down the number of pages until I am sure what I get done. Must go to work now.

Sept[ember] 20 [1938]—10:30 [Tuesday]

128-129

Yesterday did only half a day, but went back and caught up to Noah. Later went to ranch. The Stones are leaving today. Which means that we must get Steve pretty soon. Burkes are coming today to look at the house. They have really never seen it. Think I'll stay out of it. Carol handles things better than I do. I'll stay out here. Carol will cross 300 typed pages today. Poor kid is tired. Another week and she should be nearly through so that she can go on with the house and leave me to finish this book. Then later she can get back to typing and I can go on correcting. I'm still confronted with this time change, but it will iron out. I think this is harder on Carol than it is on me. Because I am so thoroughly broken in on it that it seems the normal [Ed.—routine] to me, while to her it is just work. There is no way of knowing. It is so desperately slow to do. I haven't figured out the wordage for some time. Guess I'll do it now, and then to work. Well, I figured it out, and it isn't far from 600 pages along, which is a hell of a lot of pages. And Carol isn't nearly as far along as she thought. Well, she can stop any time, but I can't. I must go on until I finish. What a long book this is. I hope it holds together. She is just at the fixing of the car [Ed.—Chapter 16] and that is a long time back. I should go to work now because the time is creeping upon me toward eleven. I bought my electric plant. I want maybe to get a little pelton wheel for lights. That would be good but would require a double wiring system but might be worth it. I'll see about it. Can't tell yet. Well anyway, the time has come to go to work. I'm sure of that. This book will be at least 800 typed pages long.

(Finished).

Entry #76
Sept[ember] 21 [1938]—10:30 [Wednesday]

130-131

I see no reason why I shouldn't fill in the pages to be written today. I have an early start. Letter from Beth—letter from [Ed.—actress Paulette] Goddard. Today it is likely that Steve will arrive. Wish we were free. It would make everything easy. But we are not free. I still can't see the end of this book. Today the dance [Ed.—Chapter 24]. And I think that will end the chapter—then south, then north. And in the north the end. But the dance will be the last I think. There isn't much to put down. Might as well get to work. And so to work without more trouble.

Entry #77
Sept[ember] 22 [1938]—10:25 [Thursday]

132-133 only half of 133 but will let it stand

Coughing pretty badly this morning. Too much excitement, too much smoking. Today we will go to the ranch and for the first time look it over without being shown. But there is work to be done first. Today the general chapter of the rotting fruit, and of the destroyed fruit and vegetables [Ed.—Chapter 25]. This should be a good chapter if I can write it. It should be fun. Well, must get to work and finish this chapter, no matter how long or short.

Entry #78
Sept[ember] 23 [1938]—11:00 [Friday]

Today is Friday. Yesterday I finished the general chapter of the rotting fruit. Today I must go on. The book is beginning to round out. I think they go to Shafter. I think. I can begin to see the end. But that time jump is bound to give me trouble. I want this book to be perfectly integrated. Well it is heading toward that now. I rather think I will spend today in contemplation. I don't know. Things are weighing on me. And time is passing. I have not heard from Pare which would indicate that his plan has not matured. But it is impossible to know and I am floundering some. There are letters to write. I really shouldn't take the time right now but I feel rather devilish about the whole thing. So many things come up and go down. The T.F. matter has undoubtedly died. I hear so many things like that die. And as for this book, it goes on and on. Pare doesn't want or need me I am pretty sure. I have lots of time to finish. Maybe I'll write to Pare today and try to get an answer out of him. Perhaps it would help. Anyway, I am fairly sure now that I shan't work today but will build on work. The Stones have left the ranch and the foundation forms of the new house are in. What a place it will be. I want to dig holes. I want to use a shovel. Did some yesterday and it made me feel fine. How I wish I were through. The time has come now to write a letter to Pare, I am pretty sure.

Entry #79
Sept[ember] 26 [1938]—11:30 [Monday]

134-135

This book has become a misery to me because of my inadequacy. Friday I took off to consider my progress, and instead I got caught in all the details of the new ranch. And I grew frightened of this property. It is so much. One person or two have not the right to have so much. Then Steve came Saturday. And Steve is a member of I AM,* a very complicated pseudo-psycho religion for people who want to dodge responsibility. That's all right if he doesn't go about conversion of us. And I am afraid that Steve is not going to be all right at all. Can't tell yet, of course. Anyway Francis* and Ritch and Tal and Ed were all up here and it was a terrific week end and it left me rather limp and raggy. And today I am still raggy and have to gather myself in. And I'm frightened that I'm losing this book in the welter of other things. The war about to break. I don't think it will, and everything. Play goes on the road. Philly Oct. 19. Must write to Annie Laurie. Neither Wally nor Brod in it and I don't care about that. A curious megalomania took them over. Rightly I guess. I hear *The Long Valley* was well reviewed* in the East. Joe hasn't touched it. Maybe he is irritated at me. I don't know. But that is his business, not mine. Carol is nearly four hundred pages along on her typing. Hope she stops pretty soon and puts up the front against the outside. I find that I am trying to get done early these days and that is entirely wrong. Today I am going to discipline myself by working all day. Can't have this time barrier up. It would ruin the book. Must throw out the world for a little time more—a month perhaps. We'll see, but I must keep it leisurely and not try to get done too fast. Must remember that. We don't have to put in a new pipe [Ed.—water line] until we want to. Just get the house ready. That's the thing. This book is my sole responsibility and I must stick to it and nothing more. This book is my life now or must be. When it is done, then will be the time for another life. But, not until it is done. And the other lives have begun to get in. There is no doubt of that. That is why I am taking so much time in this diary this morning—to calm myself. My stomach and my nerves are screaming merry hell in protest against the inroads. I won't be glad when it is done so why try to hurry it done? Now, I hope I calm down enough to start work again.

Entry #80
Sept[ember] 27 [1938]—11:00 [Tuesday]

136-137

Time again. Letters—Elizabeth saying she may come out in November. Margolies* in Brentanos again. And that's all. Hitler has pulled in his stomach a little bit. The force against him is too great, I guess, even for his craziness. Saturday is the dead line fixed. I don't think it will come to war, and neither do many. But the preparation goes on and it will take only one word to start it. The Poles can probably do it if they get rough. Lawrence here about the house and windows and stuff. Foundations are all poured at the new house. This afternoon we go up to Masson [Ed.— Martin Ray's] to look at the grapes. They aren't really ready. Won't be for a week or ten days. Must go to work now. Wire from Chaplin says he'll be here Friday.

Entry #81
Sept[ember] 28 [1938]—11:00 [Wednesday]

138-139

Well, time again to start [Ed.—Chapter 26]. Action is about to start in this book for a while. People will be led to scab and will break out of it. Will go north for the cotton and will end there. Go to the box car camp and be moved by flood waters. And the book will end there. But there is a hell of a lot to happen yet. I mustn't get impatient. I'll be lucky if another month does it. I don't care much. Yesterday I worked in the grapes and it proved how soft I am for the back hurt. Haven't seen any reviews of the shorts except for Fadiman's.* Hear there is a review in the *Chronicle** this morning. Will ask Carol to get it. Foundations are poured for the new house now. I must take my time about starting. This is the important part of the book. Must get it down. This little strike. Must win it. Must be full of movement, and it must have the fierceness of the strike. And it must be won. I can't let this thing get lost at this late date. And in my mind the story is moving again. They'll be recruited first [Ed.—to pick peaches at Hooper Ranch in Pixley], then escorted by state police, then by farm deputies. That night Tom creeps out and penetrates the lines. Meets the preacher, etc. However, I won't get them today or any where near. I'll be glad to see Chaplin. I think he'll like the winery and the grapes. I hope so. I hope so. I love it. I like the smell and the process. I'm sure he will. Funny man. Seems so dreadfully lonely. Maybe that's why he wants to come up so much. The rotisserie will make him love it. I'm sure and the bird cooking on the spindle. Now I must get to work. Three more work days this week. Finished a section yesterday. Must go on now. The tire is broken.

Entry #82
Sept[ember] 29 [1938]—11:30 [Thursday]

Late start today. Carol is gone in to San Jose. Some people just came to the gate, photographed each other in front of it and then went on. This is the most sickening thing that has happened so far. It sort of turns my stomach. I wonder about work today. Going to finish O.K. if only Pare doesn't insist. Wish I would hear from him. It will be November before I am done in any way. Might just think today. And work in the house. Today is the big meeting in Munich for the partition of the Czech republic. I don't think it is the end yet. I thought I would work today but I guess I must [indecipherable].

Entry #83
Sept[ember] 30 [1938]—11:00 [Friday]

Yesterday was an unhappy maundering bust. And today doesn't look much better. It started early. Parsons* told in her column that Chaplin was coming for the weekend and already real estate people are trying to sell stuff. This meant guarding against [Ed.— intrusions]. I am all mixed up, but this time I simply won't let myself. After all I have a book to write. Once it is written it will be all right. Then I can do things. And then I probably won't want to. This is a hell of a day. I must get down to it now and prove to myself that I can still concentrate no matter how badly. Time to go now. Get to it and fight it through.

Entry #84
Oct[ober] 3 [1938]—[Monday]

Time has come now for a resume. My book is going to pieces if I am not careful. I look at it this way. I have one more month of work. I must keep this up. One more month of good hard work will finish it. So I must put it in. Must. I intend to take today off—making a hell of a long lay-off for the purpose of getting in working trim again. And then the dash for the finish. And it will only be about as long as an ordinary short novel. But today I must get the tendency back again. Short resume of week end— Chaplin and Dan James were here. We had lots of talk and fun and very little reporter trouble. Talked a great deal. Must be sure not to go. Up for the party* and fun and talk. I'm confused by the talk yet. That's why no work today. Must shake off the confusion and then work tomorrow after a good long sleep and a dull evening. That's the necessity. And to slip back. I need that. I must have that. Now I'm simply talking and talking. But I think I have the energy now, and I think I've lost the tiredness like being away for a while. Now I can get these people back again. And a dash and I will be done. Think! Think! Like Frank W. This is going to work. I feel very good about this book now. What I am worrying about is this draft. I am convinced that Carol shall not do the dull final draft. And at the same time there must be a great deal to do with the manuscript. My hand writing is bad now. One more month—one more. And then I have it. I am just gibbering. And that is all right. I don't care. At three o'clock. What strangeness. What strangeness. Can't let things go.

FINAL.
Entry #85
Oct[ober] 4 [1938]—11:15 [Tuesday]

140-141

And now all of the foolishness and the self-indulgence is over. Now there can be no lost days and no lost time. Straight through to the finish now without loss. It must be that way. And I shall do it. Shall gather all my will together and go on. That is settled. The disintegration lately has been terrible. It can't go on. I have done that amount before and I can again. In fact, at the beginning of each day now I shall again put down the pages to be done and then they will get done. My laziness is overwhelming. I must knock it over. Don't feel right about it if I don't, and I think after this good rest it will be all right. I have the energy now. All I need is the force to go ahead. There isn't an awful lot more. But it must move slowly and truly on and on until the finish and this time there must be no hesitation. This work diary is complete thus far. Must make it final. And now the time has come. There have been delays and rests and squirms. And now such things are over. What do I care if criticism is adverse?* The book must go on to a conclusion this time. I remember the drive of the other days. And this must be a drive to the end. And now I'll read a little of the early diary and then plunge in. This time it is a GO signal and a real one. I've been looking back over this diary and, by God, the pressures were bad the whole damned time. There wasn't a bit that wasn't under pressure and now the pressure is removed and I'm still having trouble. It would be funny if my book was no good at all and if I had been kidding myself. Now forget the end and just go gradually to work. So long, diary.

(Finished).

Entry #86
Oct[ober] 5 [1938]—11:30 [Wednesday]

142-143

Late start today. I slept until 9:30. I don't know why. Defeated dreams too. I don't know why those either. But I feel fine this morning and the dreams have no effect. I don't care about the lateness of the start. I have plenty of time, plenty. And I've lost the rush feeling. Yesterday to the ranch—they have framed in the house and sheathed it. I always hate to come down again. It is so fine up there. Well before too long we'll be there, I guess. Yes. We'll be there. And in time this book will be done. All in good time. I'll get it done. Just trust in that. Pare has not made any demands on me. No one has. The demands of people to use my name. Things like that are different. They can't be helped. It is particularly fine today because the noise next door has stopped at least for the moment. No cement mixer, or pounding on pipe or things like that. Almost too good to be true. It would be funny if the absence of noise made it hard. It won't. It is delicious this silence. Absolutely delicious. And my story is coming better. I

see it better. See it better. Ma's crossing with the clerk [Ed.—
in the Hooper Ranch Company Store], and then Tom's going out—
meeting Casy—trying to move the men in the camp. Arrest and
beating. Return in secret. Move. Cotton—flood. And the end—
Tom comes back. Stolen things. Must go. Be Around. Birth. And
the rising waters. And the starving man. And the end. What
more? And now to it.

Entry #87
Oct[ober] 6 [1938]—10:30 [Thursday]

144-145

Early start this morning. Can't ever tell. Worked long and
slowly yesterday. Don't know whether it was good, but it was a
satisfactory way to work and I wish it would be that way every
day. I've lost this rushed feeling finally and can get back to the
easy method of day by day—which is as it should be. Got the
iron gate [Ed.—in exchange] for an autograph. That is a bargain.
Today I shall work slowly and try to get that good feeling again.
It must be. Just a little bit every day. A little bit every day. And
then it will be through. And the story is coming to me fast now.
And it will be fast from now on. Movement fast but the detail
slow as always. I seem to be delaying pretty badly today. Half
an hour gone already and I don't care because the little details
are coming, are getting clearer all the time. So the more I wait,
the more of this book will get written. How about the jail. Today,
the preacher and Tom and the raid on the tent and the killing of
the preacher [Ed.—Chapter 26]. Tom's escape. Kills. Goes back
to the camp to hide. Tom—half bitterness, half humane. Escapes
in the night. Hunted, hunted. Over the last pages Tom hangs
like a spirit around the camp. And in the water brings stolen
food. Must get to work now. The thing speeds up.

Entry #88
Oct[ober] 7 [1938]—11:00 [Friday]

146-147

Friday again and a short week. Has gone quickly. I think the work has been pretty good but I can't tell. I've a funny feeling about it. And a change is coming over me—a goatish sexuality. The summer has been just the opposite—very low. Now it is rising rapidly. Maybe the weather, I don't know. Maybe the burden of the work getting near an end has something to do with it. No mail of importance this morning. Not even requests for things. Today is quiet. I should be able to get my work done fairly easily. Furnace men coming this afternoon. I hope they come early. There is one fly in this room and I can't find him. I hope next week the work comes as well as this week. I think it will. And 10,000 [Ed.—words] next week instead of 8,000. Got the fly. He is the last. Now—no hurry today. Plenty of time. Yesterday, I finished early and wasted a great deal of time. Today I can't do that. Take all the time on the manuscript I want. It is Friday and I can finish gradually for the week. This leisurelyness must go on although the tempo gets faster the details must be as slow. Today the hiding of Tom and the scene with his mother [Ed.— the end of Chapter 26]. The cut in wages. Tom has to go. Getting together. The drop to starvation level of the wages. The trapped quality. Must get it in—Difficulty of getting clean. No soap. No money to buy soap. Then peaches. The rush of workers and the fight for the peaches. Fight to get them. Must get this all in. There's so damned much in this book already. I must keep it coming. Furnace men came. Means we can get in to San Jose today. Must get to work.

Entry #89
Oct[ober] 10 [1938]—11:00—Monday

148-149

Very quiet week end for a change. Mary and Bill* Saturday night and to dinner. Had fun and a good bottle of wine. Home after going up to the ranch in the moonlight. The roof is on the new house. Begins to look like a house. And another agent from Hollywood wanting to buy *The Red Pony*. Carol took it and shot it. I don't want that stuff. Nice day today and I'm in no hurry. I can take all the time I want. And that's a good way to work. Carol is going up to the ranch. And this week I want a full week's work. No short week this time or I won't even finish on the first of November as I'd planned. I'll do it. I'll get the book done if I just set one day's work in front of the last day's work. That's the way it comes out. And that's the only way it does. Writing is a little bit bigger today. It usually is at the beginning of a week. Well the time has come. Must get to it. 150 pages tomorrow.

Finished 3:30.

Entry #90
Oct[ober] 11 [1938]—10:30 [Tuesday]

150-151

I'm a little early today. A brilliant day, with an autumn snap to it. Good day for work. And the work is ready to do. Carol is going to S.F. tomorrow. I want to get down and see about the motor today. Try it on a refrigerator and see if it will start it. Time has come to get it up there. Well the work is moving along. And I don't resent it. All the growth of the fascist tendency is heart breaking. Nothing seems to work against its stupidity and one gets very tired. I think I wish I wouldn't have to think. Wish I could just let things go past but that time is gone. No one can escape it. Me least of all. I'll probably be framed before very long. As usual I'm messing around a lot before going to work so that it is now darned near eleven o'clock and me not actually at work yet. There is the problem of the flood and whether I'll include it. I think so. I think I will and I think I'll include the box car camp and the digging all night and the break through. It is really time to go to work. But today is Tuesday and I might as well fill out.* Letter from my cousin Grace—first in 22 years. Wonder what she is like. I bet I know. The Y.W. must have left its mark. And the interest is solely because of the publicity. Seems to affect every one. She'll be denying the relationship before long now. Every one will. To work.

Funny Hopper came by yesterday.

Entry #91
Oct[ober] 12 [1938]—10:45 [Wednesday]

152

I got a fairly early start today and then George Mors came and talked a while so I am a little late. I may do only half today because then I'll finish just this section this week. And it will even up the numbers. The end is peering in on me now. I can feel it. It's coming closer. But a lot of things have to happen. Also I am pretty excited now about my story. Al is going to get married and go away. Al is tough. Tom is going to go. Hint of small pox, measles. Measles for R. of S. [Ed.—Rose of Sharon], weakening. Cause miscarriage or rather birth of dead baby. Breast pump. Then the rain. Tom comes back. And he goes again. Letter from Sis.* La Follette people* are here. That may raise hell. I think the time has come and with one page. One end of a box car [Ed.—Chapter 28]

Entry #92
Oct[ober] 13 [1938]—10:45 [Thursday]

153-154

Yesterday only half a day's work, but with good reason. This blind weariness had me. I can't tell anyone about it but I am almost sick to my stomach with tiredness. The air is very heavy today. Must be going to rain. It is stifling. But it is quiet. No pounding or anything like that any more. The mail this morning—just a mass of requests. Driving me crazy. Terribly nervous today. As Carl* used to say—I'm nervous as a cat. Cats always seemed to me to be fairly placid animals. It becomes increasingly apparent that I must make a stand against joining things as I have against speaking. The mail is full of requests to use my name. Another request to be a clay pigeon. I won't do any of these public things. Can't. It isn't my nature and I won't be stampeded. And so the stand must be made and I must keep out of politics. Now these two things are constantly working at me. Criticism of me is very strong and will grow bitter but I must remember the one and the ninety-nine [Ed.—Luke 15:3–7]. And I must not stampede. I want to see.

Entry #93
Oct[ober] 14 [1938]—10:45 [Friday]

155-156 Section

Comes Friday and this time Friday and a section come at the same time. Again no mail but requests. Pat will be in S.F. early next week. If tomorrow should be a rainy day, I think I will do a page to catch up in case I lose a day next week, which I probably will. I think probably one more section or two weeks will get this done. Had I worked every day I should be done now. Yesterday was a good scene. Must repair one part of it. I'm getting excited now that the end is coming up. Rather work than not. I'll be sad when this is done. But I am glad to finish. Only two more weeks or maybe less. Depends. The last general must be a summing of the whole thing. Group survival. Yes, I am excited. Almost prayerful that this book is some good. Maybe it is and maybe not. Now let's see what we have. The marriage of Al—the birth of the baby—the general on rain and survival—the trenching and then the flight to the high land—the finding of the barn. Attempt to sell the car, it is flooded and lost. Not so much, you see, and concentrated tempo. And ending where I thought. Well—there is no reason not to go back to it now. I hope my hand doesn't shake too much any more. I guess I might as well get to it. After today an outside of 20 pages. Probably less.

Entry #94
Oct[ober] 17 [1938]—11:00 [Monday]

157-158

Monday again but because of the nearness of the ending of this book a day of excitement and the reserve was taken up also. Interesting to see if it really is a second wind. I think so. Need the energy now because there has been a great drain of energy and emotion into this book. Pat due in S.F. some time this week. Letter from Pare talking about the picture [Ed.—*In Dubious Battle*]. I really think we'll work on it when I get through. Letter from Louis.* He likes part of the manuscript. And doesn't like part. Must judge his criticism coldly as valid, but only as one man's criticism. It is very valuable. I've been so tied up that I don't know. And I don't want to know until I am finished. That is going to be difficult to get it in second draft. And I think I shall have to do another draft without fail—not Carol though. She will have done enough. I'll get a regular stenographer to do it. Probably can get one with ease. But I am sure it must be done. I think I will have to make many changes if only just of tone and word. Sorry, but I could hardly be expected to whip out finished copy. It'll work out some way. Kind of dull feeling up around the eyes. Clinical I guess. I've had a fine rest this week end. And am all ready to go, and there is no time like right now [Ed.— final section of Chapter 28].

Entry #95
Oct[ober] 18 [1938]—11:15 [Tuesday]

159

Today a single page—the general of the rain, and the last general [Ed.—Chapter 29]. And then one more very long chapter to finish. I expect Pat to call today but he hasn't so far. The month is flying away. Never saw time go so quickly as this spring and summer and yet the daily time has not been so quick. Not quick at all. I'll be glad to see Pat. I only hope he is not embarrassed or anything. I should be hurrying to work in case he calls. But I don't want to hurry this. My nerves are very shaky. Little sleep these nights. But I'm going to finish, by God. I'm sure going to finish and whether it is any good or not it will be done. I wonder how I'll feel then? Good I hope. And then the whole weight of every one who wants me to do things will fall on me. Well—that's what I must watch out for. I have the energy to work but I'm not going to be rushed.

Entry #96
Oct[ober] 19 [1938]—10:45 [Wednesday]

160-161

Wednesday today and I am a little early in starting. Play opened last Thursday in Pittsburgh. Haven't heard how well. May hear later. Wally and Brod are not in it. Then—Pat is in S.F., but very busy. We'll go up Friday to get him. Another note from Rodman. Still wanting material. I think I'll tell Pat to let him look over the manuscript and maybe take a general chapter.* I don't know. McWilliams* wires me to come to meeting in L.A. Request to serve on the board of Dramatists' Guild. Here are [indecipherable] just for the [indecipherable]. I'm not too hot for work today. Strong reluctance to finish I think. Can't give myself the allowance of laziness just now. When it is done I can—but not until then. My mind doesn't want to work—hates to work in fact, but I'll make it. I'm on my very last chapter now. The very last. It may be fifteen pages long but I can't help that. It may be twenty. The rain—the birth—the flood—and the barn. The starving man and the last scene that has been ready so long. I don't know. I only hope it is some good. I have very grave doubts sometimes. I don't want this to seem hurried. It must be just as slow and measured as the rest but I am sure of one thing—it isn't the great book I had hoped it would be. It's just a run-of-the-mill book. And the awful thing is that it is absolutely the best I can do. Now to work on it.

Entry #97
Oct[ober] 20 [1938]—12:00 [Thursday]

162

A late start. After last night it is no wonder. My nerves blew out like a fuse and today I feel weak and powerless. I wish it hadn't happened until I was through. Guess I better not press my luck. Just write today until I am tired and not force it. Got to if I don't want to collapse. About three or four more days and it will be done. Funny to think in such terms. Seems impossible that it should be so near. Maybe it shouldn't be. I hope the close isn't controlled by my weariness. I wouldn't like that. But I think this is really a good tiredness. "Tom! Tom! Tom!" I know. It wasn't him. Yes, I think I can go on now. In fact, I feel stronger. Much stronger. Funny where the energy comes from. Now to work only now it isn't work any more.

Entry #98
Oct[ober] 24 [1938]—10:00 [Monday]

Monday again and I think it is my last week. I'm almost dead from lack of sleep. Can't go to sleep. I don't know why. Just plan for the ending. Pat was here for the week end. He read the first part—400 pages. He is very volatile. Likes it very much, he said. I hope he doesn't over sell* it. Too many superlatives can spoil its chances. I hope he lays low and lets people find out about it if they will. Well any way, that's the story. Saturday and Sunday went out to the ranch. Set a lot of gopher traps. Caught four and have ten traps out now. Can gradually work them out if I keep after them. Word from Pittsburgh that M & M is playing to crowded houses. Hope it gets a little run. It could pay for the whole damned ranch if it wanted to. And also it could pay Viking out on the contract. Well enough of that. My stomach is shot to pieces with tiredness. If I could only get some sleep I'd be all right. Twelve hours I'd like. Carol is back at typing. Poor kid, but there is to be no final draft, thank goodness. Well, I might as well get to the work. No one is going to do it for me.

Entry #99
Oct[ober] 25 [1938]—11:00 [Tuesday]

163-164

I don't know whether it was just plain terror of the ending or not. My stomach went to pieces yesterday. May have been nerves. I lay down and slept all afternoon. Went to bed at 10:30 and slept all night. May be some kind of release. At any rate, I feel rested today and that is something. Don't know how many pages or days to finish. Probably three days. Must get into it today. Beautiful weather. Carol ruined her hand typing yesterday. Can't work today. I must get through so I can take all the house work. Nice weather for the finish, but I almost wish it would rain. No letters this morning. I have nothing to bother me so there is no reason at all for not continuing. And I think I have every single move mapped out for the ending. I only hope it is good. It simply has to be. Well, there it is, all of it in my mind. And I hesitate to get to it. Maybe I'm afraid I can't do it. But then I was afraid I couldn't do any of it. And just day by day I did it. So that is the way to finish it. Forget that it is the finish and just set down the day by day work. And now finally I must get to it.

Entry #100
Oct[ober] 26 [1938]—10:30 [Wednesday]

[165]

Today should be a day of joy because I could finish today—just the walk to the barn, the new people and the ending and that's all. But I seem to have contracted an influenza of the stomach or something. Anyway I am so dizzy I can hardly see the page. This makes it difficult to work. On the other hand, it might get worse. I might be in for a siege. Can't afford to take that chance. I must go on. If I can finish today I don't much care what happens afterwards. Wish—if it was inevitable, that it could have held off one more day. My fault really for having muffed on Monday oddly enough. I feel better—sitting here. I wish I were done. Best way is just to get down to the lines. I wonder if this flu could be simple and complete exhaustion. I don't know. But I do know that I'll have to start at it now and, of course, anything I do will be that much nearer the end.

Finished this day—and I hope to God it's good.

PART III:

Aftermath

(1939–1941)

. . . I must make a new start. I've worked the novel . . . as far as I can take it. I never did think much of it—a clumsy vehicle at best. And I don't know the form of the new but I know there is a new thing which will be adequate and shaped by the new thinking. Anyway, there is a picture of my confusion. How's yours?

—Steinbeck, in a letter of November 13, 1939, to Carlton Sheffield.
(In Steinbeck and Wallsten, eds., *Steinbeck: A Life in Letters*, p. 194)

Commentary

In March 1939, when John Steinbeck received copies from one of three advanced printings of *The Grapes of Wrath,* he was "immensely pleased with them," he told his editor, Pascal Covici, at The Viking Press (Steinbeck and Wallsten, eds., *Steinbeck: A Life in Letters,* p. 182). Besides achieving a memorable aesthetic and physical appearance, the result of its imposing size (619 pages long) and captivating Elmer Hader dust jacket illustration, which pictures the Joads "silent and awestruck" by their first view of a lush California valley near Tehachapi (Chapter 18), the novel also became an unprecedented commercial success. Following its official publication date on April 14, 1939, *The Grapes of Wrath* remained atop the best-seller lists for most of the year, selling roughly 428,900 copies in hard cover at $2.75 apiece. (In 1941, when The Sun Dial Press issued a hard-back reprint selling for $1.00, the publisher announced that over 543,000 copies of Steinbeck's novel had already been sold.)

The steady, unrelenting sale of the novel brought fame, notoriety, and financial success to the Steinbecks which exceeded their wildest dreams. "I don't think I ever saw so much [money] in one place before," Steinbeck told Elizabeth Otis. By October 1939, however, the dream had turned to "a nightmare," as Steinbeck confessed to his agent (Steinbeck and Wallsten, eds., *Stein-*

beck: A Life in Letters, pp. 182, 189). In addition to requests from strangers for money, there were invitations from club program chairmen and civic busybodies to speak publicly, which Steinbeck flatly refused: "Why do they think a writer, just because he can write, will make a good after-dinner speaker, or club committeeman, or even a public speaker? I'm no public speaker and I don't want to be. I'm not even a finished writer yet, I haven't learned my craft," he admonished an Associated Press interviewer in July 1939. More wrenching than that, however, there was constant vilification from the corporate agriculture industry (an August 26, 1939, United Press wire story stated that "The Associated Farmers of California, through its executive council . . . would do everything possible to tell the public that . . . 'Grapes of Wrath' . . . cannot be accepted as fact"), and vicious rumors and threats of reprisal circulated by large landowners and banks ("The latest is a rumor . . . that the Okies hate me and have threatened to kill me for lying about them," Steinbeck informed Carlton Sheffield on July 20, 1939). The "rolling might of this damned thing," the unhealthy "hysteria" of the novel's reception (Steinbeck and Wallsten, eds., *Steinbeck: A Life in Letters*, p. 188), all took their toll on Steinbeck, who became increasingly depressed and withdrawn.

As a result, the final segment of Steinbeck's journal has a very private, allusive air. It was written sporadically during a period of such chaotic emotional upheaval in his life that it sometimes reads like the notes for an unfinished romantic drama—full of turbulence, brooding signs and portents, but very little resolution. The entries vary in length, frequency, and details, Steinbeck's pace is less frantic than in the previous section, and his jottings are often more associative and deep-diving than those he made earlier. The motif of self-doubt is still prominent, but is compounded by guilt and tempered by foreshadowing, as though he were hovering on the brink of some enormous "catastrophe" (Entry #101). While the *Grapes of Wrath* section was informed by a terrible immediacy, an obsessive urgency, this section is colored by intimations of paranoia and dark fatality, all the more ominous because never fully articulated.

In fact, Steinbeck writes here as though Carol were looking over his shoulder and might at any moment discover the secret of his love affair with a twenty-year-old singer named Gwyndolyn Conger ("the other," Steinbeck cryptically calls her). His attachment to the aspiring showgirl (she was working in the chorus line at CBS studios, and in an Irene Dunne movie, *Theodora Goes Wild*) had escalated since their first meeting (instigated by "M," his childhood friend, Max Wagner) in Hollywood in June 1939. Steinbeck, physically ill, crippled by sciatica, and severely depressed, was "hiding out" from publicity at the Aloha Arms Apartments off Sunset Boulevard. Like "a half-assed Florence Nightingale," Gwyn brought him chicken soup and "sat talking with him the whole night through." Steinbeck hated chicken noodle soup, but he loved her talk and tender ministrations. "What happened between us that night was pure chemistry," Gwyn later recalled in her autobiography (Halladay, ed., " 'The Closest Witness,' " p. 36). Although their relationship proceeded slowly—now off, now on—Steinbeck was deeply hooked. Gwyn "is all woman, every bit woman," he crowed to Mavis McIntosh.

Steinbeck began these twenty-three irregular entries one year after completing his novel, while he and Carol were living at the Biddle ranch. They continue until late January 1941, when Steinbeck, on the lam in Pacific Grove with Gwyn, but getting the "horrors" regularly over Carol's unhappiness, summarily ended his reflections during the third day of writing *Sea of Cortez* with these words: "I think I'll leave this book now" (Entry #123). The distance between Los Gatos and Pacific Grove was only about sixty miles, but it might as well have been a thousand, because it was the difference—in Steinbeck's tortured view—between a settled existence of domestic attachment and financial security on the one hand, and an exciting life of uncertain future but passionate feeling on the other. (See Entries #120 and 121.) It is an old story, but one the morally conservative Steinbeck had never acted in before; as the following entries suggest, he vacillated miserably, his head in one place, his heart in another.

Mostly, Steinbeck was sick of being constrained. The two things he wanted above all others, he told Carlton Sheffield, were "freedom from respectability" and "freedom from the necessity of being consistent" (Steinbeck and Wallsten, eds., *Steinbeck: A Life in Letters*, p. 193). In fact, throughout 1939 and 1940 nearly everything associated with his public fame and private success—including, at times, his marriage—had become a repugnant "nightmare" to him; yet during the period observed in this section of his journal he couldn't bear to rectify his situation by confronting Carol directly. (The explosion occurred offstage, in April 1941; separated for two years, they finally divorced on March 18, 1943, and eleven days later John married Gwyn). Fatalistically, he wavered in his feelings, waiting for "salvations to be worked out," though he took little hand in their solution. "Trying to follow the plan I laid out," he told Wagner, "that of doing nothing" (John Steinbeck/[Max Wagner], letter, [August 22, 1939]; courtesy of Stanford University Library.) Customarily, he threw himself into a variety of writing projects, hoping to resurrect the discipline necessary to become productive again, even though several of his jobs were collaborations, a situation he never fully liked. He resolutely turned his back on the "clumsy" novel (between 1939 and 1945 he published eight books, only half of them fiction). Instead, he tried his hand at a whole new range of genres, including comic drama, documentary film, scientific prose, travel writing, and poetry. As part of his "complete revolution" Steinbeck cast off the straitjacket of novelist and took up the mantle of man of letters. It was an imperfect fit, but the new writing—especially *Sea of Cortez: A Leisurely Journal of Travel and Research*, which was immersed in his tide pool investigations and his belief that there was a "great poetry in scientific writing"—proved to be a "life saver" (John Steinbeck/Mavis McIntosh, letter [June 1941]; courtesy of University of Virginia Library).

Not all of Steinbeck's fresh departures reached their destinations on schedule. "The God in the Pipes," a satiric play written for his own pleasure, as well as that of Carol and of his sister Mary (Entry #114), gave him fits for several years, until he reluctantly gave it up entirely in 1941. "The tide pool hand book," based on a December 1939 collecting expedition with Ed Ricketts to Tomales Point and Duxbury Reef, was abandoned after Steinbeck failed twice to write a satisfactory introduction (Entries #106–108). But Steinbeck, as one might expect from a writer of profoundly ecological sympathies, rarely wasted his earlier experiences; rather, he frequently found ways to recycle them. He employed the basic metaphor of his "Pipes play"—human beings inhabiting the cast-off boilers and pipes of Monterey's cannery factories—in *Cannery Row* (1945) and its 1954 sequel, *Sweet Thursday* (Elizabeth Otis/Robert DeMott, interview, August 20, 1979). His preparatory exercises on the San Francisco Bay guidebook trained his eye and mind for *Sea of Cortez*, and found expression in his 1948 Preface to the revised edition of Ricketts's and Calvin's *Between Pacific Tides* (Entry #119). The apprentice labor on *The Fight for Life* Steinbeck performed for Pare Lorentz in Chicago (and later in Hollywood, where editing took place) gave him a foundation for his "Mexican film," *The Forgotten Village* (1941), a documentary about the clash of tribal "magic" with modern "medicine," produced and directed on location by

Herbert Kline, and simultaneously published by The Viking Press with 136 photographs from the film (Entries #119 and 120). And though Steinbeck had no way of knowing it then, even his short-lived future marriage to Gwyn (they divorced in 1948; she later summed up their "star-crossed" marriage as "tragic") would find its way into the bitter characterization of Adam and Kate Trask in *East of Eden* (1952), and—distilled even further—into the immortal words of Fauna, the bighearted madam of *Sweet Thursday*'s Bear Flag: "When a man falls in love it's ninety to one he falls for the dame that's worst for him."

While Steinbeck intermittently appeased his guilt by attempting a play for Carol, buying her a car (a Packard, just like his), and constructing a 60-by-15-foot swimming pool in their backyard (complete with a brass name plaque), he saved the spiritual part of himself for Gwyn. Steinbeck traveled often in 1940, mostly to Mexico, the setting for both *Sea of Cortez* and *The Forgotten Village*. These excursions separated him from Hollywood and Gwyn, for whom he had created an impossibly idealized role, and naturally the absences increased his heart's longing. In the autumn of 1940, between tedious bouts of revising the final script for *The Forgotten Village* and hammering out the pesky details of the film's voice-over narration, Steinbeck alleviated some of his boredom and frustration by composing—right under Carol's nose—a revealing suite of twenty-five love poems for his paramour (Entry #118). "Please tell Gwyn that I am making a song for her and I have never made a song for anyone before," he announced to Max Wagner, his Hollywood confidant and go-between, in November (Steinbeck and Wallsten, eds., *Steinbeck: A Life in Letters*, p. 217). These "songs of fulness / And fulfillment" (roughly in the manner of Petrarch's "Sonnets to Laura," but leavened with a mystical, confessional presence, like Whitman's "Song of Myself") are bursting with stock romantic notions—"nostalgia," passionate "longing," and inconsolable "ache of loneliness" be-tween the speaker and his ethereal "girl of the air," who is "young and red haired, milk skinned" (Halladay, ed., " 'The Closest Witness,' " pp. 301–27). Steinbeck's secret poetry is not lyrically even or linguistically memorable, but it does manifest the alogical coherency of emotional urgency, the quality of bright emotional promise (balanced with despair at their separation) which he projected on Gwyn. Perhaps most telling of all, the poems confer dignity on sexual attraction, and elevate the man's and the wom-an's mutual "chemistries" to a religious level: "The glory of syn-chronization of ductless glands," Steinbeck says in Poems 8 and 9, " . . . has been God in many times to many men. / And it still is God" (See Entry #109).

Steinbeck's naive propensity to idolize Gwyn suggests that his affair with her was the most intense emotional relationship he ever had; though it ultimately wounded everyone involved, there is no denying that it remained a constant touchstone of his ex-perience for the next decade. Steinbeck was fond of repeating the story of how Ed Ricketts, very much like Lleu Llaw Gyffes, "that enlightened knight in the Welsh tale" of *The Mabinogian*, "manufactured" the women he wanted. But the fact was Math conjured a woman "entirely out of flowers" for Lleu in the me-dieval *Mabinogian*, just as it was Steinbeck who "built his own woman . . . created her from the ground up. . . ." In that telling anecdote in "About Ed Ricketts" (1951), Steinbeck was actually talking about his own propensity to create Gwyn. Small wonder, then, that Carol failed to regain her husband; against Steinbeck's holy distortion and prayerful magic she didn't have a mortal's chance of success.

But significant as it was, Steinbeck's fatal attraction to Gwyn only helped move his life further along a route he was already traveling. "The world is sick now," he explained to Sheffield.

"There are things in the tide pools easier to understand than Stalinist, Hitlerite, Democrat, capitalist confusion, and voodoo. So I'm going to those things which are relatively more lasting to find a new basic picture. I have too a conviction that a new world is growing under the old" (Steinbeck and Wallsten, eds., *Steinbeck: A Life in Letters*, p. 193). With the publication of *In Dubious Battle, Of Mice and Men,* and *The Grapes of Wrath* Steinbeck concluded an integrated body of work about his native California, a triology of desire and illusion based on a notion of relatively fixed social reality that he no longer fully believed. With the world massed for war, the best minds of his generation "confused," and his own eye dazzled by a "blind tropic movement" which threatened to reduce language itself to "nonsense," Steinbeck felt compelled to look elsewhere for meaning (John Steinbeck/Wilbur Needham, letter [September 29, 1940]; courtesy of University of Virginia Library). He turned to the oceanic tide pool not as a replacement for the world of men, but rather as a place to heal his vision, to begin again at the bedrock of observation. It was not the *subject* of the tide pool that captured his attention so much as the liberating *process* of observing it, a process that required baptismal immersion in its eddying currents. Only then could he begin to understand how the laws of thought become the laws of things, or "the design" of a scientific travel book becomes "the pattern of reality controlled and shaped by the mind of the writer."

A couple of days before this tantalizing journal breaks off, Steinbeck, who had been postponing the "difficult" work for several months, plunged into the writing of *Sea of Cortez* (he finished writing it in July; the book was published in December) with those introductory words of purpose. Ed Ricketts's notes from the Gulf of California trip were close at hand, and he transformed them so effectively that Ricketts later said: "There is a dual structure of thought and beauty. Contributions from the one side are largely mine, from the other, John's. The structure is a collaboration, but shaped mostly by John. The book is the result" ("Morphology of *The Sea of Cortez*," in Hedgpeth, *The Outer Shores, Part 2*, p. 171). Actually, some of the book's most poignant statements emanated from the writer, not from the marine biologist, as, for example, this assessment of mankind: "Man might be described fairly adequately, if simply, as a two-legged paradox. He has never become accustomed to the tragic miracle of consciousness. Perhaps . . . his species is not set, has not jelled, but is still in a state of becoming, bound by his physical memories to a past of struggle and survival, limited in his futures by the uneasiness of thought and consciousness" (p. 96). It is Steinbeck, writing of himself again, almost—but not quite—from the other side of catastrophe.

Entry #101
October 16, 1939 [Monday]

It is one year ago less ten days that I finished the first draft of the *Grapes*. Then we came up here to the ranch and then my leg went bad and I had ten months of monstrous pain until the poison from the infection was gone. This is a year without writing (except for little jobs—mechanical fixings). The longest time I've been in many years without writing. The time has come now for orientation. What has happened and what it has done to me. In the first place the *Grapes* got really out of hand, became a public hysteria and I became a public domain. I've fought that consistently but I don't know how successfully. Second, we are rich as riches go. We have money enough to keep us for many years. We have this pleasant ranch which is everything one could desire. It lacks only the ocean to be perfect. We have comfort and beauty around us and these things I never expected. Couldn't possibly have expected. We have a cow and a Doberman pinscher. The war came but book sales went right on. And it is a curious kind of war, unlike any before. Its pattern will not emerge for a long time. So much for the external things. A straight line progression that can lead only to catastrophe. But let it. I have made powerful enemies* with the *Grapes*. They will not kill me I think, but they will destroy me when and if they can.

We come now to the dangerous part. Whereas a few years ago I could not sell my work—now it is so in demand that anything with my name on it would be snapped up.* And that is the worst thing of all. That is the goodness of this ranch. Here I can lose the fanfare. Here I become the little creature I really am. One cannot impress our forest.

Now I am battered with uncertainties. That part of my life that made the *Grapes* is over. I have one little job to do for the government, and then I can be born again. Must be. I have to go to new sources and find new roots. I have written simply for simple stories, but now the conception and the execution become difficult and not simple. And I don't know. I don't quite know what the conception is. But I know it will be found in the tide pools and on a microscope slide rather than in men. I don't know whether there is anything left of me. I know that some of my forces are gone. Perhaps others have taken their place. First I want to do two theses for John Cage* to set to percussion music: Phalanx and the Death of the Species. Those are to be trials. I want to do them. I wanted to go into myself in this page and to try to bring out something. But nothing of interest is there. My will to death is strengthened. In a sense, my work is done because there wasn't much to me in the beginning. But my mind ranges and ranges and searches. If only I wanted money, I could make a great deal of it. The wolves of the reformers are on me, and I think they are ego islands. I must work alone. That is necessary. I must think alone. The song of the microscope. There is something. Glass tubing—x-ray. These are poems worth writing. These are things that could make for rebirth.

Entry #102
Oct[ober] 18 [1939]—[Wednesday]

These notes, as usual, are a prelude to work. The words grow stiff and unruly, like puppies they want to go their own ways— all directions. And the sounds are rough. These notes and comments loosen up the language and make me more able to write it. I've wondered whether I could do that pipe play.* I might be lousy. Sorry I committed myself to the Washington thing. My head is humming with this cold today. But the work is crowding me a little. I wouldn't care if it didn't. Called Ed today. This is a good place to work—so far, that is. I like to sit here and have this book in front of me. I'll be glad when I have a straight-away cause. With so many things facing me I get none of them finished. It will be good when I have settled on one. This pipe deal isn't so bad. The more I think of it, the more it seems it might be fun. Now I don't know about this play—whether I want to do it, whether it would be any good if I did do it. Its one and greatest advantage would be that it would not be important. It would break this damned posterity thing that is being put on me by my contemporaries. I don't know whether I could make it. But in these damned pipes is a chance for the broadest kind of satire of nearly everything.

Entry #103
Oct[ober] 19 [1939]—[Thursday]

Sitting here every day letting my mind go galloping. And that's a good thing—unproductive but I don't have to produce until the pressure inside me does it. That's right. That's the way it always should be and never is. And if I should spend my whole life at this I don't care. I am busily fencing out the forces and people who would take my life and work over [it] for their own ends. If Chaplin can get away without ever answering a letter, so can I. And so I sit here. Nearly the end of October. That is mad. Carol is paying the bills. Life in one way is narrowing down and in another it is widening out. I'm changeable and skittish. Tasting the work I may do, and discarding. Still this huge picture. But the little comedy of the pipes—I don't know. It might be fun but I don't know whether I want that kind of fun.

Mice and Men will soon be released as a picture.* I don't know whether it is any good or not but I rather suspect it is. It doesn't make much difference really. Ed and Ritch and Tal are coming this weekend. Must talk to Tal. Carol says one mustn't play God in peoples' lives but on the other hand what if one can make the little shift which is the difference between failure and ease? Ben Abramson made it for me. I want to do it for Ritch if he wants, or rather if Tal wants him to want it. I think Tal knows more than any of us. But at least she'll know whether or not it is right to do.

These maunderings are good to do. The season is turning fast now. Already the rain clouds are beginning to form. We'll have rain within the week. And the leaves are falling, walnuts gone, box elder going, maples going. The fruit trees are still in leaf. The peaches colored and so are the pears. Apples still green. English walnuts getting kind of moth-eaten. And the ground is so covered with leaves that it does no good to rake them until they are all down. We had Steve and he was no good at all, and Ray was lots better, and now Joe is better than Ray.* We'd like to keep the two of them. Carol is writing letters today. The war is very strange. Russia is fortifying the western end and Germany is bombing British ships and France apparently is doing nothing. It's a waiting game and I don't know whether either side knows what it is waiting for. May be.

Entry #104
[October 20 or 27, or November 3] [1939]—Friday

The last two days I have had death premonitions so strong that I burned all the correspondence of years. I have a horror of people going through it, messing around in my past, such as it is. I burned it all. I think now I have left no vestige of writing except the few notes scattered through the ledgers and my work. This doesn't mean that I feel it is imminent but only that I had a sense of its occurrence strong enough to make this preparation.

Entry #105
November 10 [1939]—[Friday]

No comment.

Entry #106
Jan[uary] 4, 1940—[Thursday]
P.B.L. [Ed.—Pacific Biological Laboratory]

Came down here to try to work on the tide pool hand book.* I discover that there are no easy books to write and that this may well be one of the hardest. Besides, there is the grave and great difficulty in myself which is the real reason for the attempt to write it at all—the crash within myself. The feeling of finish, the destruction of all form and plan. This I can't explain to anyone, since no one but myself can see either the germ or the growth of it. But there it is. Carol at the ranch. Salvations to be worked out—hers and mine and ours. Maybe this is wrong or right. That it is so is more important than either. But the work is to be done and I must do it. Things are slipping. I can't stand firm unless there is something to stand on and I am attempting to find the foundation of some new discipline in this book.

Entry #107
Jan[uary] 5 [1940]—[Friday]

Yesterday I slovened out a part of an introduction. It says what I want to say but so clumsily and heavily that I think I'd better do it over again today. Carol phoned. The President doesn't like *The Fight for Life*.* Pare will be despondent. But it is right in line with the change Paul [Ed.—de Kruif] spoke of. I wonder whether our Mexican [Ed.—*Sea of Cortez*] plan will go down for the same reasons. I may have to run east and clear the lines. Hope not. This hand book is hard. It is so long since I have done any disciplined thinking. Well, I'll get to it. I wired Tracy* to come up here and received no answer at all. It is difficult to deal with such a man and maybe the whole thing should be thrown over. Well, to work.

Entry #108
Jan[uary] 10 [1940]—[Wednesday]

Last night went to Mary's [Ed.—Dekker]. Her birthday. She looked well and seemed to be happy and thoughtful. Rain constantly. It will be a big year. Must telephone Carol tonight. She is doing her garden book.* Now—lab work. Tracy's boat deal is entirely off. We wrote American Consulate in Guaymas for information regarding boats* and should have an answer before long. There has been a hell of a lot of talk about the hand book and all good. Out of it comes something, if only we get down to the writing of it. I have more introduction almost ready. Shall start on it today. Lots of good things to think of in this connection and I want to get down the nature and implications of a tide pool. So here goes.

Entry #109
Jan[uary] 12 [1940]—[Thursday]

Carol is coming down today. She has been on the ranch during the long rain. I am so glad. We'll go maybe to an auto court. The old difficulty arises. I couldn't sleep last night, but the bottom is psychic despair and then came out of it in a feeling of glory and purged. I know now why I detest my work and I know how to rectify it, I think. As to the hand book, I am constantly down about my lack of specific knowledge. And then again, I know what I know and sometimes it seems good. I don't know. But this line is set and this deduction is fixed by many factors. Strange how the years go on and some of the struggles remain the same and others change. Very strange. And strange the relationship which shifts and changes, now for the good, now for the bad, but good I think throughout. This must be. What pressures are there, or can it be that a lack of pressure after accustomed pressure is deadly? It doesn't matter. My reach for some kind of ideal happiness is chemical. I remember how grey and doleful Monday morning was. I could lie and look at it from my bed, through the rusting screen of the upstairs window. It had a quality of grey terror of its own and the washing machine clanking in the basement and Mary playing the dull scales on the piano. What was to come next I knew—the dark corridors of the school and the desks in the ill-lighted rooms shining fiercely with the grey light from the windows, and the teachers' week end over facing us with more horrors than that with which we faced them. Then the subjects in which no one was interested. And then one young teacher who aroused us all to ecstasies over economics when really we were merely aroused to sexual maturity by her light pretty figure and her own new-come maturity. M. [Ed.—Max Wagner] told me he kissed her on a horse and promptly fell off the horse. M. knew about such things while I (dope that I was) thought that I loved sociology when I loved the teacher.

This was not unique for me. Much later I saw many ladies similarly confused with Krishnamurti, and perhaps even he [Ed.— Max Wagner] was confused. I wonder what became of that teacher? She was so pretty. But the long jawed dark ones who were not pretty got no spark from us and taught us very little. At that time, knowing little about the precocity of personality I should have said that Bill Black* would have passed us all because I could not see that his very excellences were the rheostat of his mediocrity. Were I to look again and try to judge a future, I should pick a tortured child, frantic with uncertainties and unhappy in his limitations. Ed riding a milk street car from illicit fornication to stoke a furnace from then to study, cursing a day and night that had no time for sleep.* But Bill did things with ease and assurance. Good grades and the light affection of pretty girls, he ran fast but was beaten by a gnomish sufferer. He would have made good, tender tasty eating meat. And even after all these years I remember the envy at his ease. He must be having a good, thin life, and he will die a peaceful death. I wonder why I go back to this? Can it be that there is something I have not dug out of it? That must be true. Is my work over for a time, or for all time? It might be. I have no longer the great sense of rush. Yet there is immanence. I write easily now but I do not think easily. And only by little do I ever discover the top rocks of the littoral. Perhaps I can get down to the base. I hope so. Promise of what? There's the problem. I've fulfilled little promises. What can I do to large ones, if I want to? And at least I am still honest, and still not too afraid. Working with ease, toward ease. The sad, boastful girl in the bar, finding some justification in the fact that her uncle had lots of money and cursing the government because it took part in taxes. I know in a little while Carol will come rush-tumbling up the stairs, and that will be good and we'll all be merry. Or she will come slowly with troubles in her hands and we will be sad. So much always depends on Carol. She can and does make the tempo of the house. I wish she knew that. I can help, but she can really do it. I am getting so ugly these days that I shock myself.

Entry #110
Jan[uary] 16 [1940]—[Tuesday]

Now I am at home on the ranch. The whole Tracy boat thing fell through. I don't know why. Also I am withdrawing the *Red Pony* matter and will probably give it to Milly* to do. *Grapes* opens in New York in a couple of weeks. Then all hell will break loose as far as I am concerned. Or maybe not. *Mice* apparently is just dying on its feet for lack of backing. I have not heard a boo about it. Sunny, sunny day. Carol has the dumps. May be catching a cold. She went to San Jose today. She finished her seed book last night and got it off this morning. I think it is very good and that a little fortune is in the idea. We'll have to see what New York thinks of it, however. I hope to heaven it goes. Terrible feeling of change in the air. Don't know what it can be. Beautiful days, lazy days, but storm clouds all about. My sleep is over-shadowed with pain of apprehension as though some frightful thing were imminent. And I don't know what it can be. Perhaps nothing. My hunches have never been much good.

Entry #111
Jan[uary] 18 [1940]—[Thursday]

The month flies. And I don't get much done. I think a lot. Due to the tonsils coming out, I am getting fat and it depresses me so that I am starting today to lose it. It will be interesting to see whether I have any willpower. Be hard because I love to eat. Big spreads of pictures on *Grapes** which opens next week.

Entry #112
July 20 [19]40—[Saturday]

A long time between. Gulf trip over now and the film trip to Mexico [Ed.—*The Forgotten Village*]. Went to Washington* and talked about the loss of the south to the Germans. I hope I made some of it stick. Then back here [Ed.—Biddle ranch] simply to rest in the sun awhile before going back to Mexico, and in October setting out on the Gulf Marine book. And then one morning, sitting on the porch the pipe play came back but stronger and funnier. And this time I know I can't check it. I'll have to write it. I have six weeks or two months to work with. I've already started it. Monday I'm going on with it. And I feel good about it. Can be very funny. [Indecipherable] coming to dinner tonight. I'll cook steaks. Very strange—the hysteria and fear of the coming war and then it passed off in the night. We know it is coming, but we aren't afraid any more. Some singular jump in the psyche. And it isn't that we have hardened. We are as soft and sentimental as always, but the war has become a fact and we accept it. The reasons are good—we want to preserve a little of what we have and are used to—all kinds of intellectual reasons, but the great basic reason is that we have accepted war and it will be our manner of life for the next while. Perhaps treachery will cut us down, but I don't think so. In my own person I am filled with a lowness that has the physical feeling of a hang over. It bothers me in the night. I wonder what facet of my own folly is responsible for it. Tomorrow is Sunday, and then Monday I am going to work. I'll work hard but it won't seem hard. Probably won't be any good either. But I don't care. It will be fun. I'll keep the daily notes because it is good to keep them. A fair chance for the words to break loose. And all such things are good. There is no doubt that this fine old pen is better and smoother than the newer one. I think I'll keep with this good old pen. I've done a lot of writing with it. I only hope it holds up. I wonder with all the books I have now, whether I'll be able to paragraph my dialogue.* It will seem like a terrible waste of good paper to leave some of it blank. But also it will be much easier to read—much. So I'm going to try to do it any way. The sun is brilliant now. For several days there was fog. Today I ordered a vacuum cleaner for the pool. Dust was getting pretty thick on it. If this is a lot of writing in the note section, it is because I haven't done much for a long time and wish to get some words down. But I think enough has been done.

Entry #113
July 23 [1940]—[Tuesday]

The days pass and pleasantly. Carl Sandburg* came up for the
night and yesterday, a good thinking man. I liked him and got a
nice feeling from him. These are nice days, perhaps a lull-before-
storm-feeling. And the good work feeling is on me. Words and
pictures piling up. I'll have some fun with this I hope. I know I
will even if I am prevented from finishing it. I'll simply go on
the best I can. Hope I am not making the coming men an excuse
not to work. But I don't need an excuse. If I *could not* work and
be happy, I would be idle. But these pipes have just haunted me
for too long and I might just as well get them off my mind. It will
be great fun and to hell with the critics of all kinds. I'm not
working for them, but for my own full joy. A few people will like
this as well as I do, and many won't understand it at all. But I
understand it and like it. And here goes—the real and final
plunge.

Entry #114
July 24 [1940]—[Wednesday]

In the work diary which had to do with the *Grapes*, I put down
the time of going to work. There was a franticness in that effort—
a fear that time would cut me off. Now in the *Pipes* I want to
overcome that frantic quality. I want it to remain easy, leisurely,
and fun. If some days go by and I do not work, there is no
conscience penalty. If I never finish it, very little will have been
lost. This is being done for my pleasure and for Carol's and for
Mary's. And I don't care if no one else sees it. In form it is almost
like a ballet. In tone it is a serious thing, not too much over-

drawn, because the things said must be capable of being listened to even if the background were different. But above all it must be fun. The moment it stops, in that moment I will stop writing it. At this moment my first act is difficult as they always are. Bringing people on the stage is a clumsy process and one not easy to accomplish. And then, too, in spite of the slightness of this play, I have the old fear of beginning work that I have always felt. The terror that I could not bring it off. Of course, the main difficulty lies in the fact that between books I soften up both in literary and intellectual discipline, so that with each beginning I must fight soft muscles in the head and in the technique. Naturally, I am frightened. It takes some time for those muscles to harden and for what I now instinctively know about technique to assert itself. Today so far there is no war news. I won't listen to the radio until my day's work is over. It is a good, hot day, and when I finish my day's work, I will go out to the pool and swim and lie in the sun. Congress proposed a universal training act yesterday. It will not be long before I must register for military service.* It will be interesting to see how the nation as a whole reacts to this. It might create a real feeling of the wholeness of the people, and again it might draw out a sullen resentment. Must see it before one can tell. I feel that I would rather serve with common men than to try to get an "office job." But all that will come as it comes. We'll just have to see. And now to work.

Entry #115
July 26 [1940]—[Friday]

This is a lazy day. Went to dinner with the Woods.* Got home early and sober. Carol in pain from Female Complaint. She is having a hard time this time. Went to sleep before twelve and slept until ten this morning without awakening. Disgraceful. I think I'll start setting the clock for seven and going to work immediately. This play might benefit from the half sleep carry-over. Also then I would be free in the hot middle of the day. Worth trying anyway. Good letter from Duke—good and long and healthy. I'll be glad to see him if he ever gets down this way. Must write him a decent letter* soon. Today is fine and as hot as it usually gets up here. I'm keeping myself in check with this manuscript so that the words do not tumble over one another in their hurry to get out. My fingers get a little sticky in this weather so I rub alcohol on them so the pen will be slick in my hand. That seems to be important to me. I don't know why. But it does. The good feeling of the pen should be kept—should be dry and a smooth point and fine paper like this. There's something very good about this kind of affair. My room is cool and lovely. Outside a blinding sun and I at a roll top desk*—I've always wanted one and they are perfect. I never had anything nice to work at. And a swivel chair that comes to the perfect height. I can see the greenhouse from here, and the perfect pen and the perfect paper and me working on work that pleases me and has no note for the critics. Indeed, I'm going to be very careful about submitting it for publication at all. But I will have had fun doing it and that is the most important thing—And it is fun. Well the time is now to go to work and I have a good feeling about it. It is nice to be this way. Don't imagine it can go on for very long. I'm afraid of good luck more than bad.

Entry #116
July 29 [1940]—[Monday]

The trouble with being too casual about a manuscript is that you don't do it. In writing, habit seems to be a much stronger force than either willpower or inspiration. Consequently there must be some little quality of fierceness until the habit pattern of a certain number of words is established. There is no possibility, in me at least, of saying, "I'll do it if I feel like it." One never feels like awaking day after day. In fact, given the smallest excuse, one will not work at all. The rest is nonsense. Perhaps there are people who can work that way, but I cannot. I must get my words down every day whether they are any good or not. And I am a little afraid that they are not much good. However, down they go. The forced work is sometimes better than the easy, but there is no rule about it. Sometimes they come out better than at other times and that is all one can say. I am becoming very calm after the hectic quality of my recent life. Seems like a crazy dream, the other life, and the tone of it leaves slowly. But now I am feeling more slow and deliberate every day. That is a pace that seems most normal to me. I wish I could have it this way for a little while. But one can never be sure, not even for a week. So I go on with my daily stint, and if it is stopped in the middle some time—that will have to be that. I can't think of any other way just now. The good slow life won't last. Nothing to report. Swimming yesterday. It's a good sunny but cool day today. Not hot enough to drive me to the pool until I am ready to go. It is really time to go to work, and I am nearly ready for it, too. Perhaps I write too much in these notes. No way of telling. I finish out a space visually any way. And that space is finished out for today. Second scene Act 1.

Entry #117
July 27 [1940]—[Saturday]

This can't be much of a note, for this is Saturday. I'm only going to do half a day's work today and spend the rest of the time in riotous living or riotous resting. Letter from Joe [Ed.—Joseph

Henry Jackson] yesterday. Gussie has been desperately ill. Hemorrhage, etc. Joe says that they just saved her. Some curious psychological features to this. It seems very clear to me. Perhaps it isn't as simple as I think. Hard to tell. Clouds and some wind today. Perhaps the swimming will not be so good as it might be. I'll get my one page done and find out. When I think how I am not following orders to do what people think I should do, I am scared, but then I think that it is my own work, if anything, that will be remembered. I can't work for other people. I don't do good work with their ideas. So I'll go on with my own. I think probably the pipe play is lousy, but I'll go on with it just the same. And I think now is a good time to get it going. As good a time as any. So here goes.

Entry #118
Sept[ember] 29 [19]40—[Sunday]

The time goes and I live on in a mess of puzzlement—like every one else in the world. Took up flying [Ed.—at Palo Alto Airport]. Seven hours I had. Went to Washington with Knisely's idea. I don't know whether or not it will be used. It should. Then on to New York where for a week Carol and I did wild rioting in clubs and restaurants. Good worthless week. Came home tired and sad. Lack of work does it, I guess. Lorentz wants to make "Flight," Milestone *The Red Pony*. I want to finish my play and the *Sea of Cortez*. Just got home when Nosler* called. Wants me to go to Hollywood for the opening of *The Fight for Life* on Tuesday. I may do it since there are other things I want to see about. I have trench mouth. Don't know where I got it, but prosaically I'm sure. Have to go back to Mexico the 20th of October. Carol is in Monterey today. Idell and Paul* are back. Seem well but confused like everyone else. Joe [Ed.—Higashi] is worried about the Japanese situation* and so are we. It becomes very dangerous. May blow up any day. With so many things happening it is very hard to settle down. Emotionally I am pretty much messed up, too. The old trouble of restlessness. Pat wants me to finish *God in the Pipes*. Carol is feeling lone and lost. But so is every one. My own change of temperament seems pretty radical. Really feel different. But what is to happen? I don't know. One thing I know is bad but I go on with it anyway. Curious feeling that I must not be a disappointment. And I am and I don't even know whether the disappointment would be at all sharp. In fact, I am pretty sure it would not. The day is lonely today. And the world is crazy. I wonder whether it will ever be sane again. Probably not. Life for me is nearly over any way. And my head is good still and I can still write. Strange thing honor. The most sapping thing in the world. Oh! Lord, how good this paper feels under this pen. I can sit here writing and the words slipping out like grapes out of their skins and I feel so good doing it. Pat's dream was a very real dream, but I think it had to do with him not me. The lonely sun and flowers. I'm too fat again. Must start taking it off. Seven pounds at least. Well, I can do that. What has been done can be done again. At first you drink coffee when you get hungry and in a while your stomach shrinks and you are not hungry any more.

Here is a strange thing—almost like a secret. You start out putting words down and there are three things—you, the pen, and the page. Then gradually the three things merge until they are all one and you feel about the page as you do about your arm. Only you love it more than you love your arm. Some day I will be all alone and lonely—either dead and alone or alive and alone, and what will I do then? Then those things I have now and do not know will become so desperately dear that they will be aches. Then what? There will be no way to cure those aches, no way.

In that coldness nothing will come. Things are leaving me now because they came too fast—too many of them—and being unable to receive them I threw them out and soon they will not come any more. This process is called life or living or any one of a number of things like that. In other words these are the soundless words, the words that have no being at all. The grey birds of loneliness hopping about. I thought that there might be a time or a condition different from that. But I know now—there isn't any other way. But in a will toward holiness one goes on—and curiously—the holiness is often evil in a way, mischievous in a way, sometimes destructive. Must be some way. There must. If only this winter were a calm sweet time. If only. But it isn't. It can't be. The frog in the pool and the man who raises foxes. Four hundred dollars a pair. Curious man. Wants to train foxes to pull a little sled. The gay horrible life. And now I've done enough of this and I think I'll move over to the other [Ed.—love poems to Gwyn].

Entry #119
December 12, 1940 [Thursday]

My writing in this book is so irregular. A few entries and then six months with none. Back from Mexico again and this time I'm through there I hope. And back from Hollywood again and definitely not through there. I try to stay relaxed about that. It isn't possible to be more than it is, and I know that. What a fiasco that would be. And I like it and keep at it and will continue. It seems the best thing to do and surely the pleasantest in many ways, but there are stomach pains in it, too. How will it end—tragically, I imagine, but that is part of it too. I won't even run from that. I won't do anything. The years fly away now and I am mostly glad. My forces, probably due to the relaxation, increase and may continue to do so for a time at least, and I will make the most of them, too. The year is turning. Mexican film [Ed.— *The Forgotten Village*] with the exception of commentary is done, too. Now comes* only the *Red Pony* with Milestone and the "Flight" with Pare and the introduction for Ed's book second edition and the *Sea of Cortez*. I need to lose weight again. Last winter I lost 30 pounds in six weeks. Fifteen is all I need to lose now to be in good shape. I'm starting it now, too. I may not try to hit it so quickly. Depends on how hard it sticks.

Much magic* in Mexico this last time, and of the very blackest kind. Probably some of my present difficulties are due to just that magic. Things are beginning to turn and twist in my head again. I must be sure to choose which is love and which sorryness. I'm not a very good person. Sometimes generous and good and kind and other times mean and short. I'm going to load myself with [Ed.—Vitamin] B for a few days and see what the effect is. Might be interesting. Ed is in pretty good shape now. He has a girl he likes. I feel pretty fine myself except for loneliness. Have been drinking more than usual. Maybe that is good. Can't say. I'll let it go as it goes. Have yet to drink for its own sake. But in the present world of cruelty and fierceness of expectancy and greed, drinking, even if practiced as a vice, seems a very little unoffensive one. And I get sick of it very quickly, too. Accounts in the big book of rains that may come. Joe is raking and burning leaves in the vegetable garden. And I have this whole sense of coming tragedy and am so conditioned that I do not even resent it. Carol has been having some quite bad dreams. Poor darling feels insecure, too. And insecurity is every where. She doesn't know how much nor can conceive how much.

This is a new pen. I bought it for the *Sea of Cortez* job. I wonder whether I can do anything of a job on that. The little bird in the black coffin is part of the magic and a very powerful part. Now the clouds are running in fast. Sometimes, I would like so much not to have this beautiful ranch, but a tight, small house built on piers over the water so I could hear it moving and breaking all the time. I am so restless. What will come of this restlessness? I don't know.

Entry #120
Jan[uary] 20 [19]41 [Monday]

Now back from Hollywood and the Mexican film done as far as I can do it. It isn't anything I am going to be very proud of, but other people will probably like it. Stayed in the Aloha Arms two weeks. An apartment with four beds. Worked and came back to bed. Only thing to do. And had little quarrels with Herbert,* my own smallness mostly and being bored with the film. No open quarrels. The other, I think, might be over or nearly. [Ed.— affair with Gwyn] Just a feeling and I hope it is true, really, deeply, I hope so. Can't really see anything good in it in any future. Now I am home for a few days. And Carol is feeling badly because it rains all the time. She lives on sun more than on food. I'll try to get her to go get the southern sun, if she will. A boat trip would do her good if it went south. I am going to Pacific Grove to work on the gulf book and it will be pretty rainy there, too. I want her to be healthy and happy.

Strange how the strangeness is. I'll stay at Esther's house* in the woods in Pacific Grove. It will give me the privacy to write at the same time as the work at Ed's. Waiting, always for something. I'm going to look for a [indecipherable] to see within myself whether this is generalized or personal. Can't tell except that the other urges do not come. I'll try though—to see. I'll fill this book this time I hope. There's nothing else to do. And the world we know crumbles slowly and melts away, and the powerful voices of hysteria and terror are in the air.

Entry #121
Jan[uary] 28 [1941]—[Tuesday]

I am down at P. G. at Esther's house and just starting the gulf book. Last night Ed and Toby* and I drank too much and caroused about. Finally even got a little mischievous. But oddly enough no hang-over. [Indecipherable] child's letter. No happiness there but still a fervent belief in it. Carol was to go to Santa Cruz yesterday. Don't know whether or not she did. It is sunny and clear down here but I don't know for how long. Now the old laziness but I don't think it will hold me long. This is a comfortable house, with a rather good fireplace. I must not get into the difficulty of drinking as every one down here does. This is the up-hill fight with no end but clarity and no reward except the feeling that a decent job has been done. I wonder whether I can do it. My back aches a little bit with that old ache that plagued me so and that is a little frightening, but if it is another focus of infection we can cure that. Shouldn't be hard to locate this time. Writing the little daily journal is fun. I have set my usual two pages of writing as the day's work. Don't know whether I can keep this up from the beginning, but I will try. I must if I can.

Lord! I forgot to wire Lon Stewart that I could not come to dinner in L.A. I must also write to Max and send him the article to give to Herb. And these things must be done today. I'm sitting here wallowing in beginnings. Hard things beginnings—very hard. But I must do them. And I can. It will be easy when once the start is made. And that start is going to be made, and that today. It should not be hard. I think I am going to enjoy just sitting here and writing. I'm pretty sure I am. It is comfortable and quiet. At night I can draw the curtains and it will be warm and nice. The inevitable thing happens. My busy little mind thinks up a hundred things I ought to do rather than the writing. I should think at my age it wouldn't try to do that any more. Time is running out and at the end of this page I will go to the opening. And the opening should be good—very good.

Entry #122
Jan[uary] 29 [1941]—[Wednesday]

And the opening was good, I think. Ed thinks so too. In fact, he thinks it is better than I do. Last night I went to bed by 9:30 and dreamed strangely. Woke up early. Still the back ache and stomach ache. Maybe I have the flu again, too, but I don't think so. The pen writes a little thickly. I hope this isn't a psychic pen. I'm having enough trouble with such things. Visitations so definite that I don't see how I can imagine them. Perhaps I am just crazy. I've never been sure I am not. Called Carol last night. She is low and mourning. I wonder if she is ever going to be even reasonably happy. It isn't fair that she has so much unhappiness. It is becoming almost her usual state of mind. She used to blame it on other things. Now she blames herself and that is worse and she mourns more. I just don't know what to do. Poor darling, I want so much for her to be happy. No sun today. It is 10:30 and I feel the crowding of work and the urge to hurry. But why? I have all day. I can work as long or as little as I want. The work flows easily and is fun. Why should I hurry? I'll stay relaxed if I can. I hope this can be a relaxed book. There are so few of them now and the world really needs them for the world is tight and knotted now. A good fire is burning in the fire place and the room is warm. And I can even work at night if I want to. I can do anything, but I usually wind up doing the same things every time. There isn't very much variation in a given man. I haven't been or felt so quiet in years. Of course, the birth of other peoples' unease are in me but of myself I am at peace. Perhaps a kind of anaesthesia. I don't know. But I seem to be aware at least. Back still hurts and stomach ache has come to join it nicely now. Maybe it really is the flu. Can't tell, don't even want to. I'll just sit here by the fire and set down words. Nothing wrong with that. I should be opening the page for the book work of today. There are so many things to go into this book. An astonishing number of things. But I'll get them all in if I just relax and get them in day by day and only worry about the 2000 words of each day's work. That's the only way to do it, I have found. But damn it, I have to learn it over again every time. And that's all for this section for today.

Entry #123
Jan[uary] 30 [19]41—[Thursday]

Now the third day of writing. I don't know how well, but rather imagine not too well. I am ill—ill in the mind. My head is a grey cloud in which colors drift about and images half-form. I'm bludgeoned and feel beaten by many little things. And I can't figure answers to them. Maybe some people think clearly all the time and make nice decisions. I don't know. But I feel very lost and lonesome. And no other way—for me, I mean. It is so curious. I think I use that word far too much, but it is I guess an indication of a staggered mind. The terrible thing to contemplate is that badly as I am thinking, so many others are thinking much more badly. Much more. And I am held in to this by a flogging head and increasing weight and everything like that. I don't seem to have the knack of living any more. The clock is running down, my clock. This book has to be written. It should be good. I think it is my book. Maybe those people who say that I should never deal with thinking subjects are correct. I don't know. It is impossible to say. Now the sun is gone again. Haven't heard from Carol. I hope she isn't feeling so lonely as she was. She was so low. I think I'll leave this book now.

Notes
and Annotations:
A Bibliographical Preface

Although he cultivated reclusiveness and solitude, John Steinbeck was a writer immersed in and moved by the events, personalities, and conditions of his time. The indispensable primary accounts of the novelist's multifarious life and career are: Elaine Steinbeck and Robert Wallsten, eds., *Steinbeck: A Life in Letters* (New York: The Viking Press, 1975); Jackson J. Benson, *The True Adventures of John Steinbeck, Writer* (New York: The Viking Press, 1984); and Adrian H. Goldstone and John R. Payne, *John Steinbeck: A Bibliographical Catalogue of the Adrian H. Goldstone Collection* (Austin: Humanities Research Center, 1974). Equally valuable are: John Steinbeck, *The Log from the* Sea of Cortez (New York: The Viking Press, 1951), which includes "About Ed Ricketts"; John Steinbeck, *Journal of a Novel: The* East of Eden *Letters* (New York: The Viking Press, 1969); Florian J. Shasky and Susan F. Riggs, eds., *Letters to Elizabeth: A Selection of Letters from John Steinbeck to Elizabeth Otis* (San Francisco: The Book Club of California, 1978); Thomas Fensch, *Steinbeck and Covici: The Story of a Friendship* (Middlebury, VT: Paul S. Eriksson, 1979); and K. Nakayama and H. Hirose, eds., *Selected Essays of John Steinbeck* (Tokyo: Shinozaki Shorin, 1984).

Professor Benson's great book makes everyone else's seem like a footnote, though occasionally shiny nuggets still turn up that don't appear in his biography. These other works are original and helpful: Lewis Gannett, *John Steinbeck: Personal and Bibliographical Notes* (New York: The Viking Press, 1939); E. W. Tedlock and C. V. Wicker, eds., *Steinbeck and His Critics: A Record of Twenty-Five Years* (Albuquerque: University of New Mexico Press, 1957); Peter Lisca, *The Wide World of John Steinbeck* (New Brunswick, NJ: Rutgers University Press, 1958); Richard Astro, *John Steinbeck and Edward F. Ricketts: The Shaping of a Novelist* (Minneapolis: University of Minnesota Press, 1973); Nelson Valjean, *John Steinbeck: The Errant Knight* (San Francisco: Chronicle Books, 1975); Joel Hedgpeth, *The Outer Shores, Parts 1 and 2* (Eureka, CA: Mad River Press, 1978, 1979); Terry G. Halladay, ed., " 'The Closest Witness': The Autobiographical Reminiscences of Gwyndolyn Conger Steinbeck" (MA Thesis, Stephen F. Austin State University, 1979); John Gross and Lee Richard Hayman, *John Steinbeck: A Guide to the Collection of the Salinas Public Library* (Salinas: Salinas Public Library, 1979); Susan F. Riggs, *A Catalogue of the John Steinbeck Collection at Stanford University* (Stanford: Stanford University Libraries, 1980); Bradford Morrow, *John Steinbeck: A Collection of Books & Manuscripts Formed by Harry Valentine of Pacific Grove, California* (Santa Barbara: Bradford Morrow Bookseller Ltd., 1980); Carlton Sheffield, *Steinbeck: The Good Companion* (Portola Valley, CA: American Lives Endowment, 1983); Joseph Millichap, *Steinbeck and Film* (New York: Frederick Ungar, 1983); Robert DeMott, *Steinbeck's Reading: A Catalogue of Books Owned and Borrowed* (New York: Garland, 1984); Robert H. Woodward, *The Steinbeck Research Center at San Jose State University: A Descriptive Catalogue* (San Jose: *San Jose Studies*, 1985); Bruce Ariss, *Inside Cannery Row: Sketches from the Steinbeck Era* (San Francisco: Lexikos, 1988); and Jackson J. Benson, *Looking for Steinbeck's Ghost* (Norman: University of Oklahoma Press, 1988).

For specific analysis of and background to Steinbeck's most famous novel, the following are recommended: Joseph Henry Jackson, Preface (originally printed as "Why Steinbeck wrote *The Grapes of Wrath*") to the two-volume, Thomas Hart Benton illustrated deluxe edition of *The Grapes of Wrath* (New York: Limited Editions Club, 1940); Warren French, ed., *A Companion to* The Grapes of Wrath (New York: The Viking Press, 1963); Agnes McNeill Donohue, ed., *A Casebook on* The Grapes of Wrath (New York: Thomas Crowell, 1968); Peter Lisca, ed., The Grapes of Wrath, *Text and Criticism* (New York: The Viking Press, 1972); Warren French, *Filmguide to* The Grapes of Wrath (Bloomington: Indiana University Press, 1973); Robert Con Davis, ed., *Twentieth Century Interpretations of* The Grapes of Wrath (Englewood Cliffs, NJ: Prentice-Hall, 1982); and John Ditsky, ed., *Critical Essays on* The Grapes of Wrath (Boston: G. K. Hall, 1989).

I have frequently, but sometimes silently, relied upon all these groups of books for guidance, information, inspiration, and verification. The following notes to *Working Days*, then, much as they seem like poor relatives at a rich person's feast, are intended to perform an erstwhile service by sketching some of the private allusions and public references found in Steinbeck's journal. The annotations are drawn from many published and unpublished sources, and of the latter, notably Steinbeck's personal and professional correspondence with the staff of his agency, McIntosh and Otis, especially the fabulous cache of letters to and from Annie Laurie Williams, which until 1987 were restricted from public view. In addition, I have supplemented these with personal interviews and various archival documents. The aim, as Steinbeck once said, has been to create a whole picture, a unified field of facts and intimations, "where everything is an index of everything else."

NOTES: PART I

ENTRY #1

Gene. Eugene Ainsworth married one of Steinbeck's older sisters, Elizabeth (b. 1894). They were living in Stockton with their three children when he died on January 22, 1938, of strep infection.

Visalia and Nipomo. The former is the seat of Tulare County, located between Fresno and Bakersfield in the San Joaquin Valley, which itself is the southern part of the great Central Valley of California. The plight of 5,000 stricken migrant families, in the flooded country around Visalia, fully engaged Steinbeck's attention and compassion. What he witnessed there became the backdrop for the final scenes of *The Grapes of Wrath*. For three years running the latter, a small town north of Santa Barbara, had been the scene of starvation and misery among migrant pea pickers whose numbers (lured by inaccurate labor estimates and unscrupulous contractors) were far larger than needed to get in the crop. In February and March 1938, several hundred families were marooned in Nipomo.

NOTES: PART II

ENTRY #2

Work goes well. Steinbeck, at work since May 26, had already written what would become Chapters 1 and 2 of the published novel. Here, he is about to write 3, the symbolic intercalary chapter on the land turtle's determined progress across "the concrete highway." It became one of his favorite sections, and he frequently read it aloud to friends. For clarity and uniformity, subsequent references to episodes, scenes, sections, and/or chapters of the novel will be to the first published version, *The Grapes of Wrath* (New York: The Viking Press, 1939), and will be, wherever possible, incorporated parenthetically within brackets in the text of Steinbeck's entries. With the exception of minor differences in chapter numbering (in the early going Steinbeck numbered the "general," or intercalary, chapters alternately, not consecutively, with the "particular" chapters on the Joads—see his Entry #9 below) the sequence and arrangement of the holograph manuscript and the published version are precisely the same.

ENTRY #3

Duke. Carlton "Duke" (or "Dook") Sheffield, Steinbeck's Stanford University classmate (they roomed together in Encina Hall from January to June 1923, when Sheffield graduated). A lifelong friend, the independent, Thoreauvian, Sheffield was at various times a teacher, a graduate student in English at Stanford, and a newspaperman. In 1938 he was working as a journalist for the Marysville (CA) *Appeal-Democrat*. During his visit (he arrived in Los Gatos on the afternoon of June 2— see next Entry) Steinbeck read aloud "with restrained glee the chapter on the turtle" (C.A. Sheffield/Robert DeMott, letter, July 1, 1985).

Pauls. The novelist Louis Paul (aka Leroi Placet) and his wife Mary had moved from New York to Palo Alto, close enough (about twenty miles from Los Gatos) for the two couples to continue a felicitous and frequent friendship that had started in 1937 in New York City (John Steinbeck/Louis and Mary Paul, letter, August 15, 1937; courtesy of University of Virginia Library). Like Steinbeck, Paul (1901–1970), an Army veteran and ex-San Francisco longshoreman, preferred experience over education as preparation and background for writing fiction. During the period of this journal, Paul published four of his fourteen novels: *The Man Who Left Home* (Chicago: Black Cat Press, 1938), *The Wrong World* (New York: Doubleday, Doran, 1938), *A Passion for Privacy* (New York: Alfred Knopf, 1940), and *The Reverend Ben Pool* (New York: Duell, Sloan and Pearce, 1941). See DeMott, *Steinbeck's Reading* (pp. 89–90, 167–68). Starting with his appreciation of "No More Trouble for Jedwick" (first prize in the *O. Henry Memorial Award: Prize Stories of 1934*, which also included Steinbeck's "The Murder"), Steinbeck's enthusiasm for and encouragement of Paul's work remained constant until the early 1940s, when Steinbeck, following his separation from Carol, and his move from Los Gatos, appears to have lost touch with Paul. However, Paul, who had published a glowing review of *Of Mice and Men* in the New York *Herald Tribune Book Review* (February 28, 1937), eventually became perplexed by the boldly symbolic and elevated quality of *The Grapes of Wrath*. Steinbeck inscribed a gift copy of the Covici-Friede limited edition *The Red Pony* (1937), "For Louis and Mary with still increasing affection"; and a first edition of *The Grapes of Wrath*, "For Louis and Mary in gratitude."

Rays. Martin Ray (1905–1976), ex-stockbroker turned pioneering, celebrated, and iconoclastic vintner, lived with his first wife, Elsie (d. 1951), on Mount Eden, above Big Basin in Saratoga, northwest of Los Gatos. In 1936 Martin Ray bought the Santa Cruz Mountain vineyards of Paul Masson's Champagne Company, where he produced brilliant, exorbitantly priced vintages. He sold out to Seagram's in 1943, but shortly afterward started the smaller Martin Ray Vineyards. Steinbeck and Ray were temperamentally akin—both were aloof from society, self-sufficient, demanding of themselves and others, individualistic, and thoroughly dedicated to their art (Mrs. Eleanor Ray/Robert DeMott, telephone interview, June 4, 1985).

ENTRY #4

Paul Jordan Smith. Smith (1885–1971), a writer and former English instructor at UCLA, served from 1933 to 1958 as the influential Literary Editor for the Los Angeles *Times*. He not only reviewed Steinbeck's books favorably (he later called *The Grapes of Wrath* one of the "most thrilling" reading experiences he ever had) but had tried—unsuccessfully—to arrange publication of Steinbeck's 1920s' apprentice fiction. Presumably Smith never made it to see Steinbeck that summer.

ENTRY #5

The Long Valley. Steinbeck's only collection of short fiction, originally intended to be published by Covici-Friede in 1938. When the firm (Donald Friede had left in 1935) went bankrupt, The Viking Press hired Pascal Covici as an editor and bought Steinbeck's contract, so that the book was issued in September 1938, without a hitch, and to very strong reviews. (See Entries #49, 70, 79, and 81 below.) The book gathered short stories which appeared from 1933 to 1937 in such periodicals as *Harper's*, *Esquire*, and *Atlantic Monthly;* it also included the first appearance of "Flight,"as well as the complete publication of *The Red Pony*.

Tolertons. Like the Steinbecks, David Tolerton, a sculptor, and his wife, Lavinia, a painter, were part of the liberal artistic/intellectual community of the otherwise conservative Los Gatos. According to Benson, *True Adventures of John Steinbeck* (p. 351), the year before, David Tolerton had been directly instrumental in the San Francisco Theatre Union's production of *Of Mice and Men*. See Entry #49 below.

Bob C. Robert Cathcart, a classmate of Steinbeck's at Stanford (AB, 1930; LLB, 1934), was a close friend and confidant, especially during the 1920s, when the two men corresponded frequently. In 1938 Cathcart was practicing law in San Francisco.

Margery Bailey. The formidable Dr. Margery Bailey (1891–1963), an exciting teacher and an early mentor to Steinbeck, taught in the English Department at Stanford and was a major force in the English Club, where Steinbeck first encountered her. They had a strong, but rocky, personal relationship thereafter, partly because Bailey disliked Steinbeck's propensity for sentimentality. See Susan Riggs, "Steinbeck at Stanford," *The Stanford Magazine*, 4 (Fall/Winter 1976), p. 17. See Entry #55 below.

ENTRY #7

Lack of solitude. The one-story Steinbeck house, designed by Carol, built in mid-1936 on a secluded, heavily wooded 1.7-acre plot (purchased in May from Eleanor Bowdish) on Greenwood Lane, Los Gatos, was only about 800 square feet in size. Even with the later addition of a guest house, the five-room cottage was still so small that Steinbeck was continually subjected to interruptions from within and, with increasing new home construction in the area, from without as well. Most of the time, he wrote in a spartanly furnished 8-by-8-foot room, but at other times worked in the guest room, or, if weather permitted, on the porch deck (Connie Skiptares [With Assistance of Robert DeMott], "Garlic Gulch," San Jose *Mercury News*, March 12, 1986, Extra 4, pp. 1–3). For more on Steinbeck's Greenwood Lane house, see James P. Delgado, "Garlic Gulch: John Steinbeck in Los Gatos, 1936–1938," *The Book Club of California Quarterly News-Letter*, XLVI (Summer 1981), 59–64.

Music. Carlton Sheffield recalled the "simple" plan of the Steinbeck house included a speaker system ". . . set into the upper wall of the big room to carry music from a specially designed record player for their growing collection of good music." Sheffield, *Steinbeck: The Good Companion* (p. 214). See also Entry #20 below for the specific importance Steinbeck placed on listening to music.

ENTRY #8
Rodman. The American poet and anthologist Selden Rodman (b. 1909) was an editor and founder (with Alfred M. Bingham) of *Common Sense* (1932–1943), a monthly political/literary magazine published in New York City. Like several other literary editors during this period Rodman wanted Steinbeck to submit work to his magazine; the novelist had nothing on hand to send, though later he helped his friend Richard Lovejoy publish there.

ENTRY #11
Crawford . . . Ford. Broderick Crawford (1912–1986) and Wallace Ford (1898–1966) had won acclaim starring as, respectively, Lennie Small and George Milton in the George S. Kaufman production of *Of Mice and Men*, which, after closing its Broadway run on May 21, 1938, was being readied for an American tour, featuring a slightly toned-down script. At the cast party on closing night Steinbeck's drama agent, Annie Laurie Williams, presented each player with a first edition of the play, including a personal dedication from Steinbeck tipped in. To Ford, he wrote, "For God's sake stick with this play you have helped to make so much better than it is"; to Crawford, he wrote, "Your playing of this difficult part must be a work of great genius. I wish I could indicate to you my gratification. You are a great actor. One must be to play simply." (Courtesy of Annie Laurie Williams Papers, Rare Book and Manuscript Library, Columbia University.) Both men visited Steinbeck during the summer of 1938.

Good work. "New book moves and I like it," Steinbeck told his literary agent. "Goes easily. It used to worry me when they came so easily, but counting the two years of fighting with it, I guess it isn't so easy" (John Steinbeck/Elizabeth Otis, letter, June 10, 1938; courtesy of Stanford University Library).

ENTRY #13

Champagne. Martin Ray continued the Paul Masson tradition in champagnes and sparkling wines, a fact not lost on the chastened Steinbeck, who noted their wrathful effect in the left-hand margin of this entry: "Couldn't Concentrate" and "NO WORK HANGOVER." He needed one more day to complete Chapter 6.

ENTRY #15

Beth. Elizabeth Ainsworth (b. 1894), Steinbeck's sister. Between 1933 and 1938, one of her sons, as well as her father, mother, and husband, died. She was understandably "washed out" (Mrs. Eugene Ainsworth/Robert DeMott, letter, July 12, 1985). Steinbeck was thoroughly moved by "remarkable" Beth's strength during this period. He later dedicated *The Winter of Our Discontent* (New York: The Viking Press, 1962), "To Beth, my sister, whose light burns clear." See also Entry #20.

Fred S. . . . Dick's job. Frederick R. Soule, whom Steinbeck had known since 1936, was Regional Information Advisor (in San Francisco) for the Farm Security Administration (formerly the Resettlement Administration); Dick Oliver, a friend of Steinbeck's, then living in New York, applied for a position with the F.S.A. in Washington. Steinbeck wrote directly to Pare Lorentz, who—about to become Director of the newly created United States Film Agency, another progressive New Deal organization, housed temporarily with the F.S.A.—had some clout in the capital. Steinbeck's action was partly altruistic, partly self-protective—the more friends he had in the F.S.A., the more advocates he would have for the veracity of the book he was writing, which, he rightly predicted, would come in for a storm of attack from conservative groups of all kinds, especially the Associated Farmers.

ENTRY #16

Tristram Shandy. *The Life and Opinions of Tristram Shandy, Gentleman* (1767), novel by Laurence Sterne (1713–1768).

Dad. In 1910 or 1911 Steinbeck's father, John Ernst Steinbeck (1862–1935), opened a feed and grain store, The J. E. Steinbeck Feed Store, at 352 Main Street, Salinas. When the store went under, the elder Steinbeck worked briefly as a bookkeeper at the Spreckels Sugar

Refinery, then, from 1924 until his death, as Treasurer of Monterey County, his office located in the county courthouse, West Alisal Street, Salinas (Pauline Pearson/Robert DeMott, interview, May 1984). Except for the following 1951 reminiscence, Steinbeck wrote very little about his father: "My greatest fault . . . is my lack of ability for relaxation. . . . Even in sleep I am tight and restless. . . . I think I got this through my father. I remember his restlessness. It sometimes filled the house to a howling although he did not speak often. He was a singularly silent man. . . . He was strong rather than profound. Cleverness only confused him—and this is interesting—he had no ear for music whatever. Patterns of music were meaningless to him. . . . In my struggle to be a writer, it was he who supported and backed me and explained me—not my mother. She wanted me desperately to be something decent like a banker. She would have liked me to be a successful writer like [Ed.—Booth] Tarkington, but this she didn't believe I could do. But my father wanted me to be myself. . . . He admired anyone who laid down his line and followed it undeflected to the end. I think this was because he abandoned his star in little duties and let his head go under in the swirl of family and money and responsibility. To be anything pure requires an arrogance he did not have, and a selfishness he could not bring himself to assume. He was a man intensely disappointed in himself. And I think he liked the complete ruthlessness of my design to be a writer in spite of mother and hell." See Steinbeck's *Journal of a Novel: The* East of Eden *Letters* (p. 103).

ENTRY #17
Doc Bolin. Dr. Rolf L. Bolin (1901–1973), ichthyologist, oceanographer, and Assistant Director at Stanford's Hopkins Marine Station (on the Monterey Peninsula's Point Cabrillo in Pacific Grove; Steinbeck had taken a class there in the summer of 1923) was a lover "of true things," who later prompted two humorous anecdotes in Steinbeck's and Ricketts's *Sea of Cortez: A Leisurely Journal of Travel and Research* (New York: The Viking Press, 1941), pp. 31 and 215. The Steinbecks did not make it to Hawaii the next winter, though Carol vacationed there alone in 1941.

ENTRY #19

Mrs. Gragg . . . Josh Billings.   Steinbeck often turned the oral stories and local tales of Monterey he heard from friends into fiction: the second edition of *Tortilla Flat* (1935) is dedicated to Susan Gregory, who provided much colorful information; Salinas childhood friends Max and Jack Wagner's mother inspired "How Edith McGillcuddy met R. L. Stevenson" (1941). American humorist Josh Billings (aka Henry Wheeler Shaw, 1818–1885) died of a stroke in the Del Monte Hotel. Harriet Gragg's tale of the unceremonious treatment of his intestines after being embalmed by a doctor (his body was returned to Massachusetts) is told in Chapter 12 of *Cannery Row* (New York: The Viking Press, 1945). Steinbeck's premonition was unfounded—according to Benson's *True Adventures of John Steinbeck* (p. 612), he consulted Mrs. Gragg and her daughter, Julia Breinig, again in 1948 when he was researching *East of Eden* (1952).

ENTRY #20

The Swan.   Russian composer Peter Tchaikovsky's ballet *Swan Lake* (1876). Steinbeck sometimes composed his novels under the influence of music, especially at the beginning of each week's work, or after hiatuses in his writing. He listened repeatedly, for instance, to Anton Dvorak's Symphony Number 9, "From the New World" (1893), when he was writing *Cup of Gold* (1929). The "pure and effective religion" of Bach was Steinbeck's "narcotic" during the final draft of *To a God Unknown* (New York: Robert O. Ballou, 1933). During the writing of his as-yet-unnamed novel Steinbeck was influenced by "the mathematics of musical composition." See Shasky and Riggs, eds., *Letters to Elizabeth* (p. 11). See also Entry #6 above.

ENTRY #21

Letter in the *Record*.   The June 1938 issue of *Monthly Record*, a magazine devoted to inmates of the Connecticut state prison system, published a solicited inspirational letter from Steinbeck (written in April): "There is a gradual improvement in the treatment of man by man, but that isn't a . . . lot of joy to a man who isn't going to live even to see the turn of the century. There are little spots of kindness that burn up like fire and light the whole thing up. But I guess the reason they are so bright is that there are so few of them. . . . [I]n our agricultural valleys, I've seen a family that was hungry give all its food to a family that was starving. I suppose that is inspiration. It and things like it only make me feel like a rat" (p. 3).

ENTRY #23

John Street. The father of Webster Street (one of Steinbeck's closest friends and later his divorce lawyer) was in the Palo Alto hospital.

Le Roy. Mervyn Le Roy, Hollywood film director, best known for *Little Caesar* (1931). Earlier in the year Steinbeck refused to work for him (Le Roy wanted to change the ending of *Of Mice and Men* to keep Lennie Small from killing Curley's Wife), but was here proposing a screen writing job for Louis Paul, who had not done any Hollywood script work since 1935.

ENTRY #25

Pat. Rumanian-born Pascal Covici (1888–1964) had entered publishing in 1922 in Chicago. In 1928 Covici and Donald Friede started Covici-Friede Publishers, which Friede left in 1935, as he recalls in *The Mechanical Angel* (New York: Alfred Knopf, 1948). The firm always had a precarious financial existence and was taken over by creditors, led by Colonel Arthur W. Little, in 1938. Introduced to Steinbeck's books by Ben Abramson (see Entry #60 below), Covici made immediate plans to publish the novelist's work, and almost single-handedly brought a number of Steinbeck's books into the public eye: *Tortilla Flat* (1935), *In Dubious Battle* (1936), *Saint Katy the Virgin* (1936), *Of Mice and Men* (1937), and *The Red Pony* (1937) all appeared originally with the Covici-Friede imprint; from 1935 to 1936, Covici also reissued *Cup of Gold* (1929), *The Pastures of Heaven* (1932), and *To a God Unknown* (1933). In 1938 Covici moved to The Viking Press, where he worked as a senior editor for the remainder of his life, responsible for Steinbeck and later for Joseph Campbell, Lionel Trilling, Arthur Miller, and Saul Bellow. Despite his early financial record, Covici was—at least in Steinbeck's case—sometimes more adept with commercial aspects of book publishing than with the creative editorial scrutiny of the novelist's texts. In fact, it isn't clear how deeply Covici really understood Steinbeck's authorial intentions, as their squabble over the ending of *The Grapes of Wrath* suggests. Nevertheless, though their sensibilities were different, Covici's legendary generosity, optimism, enthusiasm, and support endeared him to Steinbeck, who dedicated *The Moon Is Down* (1942) and *East of Eden* (1952) to his editor. At Covici's funeral Steinbeck said: "Only a writer can understand how a great editor is father, mother, teacher, personal devil, and personal god. For thirty years Pat was my collaborator and my conscience. . . ." "In Memoriam," in *Pascal Covici: 1888–1964* ([New York]: Written and Printed for and by his Friends, 1964), pp. 19–20. See also Charles A. Madison, "Pascal Covici and John Steinbeck," Chapter 24 of his *Irving to Irving: Author-Publisher Relations 1800–1974* (New York: R. R. Bowker Company, 1974), pp. 205–12. The commentary is impressionistic, but much of the Steinbeck–Covici correspondence from 1939 to 1964 is conveniently and chronologically arranged in Fensch, *Steinbeck and Covici: The Story of a Friendship* (pp. 19–231).

Good Ed. Although the mark of his personal influence is less apparent on *The Grapes of Wrath* than on other works by Steinbeck (notably the 1936 novel *In Dubious Battle*), Edward F. Ricketts (1897–1948)—marine biologist, author (*Between Pacific Tides*, with Jack Calvin), ecologist, philosopher, nonteleological thinker, and owner of Pacific Biological Laboratories, Inc.—was (until his death in an auto/train wreck) Steinbeck's closest friend and spiritual partner. In 1938, to prevent Ricketts's bankruptcy, Steinbeck paid off the lab's bank loan. By doing so, Steinbeck became an officer and shareholder of the corporation and a silent partner in the business, one of whose specialties was the preparation of specimens for sale to schools and institutions. "Once, in getting a catalogue ready, he wanted to advise the trade that he had plenty of hagfish available," Steinbeck recalled in his memorial essay, "About Ed Ricketts." "Now the hagfish is a most disgusting animal both in appearance and texture, and some of its habits are nauseating. It is a perfect animal horror. But Ed did not feel this, because the hagfish has certain functions which he found fascinating. In his catalogue he wrote, 'Available in some quantities, delightful and beautiful hagfish.'" With their joint effort on *Sea of Cortez* (1941), Ricketts also became Steinbeck's most important intellectual collaborator. Doc, the protagonist of Steinbeck's novel *Cannery Row* (1945), and its sequel, *Sweet Thursday* (New York: The Viking Press, 1954), was based directly on the personality, ideas, and character of Ricketts. "Knowing Ed Ricketts was instant," Steinbeck said in "About Ed Ricketts." "After the first moment I knew him, and for the next eighteen years I knew him better than I knew anyone. . . . He was different from anyone and yet so like that everyone found himself in Ed, and that might be one of the reasons his death had such an impact. It wasn't Ed who had died but a large and important part of oneself." See *The Log from the* Sea of Cortez (New York: The Viking Press, 1951), pp. vii–lxvii. The pioneering investigation of the complex Steinbeck–Ricketts relationship is in Astro, *John Steinbeck and Edward F. Ricketts: The Shaping of a Novelist* (pp. 3–75 and 119–140); the most succinct and in many ways the most perceptive account, however, is in Benson, *True Adventures of John Steinbeck,* Chapter XI, and passim.

Ritch and Tal. Ritch (1908–1956) and Natalya (1908–1968) Lovejoy, of Pacific Grove, had been friends of the Steinbecks since 1930, and were intimate members of the progressive group associated with Ed Ricketts's laboratory, all of whom displayed liberal—even radical—intellectual and political tendencies, equally boisterous senses of humor, a love of good conversation, and abiding interest in odd characters of all sorts (Virginia Scardigli/Robert DeMott, interview, April 1984). The multitalented Ritch Lovejoy, who had owned and edited (with Tal) a newspaper in Alaska, and had worked at a radio station and for the F.S.A. in the Central Valley, was at this time illustrating Ricketts's and Calvin's *Between Pacific Tides* (published in 1939 by Stanford University Press), writing advertising copy for Holman's Department Store (later the setting for some scenes in *Sweet Thursday*), and trying to launch a career as a poet and fiction writer. He became a popular, respected journalist with the Monterey *Peninsula Herald*. In early 1939 Steinbeck acted as an informal literary agent for Lovejoy by sending his poems to Selden Rodman at *Common Sense*, who responded enthusiastically (Selden Rodman/John Steinbeck, letter, March 14, 1939; courtesy of Bancroft Library, University of California, Berkeley), eventually publishing a section of "The Short Road" and "Tidepool" in the July 1939 and March 1940 issues. Steinbeck debated with himself about "playing God" in Lovejoy's behalf (see Entry #103 below), but decided it was justified. To further encourage Lovejoy's writing career—and to continue a legacy Steinbeck felt had originated with his own father (who once gave his son a thousand dollars to support him while he wrote)—Steinbeck generously signed over the thousand-dollar Pulitzer Prize check he received for *The Grapes of Wrath* ("Lovejoy Gets Pulitzer Check," Monterey *Peninsula Herald*, June 14, 1940, p. 3).

ENTRY #26

Dick. G.   Before he finished *To a God Unknown* (1933), which he later told Wilbur Needham was about the "powerful, fruitful and moving Unconscious" mind (letter, April 4 [1934]; quoted in DeMott, *Steinbeck's Reading* (p. 63), Steinbeck discussed Jungian psychology and theories of myth and archetype with Ed Ricketts, Joseph Campbell, Dr. Evelyn Ott, a Carmel psychologist, and with Richard Gregerson, who had studied with Carl Jung.

ENTRY #27

Dedicating new book.   Louis Paul's novel, *The Wrong World*, published in 1938, carries this dedication: "To the author of *The Pastures of Heaven* affectionately."

ENTRY #28

Partisan.   Steinbeck's advocacy and compassion for a portion of America's disenfranchised population remained unwavering during this period, as he reminded San Francisco journalist John D. Barry. (See Entries #31 and 36 below.)

ENTRY #29

Original cast.   As it turned out, despite much jockeying and politicking by the stars, neither Broderick Crawford nor Wallace Ford were hired for the *Of Mice and Men* road show, which opened in Pittsburgh in October. The West Coast production, however, which Steinbeck alludes to, was another matter. It opened April 24, 1939, at San Francisco's Geary Theatre, then went on to Los Angeles; Wallace Ford reprised his role as George, and also served as producer.

Moore . . . critique.   Harry Thornton Moore, a native Californian then living in Chicago and working as a writer and editor (he later became Professor of English at Southern Illinois University), wrote the first book-length study of Steinbeck, *The Novels of John Steinbeck* (Chicago: Normandie House, 1939). For his monograph, Moore had the direct cooperation of Chicago bookseller Ben Abramson (Steinbeck's first advocate), of Steinbeck himself, and of Carlton Sheffield, who provided biographical and background information. After reading the book (it was published the same month as *The Grapes of Wrath*—April 1939—so Moore had very little to say about the novel) Steinbeck told Sheffield only that Moore's "hill valley fixation" in his discussion of *To a God Unknown* was a "little disgusting," and that "Freudian criticism has always seemed a kind of a waste of time. I can still look at a valley without getting an erection" (John Steinbeck/Carlton Sheffield, letter, June 23, 1939; courtesy of Stanford University Library). Moore's book was reissued with an unflattering and cranky Contemporary Epilogue in 1968 by the Kennikat Press, Port Washington, New York.

Norwegian translation. *Dagdrivergjengen (Tortilla Flat)*, translated by Haakon Bugge Mahrt (Oslo: Gyldendal Norsk Forlag, 1938). Courtesy of Steinbeck Research Center, San Jose State University.

All done. After completing Chapter 12 in one sitting, Steinbeck told Annie Laurie Williams, his drama and film agent, "I am quite sure no picture company would want this new book whole and it is not for sale any other way. It pulls no punches at all and may get us all into trouble but if so—so. That's the way it is. Think I'll print a foreword warning sensitive people to let it alone. I took three days off over the fourth. Getting back to work today. I've just scratched the surface so far. Carol thinks it is pretty good. . . . I'm sick of holding a pen. I've done 2,200 words today." [July 5, 1938], in Steinbeck and Wallsten, eds., *Steinbeck: A Life in Letters* (p. 168).

ENTRY #30

Review of my work. Steinbeck is apparently referring to Martin Bidwell's "John Steinbeck (An Impression)," which appeared in the University of Nebraska's academic/literary journal, *Prairie Schooner*, 12 (Spring 1938), 10–15. The piece is not a review at all, but rather a melodramatic account of Bidwell's 1933 visit with John and Carol Steinbeck, then living in Pacific Grove. The naive Bidwell, struggling with his first novel, hoped to get advice from Steinbeck. Instead, Steinbeck accused Bidwell of "selling out," of being "dishonest," for trying to please his literary agent rather than writing for himself. They also disagreed about Dostoevsky. Bidwell thought the Russian's characters were "abnormal"—certainly the wrong thing to say to a writer who not only considered *Crime and Punishment* (1866) one of his favorite novels, but who himself had created Tularecito in *The Pastures of Heaven* (New York: Brewer, Warren, and Putnam, 1932) and Joseph Wayne in *To a God Unknown* (1933). For Steinbeck, Dostoevsky's characters always represented the "essence" or "over-essence" of mankind, a mythic dimension he was consciously striving to create in *The Grapes of Wrath*, and one—among other things—he felt most critics never adequately grasped.

ENTRY #31

Word from Barry.　John D. Barry (1866–1942), a prolific writer of journalism, novels, plays, drama criticism, essays, and a noted peace worker, had written the Introduction to Steinbeck's pamphlet, *Their Blood Is Strong* (San Francisco: Simon J. Lubin Society, 1938), wherein he effusively claimed: "Steinbeck is a unique figure. He has come forward at a time when revolutionary changes are going on in the world. He will be a factor in those changes . . . [because his sympathies] . . . are not with the special people, but with those at a disadvantage, sorely in need of a gifted and valiant literary champion." The booklet added to the growing Steinbeck legend; by June it had gone through three of its four printings and many thousands of copies (at 25 cents each). Its contents were originally printed from October 5 to 12, 1936, in the progressive San Francisco *News* (one of the few pro-labor papers in the state), where Barry had worked as a daily columnist since 1926. The nonprofit Simon J. Lubin Society, headquartered in San Francisco, was named for the first chairman (1876–1936) of the California Immigration and Housing Authority, founded in 1913.

Who's Who.　Albert Nelson Marquis, ed. *Who's Who in America* (Chicago: A. N. Marquis, 1938), Volume 20 (1938–39), p. 2361: "Steinbeck, John Ernst, writer: *b.* Salinas, Calif., Feb. 27, 1902; *s.* John Ernst and Olive (Hamilton) S.; grad. Salinas High School, 1918; student Stanford U., 1919; *m.* Carol Henning, of San Jose, Calif., 1930. *Author:* Cup of Gold, 1929; Pastures of Heaven, 1932; To a God

Unknown, 1933; Tortilla Flat, 1935; In Dubious Battle, 1936; Of Mice and Men, 1937; Red Pony, 1937; dramatization of Of Mice and Men, 1937. *Address:* care of McIntosh & Otis, 18 E. 41st St., New York, N.Y."

Swedish translation. *Riddarna Kring Dannys Bord (Tortilla Flat),* translated by Sven Barthel (Stockholm: Bonniers, 1938). Courtesy of Steinbeck Research Center, San Jose State University.

ENTRY #32

In progress. *Des Souris et des Hommes (Of Mice and Men),* translated by Maurice Coindreau (Paris: Gallimard, 1939); *En un Combat Douteux (In Dubious Battle),* translated by Ed. Michel-Tyl (Paris: Gallimard, 1940). Courtesy of Steinbeck Research Center, San Jose State University.

First draft. Louis Paul's novel, *A Passion for Privacy,* which Steinbeck notes wistfully here, was published in 1940 and never heard from again. It is a social satire, a comedic lampoon of the clash between members of upper and lower social strata, and about as far from the tone and subject of *The Grapes of Wrath* as one could get.

ENTRY #33

Rodeo. The Salinas Rodeo, one of the largest in the state, was an annual, week-long social and cultural event. As a child, Steinbeck rode his pony, Jill, in the Rodeo parade; later, in "The Promise" (the third part of *The Red Pony*) the young protagonist, Jody Tifflin, dreams of participating in the Rodeo's steer-roping contests. The liberal-leaning Steinbeck did not always attain such felicitous relationships with his conservative home town, however. Beneath the town's "strange" "social structure," innocently recollected in his essay, "Always Something to Do in Salinas," *Holiday Magazine,* 17 (June 1955), 58–59, 152–53, 156, there lurked a capacity for violence and anti-intellectualism, symbolized by the vigilantism used to quell the Salinas lettuce strike of 1936. During this period of his life Steinbeck never understood or gained perspective on that brutishness, because he took such violations as personal affronts, as Jackson Benson rightly avers in *True Adventures of John Steinbeck.* See also Entry #38 below. Ironically, Salinas (where Steinbeck's books were burned on a couple of occasions, and where some ultraconservatives told him they were glad his parents were no longer alive to endure the shame of so "vile" a book as *The Grapes of Wrath*) has performed a complete turnaround—in 1969 the public library on West San Luis Street was named for the novelist, who is now honored in a five-day literary/cultural festival each summer, and even the Chamber of Commerce, which once repudiated him, has gotten into the act with an informative pamphlet on self-guided tours to "Steinbeck Country."

ENTRY #34

Request from CIO. The Congress of Industrial Organizations was formed in 1936 as a separate group from the American Federation of Labor. The CIO sought union representation among farm workers by chartering, in 1937, the United Cannery, Agricultual, Packing and Allied Workers of America. Through his affiliation with the Lubin Society (which supported the UCAPAWA), Steinbeck—fast coming to be considered an "expert" on farm labor issues (a role he did not voluntarily promote)—was being asked to help raise money to recruit members. Skeptical reaction from Tom Collins made Steinbeck change his mind about heading the committee, though he agreed to lend his name. The "Steinbeck Committee to Aid Agricultural Organization" was chaired first by lawyer and civil rights author Carey McWilliams (see Entry #96 below), then by actress Helen Gahagan Douglas. According to Walter J. Stein, *California and the Dust Bowl Migration* (Westport, CT: Greenwood Press, 1973), the committee issued a pamphlet in 1938, *What Is the John Steinbeck Committee to Aid Agricultural Organization?* (p. 274). The group was active during a November 1938 cotton strike in Bakersfield. A documentary record is available in the two-volume work by Howard M. Levin and Katherine Northrup, eds., *Dorothea Lange: Farm Security Administration Photographs, 1935–1939* (Glencoe, Illinois: The Text-Fiche Press, 1980), and in Roy Emerson Stryker and Nancy Wood, *In This Proud Land: America 1935–1943 as Seen in the FSA Photographs* (New York: Galahad Books, 1973), where one of Lange's brilliant photographs of the committee meeting appears on p. 172. On Christmas Eve 1938, the group, with support of many Hollywood liberals and artists, organized an enormous Christmas party at Shafter for 5,000 children of migrant worker families. In his announcement of the event, "The Stars Point to Shafter," *Progressive Weekly*, 2 (December 24, 1938), p. 2, Steinbeck wrote: "Movie stars, businessmen, farmers, writers are backing this program. . . . A radio nationwide hookup with such speakers as Edward G. Robinson, Melvyn Douglas, and other stars will place squarely before our country the problem of these courageous but destitute men and women and children who want to work and eat and live and yet are being denied those elementary principles of civilization."

Soule phoned. Frederick Soule had been contacted on July 6, 1938 by John Fischer, Director of the Farm Security Administration's Division of Information in Washington, to arrange a meeting between Steinbeck and President Franklin D. Roosevelt to discuss "Migrant Problem." Soule wired to a correspondent on July 11: "STEINBECK FIFTY MILES DOWN COUNTRY BUSY ON BOOK BUT WILLING TO COOPERATE IN ANY PLAN." (Courtesy of F.S.A. Files, National Archives, San Bruno, California; forwarded to me by Susan Shillinglaw). Roosevelt was on a hectic cross-country rail junket to gauge public sentiment and to drum up support for New Deal candidates in upcoming state elections. (Roosevelt's advocacy helped Culbert L. Olson, a proponent of labor reform, win election as the first Democratic governor in California in the twentieth century). He spoke on July 14 at the Administration Building of San Francisco's Golden Gate International Exposition on Treasure Island, where he expressed hope for world peace and extolled the positive virtues of the WPA. Nothing was said of migrant conditions. Their meeting fell through, but Steinbeck later called officially on Roosevelt in Washington in 1940. (See Entries #112 and #118 below.) On September 6, 1938, Soule asked Steinbeck to appear on a radio show with John Franklin Carter to discuss F.S.A. relief camps. Pare Lorentz, knowing Steinbeck's antipathy to public speaking of any kind, put friendship above politics and advised Steinbeck not to appear. (See Entries #66–68.)

ENTRY #35

That ranch. Carol's father, Wilbur Henning, a San Jose realtor, had found a forty-seven-acre homestead, known locally as the "Old Biddle Ranch" (settled originally around 1850). It was located in an isolated area off the Santa Cruz Highway near the Summit, about five miles out of Los Gatos. Edna B. Stone, the owner, was asking $16,000. The Steinbecks considered her price too steep and began negotiating to lower it, a process that consumed a great deal of attention and emotion during the coming weeks. Views of the Biddle ranch site are available in Anne-Marie Schmitz, *In Search of Steinbeck* (Los Altos, CA: Hermes Publications, 1978), pp. 11, 12, 15, 16; and in Don Herron, *The Literary World of San Francisco & Its Environs* (San Francisco: City Lights Books, 1985), p. 221. In 1985, the ranch, with about twenty acres of intact land, was selling for over $500,000.

ENTRY #36

My letters.   Steinbeck's letters appeared in John Barry's San Francisco *News* column, "Ways of the World," on Wednesday, July 13, 1938, p.14; they are reprinted here for the first time in fifty years. Barry, a founding member of the newly convened Bay area Citizens Committee for a Public Forum on Labor Problems, asked Steinbeck to cooperate in a nonpartisan forum between labor and capital designed to "help in the important work of ending those [recent] strikes that have done so much harm in the past and threaten the future." Steinbeck replied: "Forgive me for not answering your letter sooner than this. I am working very hard now and could not possibly take part in a forum. As to the use of my name—I should be very glad to have it used under certain circumstances. In the first place, I am not in favor of ending those strikes that have done so much harm until the abuses, on the part of the employer groups which have caused the strikes, are removed. In the second place, I am alarmed by the tendency of liberal forums to be liberal for a very short time. Such a liberal group as the Committee of 43 is absurd. Let us put it this way: If on the steering or executive committee of this forum, militant organized labor (not Vandeleur, AFL) is represented in strength sufficient to block a reactionary tendency, or if not able to block, at least to expose such a tendency, then I will very gladly offer my name, but if such labor representation is not there, I would not allow my name to be used." Steinbeck's decisiveness prompted Barry to re-emphasize his group's unbiased stance in promoting a "public hearing." His note brought forth a second, even more direct, letter (written on June 30, 1938—see Entry #28) from Steinbeck: "Your card alarms me, although I suppose it shouldn't. I am afraid of that word non-partisan. The Committee of 43 is non-partisan. The Associated Farmers are non-partisan. In fact, the word non-partisan describes one of two kinds of people: 1.—Those who through lack of understanding or interest have not taken a side, and, 2, those who use the term to conceal a malevolent partisanship. I am completely partisan. Every effort I can bring to bear is and has been at the call of the common working people to the end that they may eat what they raise, wear what they weave, use what they produce, and in every way and in completeness share in the works of their hands and their heads. And the reverse is also true. I am actively opposed to any man or group who, through financial or political control of means of production and distribution, is able to control and dominate the lives of workers. I hope this statement is complete enough so that my position is not equivocal. And please let me repeat—I shall not want my name used unless organized labor is strongly represented in the governing body of your group. I am writing this once for all to put to an end any supposition that I am non-partisan." Chastened, Barry thanked Steinbeck for giving him a lesson in "language."

ENTRY #38

My map. Probably a map Steinbeck had used when, in 1937, he and Carol had driven back to California from New York, following Route 66 through Oklahoma and the Southwest.

ENTRY #42

Reprint of M & M. Burns Mantle, one of the New York Drama Circle Critics, wanted permission to reprint *Of Mice and Men* in his annual series. It appeared in *The Best Plays of 1937–38* (New York: Dodd, Mead, 1938), pp. 31–66.

ENTRY #43

Henning. Carol's father, Wilbur Henning, had written concerning negotiations for the Biddle property. Later in the day Steinbeck replied: "We have a definite price that we can pay. You know that we never borrow money under any circumstances. . . . If Mrs. Stone will understand that we are not investing money in property but are looking for a place to live, and if she does not find it necessary to adhere to the stated price, which, frankly, seems exorbitant to us, we shall definitely be interested, but if she cannot make some price concession . . . our interest will be only a sad and regretful one." (July 25, 1938; courtesy of Steinbeck Research Center, San Jose State University). Steinbeck's frankness turned the trick—Henning sent his son-in-law's letter, and one of his own, to Mrs. Stone, who eventually dropped the selling price from $16,000 to $10,500.

O'Brien guy.   Edward J. O'Brien, editor and anthologist, wanted permission to reprint "The Chrysanthemums" (originally in *Harper's*, October 1937). O'Brien had already chosen it once for *The Best Short Stories 1938* (Boston: Houghton Mifflin, 1938), pp. 277–87; he now wished to include it in a forthcoming prize collection. Already one of Steinbeck's most popular stories, "The Chrysanthemums" appeared in O'Brien's *50 Best American Short Stories: 1915–1939* (New York: Literary Guild of America, 1939), pp. 783–95.

Cerf.   Bennett Cerf (1898–1971), President of Random House (whose Modern Library imprint had issued *Tortilla Flat* and *Of Mice and Men*) wired to say that he was willing to take over Steinbeck's contract (for $7,000) and help Covici out of his immediate financial difficulties by publishing *The Long Valley*. (Cerf could not, however, offer Covici an editorial job at Random House.) In the margin of this entry, Steinbeck later noted, "It didn't work." Two days later, on July 27, 1938, hoping to press an advantage, Cerf claimed, "I can tell you, in all honesty, that I'd rather add you to the Random House list than any other author in America today." Steinbeck was flattered, but wrote back to remind Cerf that he would "not interfere with [his agents'] negotiations." When the dust settled, and Steinbeck and Covici had joined The Viking Press, Cerf sent congratulations on August 18, 1938: "Viking is a fine house and I know they will do a brilliant job for you." (All communications courtesy of Random House Files, Rare Book and Manuscript Library, Columbia University.)

Three days . . . lost.   Steinbeck added this small paragraph on July 28. With the week's many distractions—Carol's tonsilectomy chief among them—his concentration broke and he had been unable to work on the novel since the twenty-fifth of July. He managed a commiserative letter to Elizabeth Otis, though, on whose shoulders he was sure the burden of "carrying" Covici-Friede and fielding the offers of several other interested publishing houses had fallen. Despite weariness and fears "about whether all of it is getting over," he promised the book would be ready by Christmas, and warned: ". . . this is a rough book, as rough as the people it deals with. It deals with them in their own terms. So in choosing a publisher (if you must) be sure there are neither moral traits nor reactionary ones, because a revolution is going on and this book is revolutionary. And I wouldn't want it changed to fit the policy of an old house" (John Steinbeck/Elizabeth Otis, letter [July 28, 1938]; courtesy of Stanford University Library).

ENTRY #44

Brod Crawford. The actor, who had a reputation for being "difficult," arrived unannounced into a chaotic Steinbeck household, which Steinbeck was trying to manage single-handedly. Steinbeck "took him out to meals and he was very nice." (John Steinbeck/Elizabeth Otis, letter [August 4 and 5, 1938]; courtesy of Stanford University Library).

Stanford. Steinbeck attended Stanford University intermittently from the fall of 1919 through the spring of 1925. At least twice—in the spring of 1920 and again in the fall of 1920—he fell behind and had to withdraw. He never received a degree. (Stanford University Undergraduate Transcript).

ENTRY #45

Nearly crazy. Steinbeck wanted "to kill" Wallace Ford because newspaper reporters had been told that Ford was staying with Steinbeck. "I haven't seen Ford, but I've talked to a lot of reporters for him." (John Steinbeck/Elizabeth Otis, letter [August 4 and 5, 1938]; courtesy of Stanford University Library.)

ENTRY #47

Threat to . . . printers. A few weeks earlier Steinbeck and Louis Paul had been discussing the injustices of the royalty system, in which the writer is paid only "after every other claim has been retired" (John Steinbeck/Elizabeth Otis, letter, [August 1, 1938]; courtesy of Stanford University Library). With Pat Covici in debt to them for an enormous sum, the printing firm of J. J. Little & Ives was threatening to take over his company, which meant, of course, that their accounts would be settled before Steinbeck ever saw a cent in royalties, if indeed he saw any at all. Relying on the legal power of his contract as leverage, Steinbeck sent a "brutal" threat—through Elizabeth Otis—that the printers settle fairly, or he would abrogate his relationship with them by submitting unprintable books that could not be marketed. He also cooked up an equitable scheme of royalty payment, featuring monthly accounting (John Steinbeck/Elizabeth Otis, letter, [August 4 and 5, 1938]; courtesy of Stanford University Library). See Entry #49 below.

George and Gail. George Mors, a close friend from Steinbeck's student days at Stanford (AB, 1924), and his wife, Gail, lived in Los Gatos. They took Carol to "the City"—San Francisco—about fifty miles north.

ENTRY #48
Muni. The actor Paul Muni wanted to acquire the movie rights to *Tortilla Flat* (1935), and wanted Steinbeck to write the film script. The deal fell through, however, because Steinbeck made several ironclad "conditions": ". . . 1 That I must finish this book first[.] 2 That I would not go to Hollywood but must do the work here. 3 That I have the help of a scenarist (shall specify Louis Paul). 4 That it will cost them a lot of money. . . . It would be a salary job" (John Steinbeck/Elizabeth Otis, letter, August [10 and 11] 1938; courtesy of Rare Book and Manuscript Library, Columbia University). The movie—written by John Mahin and Benjamin Glaser, and directed by Victor Fleming—eventually appeared in 1942, with Spencer Tracy, John Garfield, and Hedy Lamarr in leading roles. See Millichap, *Steinbeck and Film* (p. 196).

ENTRY #49
Viking Press. *Time* magazine reported in their August 29, 1938, issue: "Owing somewhere around $170,000, the ten-year-old publishing house of Covici-Friede last week was taken over by its printers, J. J. Little & Ives, who alone were in for a reported $103,000. Main asset of interest to creditors was Novelist John Steinbeck, ex-laborer and re-porter whose tender tale of proletarian brutality, *Of Mice and Men*, had netted Covici-Friede about $35,000. How much Steinbeck was consid-ered to be worth by publishers was disclosed last week when his contract was sold for $15,000 to Viking Press, which in addition gave Publisher

Pascal Covici a job. . . ." (p. 47). Elizabeth Otis was responsible for "breaking things open" during the negotiations and securing the favorable contract. ". . . the new agreement sounds fine," Steinbeck told her. "You'll never know how glad we are to have you" (John Steinbeck/Elizabeth Otis, letter, August [10 and 11] 1938; courtesy of Rare Book and Manuscript Library, Columbia University).

Wellman Farley.   Farley was president of the San Francisco Theatre Union, a group of "committed" actors (all of whom held outside jobs) devoted to presenting works with strong social themes. He starred as Lennie Small in their May 1937 production of *Of Mice and Men*, which—even though it was more like a dramatic reading of the novel—predated by six months the phenomenally successful George S. Kaufman Broadway production. Farley wanted to be hired for the touring production of the play. Though Steinbeck had not seen either the San Francisco or Broadway production, he had been told (by John Hobart, the San Francisco *Chronicle*'s drama critic) that ". . . Farley was far finer in the part than Crawford. . . . [I]f the question ever arises and you have a say, please note that I would like Wellman to play . . . Lennie on the road" (John Steinbeck/Annie Laurie Williams, letter, pm May 28, 1938; courtesy Rare Book and Manuscript Library, Columbia University).

Trouble . . . in M & M.   In the ledger he kept while writing *The Long Valley* stories and *Of Mice and Men*, Steinbeck recorded similar daily arguments, notes of self-loathing, and wishes for death, all of which temporarily paralyzed his "resolution of will." (Courtesy of Steinbeck Research Center, San Jose State University).

ENTRY #51
Mother and dad . . . ill.   Steinbeck's *Long Valley/Of Mice and Men* ledger book carries this entry, dated August 1934: "What a year this has been. . . . A year and three months ago we came north to find mother ill. Then ten months of paralysis. Then Dad slipping and slipping. . . ." (Courtesy of Steinbeck Research Center, San Jose State University). Steinbeck's mother, Olive Hamilton Steinbeck (b. 1867), died in 1934, while her son was writing *Tortilla Flat*. His father (see Entry #16 above), "that poor silent man," died in May 1935, during the final stages of *In Dubious Battle*. It should have been a far darker

time for Steinbeck than the one he was currently witnessing, though it isn't always clear that he saw it that way. See his letters to George Albee in Steinbeck and Wallsten, eds., *Steinbeck: A Life in Letters* (pp. 83, 93).

ENTRY #52

Joe and Charlotte.   Writer, editor, and critic, Joseph Henry Jackson (1894–1955), and his wife, Charlotte, carried on a lively intellectual and artistic household in Berkeley, across the Bay from San Francisco where Jackson reigned for a quarter of a century (from 1930 until his death) as the influential and judicious Book Editor of the San Francisco *Chronicle,* and the originator of a weekly Pacific Coast radio program, "Bookman's Guide." Jackson had a particularly strong interest in the literature and lore of California, about which he wrote and/or edited several books, among them an anthology, *Continent's End: A Collection of California Writing* (New York: McGraw Hill/Whittlesey House, 1944), which included a selection from *In Dubious Battle.* The Jacksons and the Steinbecks had been friends and traveling companions for several years. Jackson's book, *Mexican Interlude* (New York: Macmillan, 1936; rev. ed., 1937), includes a brief scene, in Chapter XV, of the Steinbecks in the market at Huejotzingo. Inscribing a copy of the first edition, Jackson wrote: "For John and Carol Steinbeck, who helped us see Mexico. Especially to John for the kind things he said about this book, and for his graciousness in accepting without comment his appearance as an actor in its pages. . . ." Quoted in DeMott, *Steinbeck's Reading* (p. 59). Steinbeck's "kind words" occurred in one of the only book reviews he ever wrote, "A Depiction of Mexico, by an Author with No Pattern to Vindicate," San Francisco *Chronicle,* May 31, 1936, Section D, p. 4. Although Steinbeck grenerally disliked critics and reviewers, he trusted and admired Lewis Gannett (New York *Herald Tribune*), Wilbur Needham (Los Angeles *Times*), and Jackson. In response to Jackson's essay, "John Steinbeck: A Portrait," *Saturday Review of Literature,* 16 (September 25, 1937), 11–12; 18—one of the first serious national exposures for Steinbeck—the novelist said: "It's a nice article, Joe, but what pleases me more than the article is that around it and through it is the feeling that you genuinely do like us and that is very important to us." (John Steinbeck/Joseph Henry Jackson, letter [October

1937]; courtesy of Joseph Henry Jackson Papers, Bancroft Library, University of California, Berkeley). Jackson not only reviewed Steinbeck's books favorably, but—drawing on his familiarity with Steinbeck's personal and intellectual life—also wrote informative introductions to the two-volume *The Grapes of Wrath* (New York: Limited Editions Club, 1940), and to *The Short Novels of John Steinbeck* (New York: The Viking Press, 1953). His widow recalled that Steinbeck was always pleased with her husband's work (Charlotte Jackson/Robert DeMott, telephone interview, July 17, 1980).

ENTRY #53

Thesis. Merle Danford, a graduate student at Ohio University, was planning a master's degree thesis on Steinbeck. Her English Department advisor, C. N. Mackinnon, wrote ahead to see if Steinbeck would mind being interviewed for the thesis. In reply, Steinbeck wrote: "Let your young woman write, but let her beware. I'll lie—not because I want to lie, but because I can't remember what is true and what isn't. I'm reasonably sure that my biography, particularly when it is autobiography, is the worst pack of lies in the world. And the awful thing is that I don't know which are lies and which aren't. Compensation maybe, I don't know. It's so bad that my wife, who is a truthful person, really likes the truth, I mean, and puts some store in it, is all confused, too. For years she struggled to keep her head above water, but she is sinking finally. I'm really sorry about this, but your candidate will just have to take her chance. I'm not trying to be funny—this is a tragic truth" (John Steinbeck/C. N. Mackinnon, letter, ca. late July 1938). Armed with this caveat, Danford sent Steinbeck a five-page questionnaire which he managed to fill out without being very specific or informative. Steinbeck's answers are appended to Danford's "A Critical Survey of John Steinbeck: His Life and the Development of his Writings" (Ohio University, 1939), and reprinted, with commentary by Robert DeMott, " 'Voltaire Didn't Like Anything': A 1939 Interview with John Steinbeck," *Steinbeck Quarterly*, 19 (Winter–Spring 1986), 5–11.

ENTRY #54

Chaplin. Charlie Chaplin (1889–1977), writer, director, actor, romantic and screen legend, was one of the most celebrated and entertaining men in the world. Charles Chaplin, Jr., in *My Father, Charlie Chaplin* (New York: Random House, 1960), claims Chaplin "was fascinated by Steinbeck's books and used to drive around the countryside where his stories were laid, trying to place the characters in the books in their proper locations" (p. 185). With Dan James, Chaplin drove up from his home in Pebble Beach, south of Carmel, to visit and to discuss politics, filmmaking, and social issues. Their friendship was immediate—"spontaneous, generous, gabby, confidential"—as Alistair Cooke said of Chaplin in *Six Men* (New York: Alfred Knopf, 1977), p. 250. Of these excursions Chaplin himself recalled that he and Steinbeck disagreed about communism (one of Chaplin's infatuations), and that "The Steinbecks had no servants; his wife did all the housework. It was a wonderful menage and I was very fond of her." See *My Autobiography* (New York: Simon and Schuster, 1964), p. 389. Sometime during their three 1938 visits (see Entries #56 and #84 below) Steinbeck and Chaplin discussed publishing the script for his Hitler satire, *The Great Dictator* (1940), then in planning stages. In early 1939 Steinbeck reported to Elizabeth Otis, "I haven't heard from Charlie so don't know whether he has thought more about *The Dictator* as a book or not. But . . . I wrote to him, reminding him of the discussion, saying I thought it important to edit, preface or any damn thing just so it got out." In Shasky and Riggs, eds., *Letters to Elizabeth* (pp. 11–12). Jackson Benson, *True Adventures of John Steinbeck* (pp. 383–84, 393–95, 464–65) is quite helpful on the Steinbeck/Chaplin connection.

ENTRY #55

Great trouble. The parallels with his writing life of two and three years earlier kept striking Steinbeck forcefully during this difficult stretch. At worst they aroused his self-pity; at best they reminded him that he was capable of overcoming enormous obstacles when his discipline was fully engaged. His current preoccupation with the Biddle place called up memories of a former "test"—trying to write *Of Mice and Men* while the Greenwood Lane house was being erected. (Again, from his unpublished *Long Valley/Of Mice and Men* ledger book; courtesy of Steinbeck Research Center, San Jose State University.)

ENTRY #60

Abramson. Ben Abramson (1898–1955), one of Steinbeck's earliest champions, owned the Argus Book Shop in Chicago, and, in Steinbeck's words, "made it for me" (See Entry #103 below). Besides being personally responsible for introducing Pascal Covici to Steinbeck's books in 1934, Ben Abramson wrote the very first bibliographical appreciation of Steinbeck, which appeared in the inaugural issue of his monthly review of rare and recent books, *Reading and Collecting*, I (December 1936), pp. 4–5, 18. Abramson worked zealously to create an audience for Steinbeck's books, and on several occasions tried Steinbeck's patience and indebtedness by prevailing upon the novelist to sign first editions of his work. Steinbeck, who disliked most book merchants, usually complied with Abramson's requests, even when it meant signing 150 copies of *Of Mice and Men* the year before, or, this time, 75 copies of the forthcoming *Long Valley*. But in 1940 a breach occurred when Abramson agreed to act as broker for Harry T. Moore and sell the private correspondence Moore received from Steinbeck when he was writing *The Novels of John Steinbeck*. (See Entry #29 above.) To Steinbeck, it was a betrayal of the first order; he never communicated with Abramson again. See D. B. Covington's *The Argus Book Shop: A Memoir* (West Cornwall, CT: Tarrydiddle Press, 1977), pp. 108–14, for his daughter's somewhat antiseptic account.

ENTRY #61

John Collier. John Collier, Jr. (b. 1913), was a commercial photographer in San Francisco, who—on the suggestion of his close friend Dorothea Lange—later joined the staff of documentary photographers working for Roy Emerson Stryker, Director of the Historical Unit of the F.S.A. in Washington.

ENTRY #62

Pounding. Years later, a more settled, less frenetic Steinbeck wrote in his *East of Eden* diary: "Today the house is full of pounding. I remember in the Grapes of Wrath book how I complained about the pounding. . . . I always felt that [it] was definitely designed to disturb me." See *Journal of a Novel: The* East of Eden *Letters* (pp. 13–14).

ENTRY #63

The chapter.   Because of the many recent distractions Steinbeck had been working since August 18 on what would become Chapter 20. The chapter covered fourteen handwritten pages; at the end of it, on page 109, he wrote, "long son of a bitch too."

Marvelous title.   Carol's discovery of the title, in Julia Ward Howe's "Battle Hymn of the Republic" (1862), was cause for rejoicing. Within a few days Steinbeck wrote to Louis Paul, Elizabeth Otis, Annie Laurie Williams, and Pascal Covici about the discovery. Otis may or may not have known about Mary Harriott Norris's *The Grapes of Wrath: A Tale of North and South* (Boston: Maynard, 1901), or Boyd Cable's novel, *Grapes of Wrath* (New York: E. P. Dutton, 1917), which, according to Morrow, *John Steinbeck: A Collection of Books & Manuscripts Formed by Harry Valentine* (p. 34), reprints lyrics of Julia Ward Howe's "Battle Hymn of the Republic" at the beginning of its text. In any event, in a return letter Otis did nothing to discourage Steinbeck's choice. On September 10 Steinbeck fired back: "About the title—Pat wired that he liked it. And I too am glad because I like it better all the time. I think it is Carol's best title so far. I like it because it is a march and this book is a kind of march—because it is in our own revolutionary tradition. . . ." In Steinbeck and Wallsten, eds., *Steinbeck: A Life in Letters* (p. 171).

ENTRY #64

House is sold.   On September 16, 1938, the Los Gatos *Mail-News* ran the following notice: "John Steinbeck's home on Greenwood Road has been sold to Miss Barbara Burke of the Burke Finishing School in San Francisco, it was announced . . . by Effie Walton, realtor through whose office the sale was made. Steinbeck has purchased the old Biddle home on the road to Montezuma School. The noted author is seeking greater seclusion" (p. 11). Local lore held that the Steinbecks vacated immediately for the new owners, but that is erroneous, as his next entry reveals.

ENTRY #65

111–112.   Steinbeck abandoned the division of the novel into books. Beginning with this entry Steinbeck filled in the number of the manuscript pages he had finished that day. Here, he had just completed the first two pages of "Ch. 10," eventually to become Chapter 22 in the published version.

New house. From the outset of their negotiations for the Biddle ranch the Steinbecks knew that building a new house on the property would be more practical and less expensive than restoring the dilapidated original homestead. Lawrence Smith, a local contractor, poured the new foundation and built the house to John and Carol's specifications. Steve (last name unknown), a local carpenter, did finish and trim work, and took care of the grounds. (See Entry #103 below.) Steinbeck bought a portable generator so the contractors would have electricity. By November—the new house and the new typescript of the novel still unfinished—the Steinbecks camped in a few rooms of the old house. In 1974 Carol told Marjorie Pierce, "I cooked over a wood stove; there were no floors, no inside water and at night the rats ran back and forth in the attic. . . ." Quoted in Ludmilla Alexander, "John Steinbeck, The Los Gatos Years," *Los Gatos Weekly*, October 17, 1984, p. 16.

ENTRY #68

Admission Day. September 9 is a state holiday, commemorating California's entry into the United States in 1850 as the thirty-first state.

Letter. Probably in response to a note Steinbeck had sent: "D--R. & T.: H-w h-v- y-- b--n. W- -r- f-ne. H-p- y-- a-e f-ne t-o. Haven't heard from Ed for a long time. Should have his store teeth by now. You must come up as soon as the people are off and see our new ranch. It is beautiful. You will love it. . . . Write us a note how you are, huh?" (John Steinbeck/Ritch and Tal Lovejoy, postcard, [early September 1938]; courtesy of Bancroft Library, University of California, Berkeley).

Valuable Ma. Steinbeck's determination to show Ma Joad in cooperative relationship with society suggests the influence of anthropologist Robert Briffault's *The Mothers: The Matriarchal Theory of Social Origins* (New York: Macmillan, 1931), which Steinbeck had read several years earlier (John Steinbeck/Carlton Sheffield, letter, June 30, 1933; quoted in DeMott, *Steinbeck's Reading*, p. 18). Carol Steinbeck later claimed Ma Joad was "pure Briffault." (Quoted in Astro, *John Steinbeck and Edward F. Ricketts*, p. 133). Consult Warren Motley, "From Patriarchy to Matriarchy: Ma Joad's Role in *The Grapes of Wrath*," *American Literature*, 54 (October 1982), 397–412, for a discussion of the subject.

ENTRY #69

Hitler. Adolph Hitler was expected to close the German National Socialist Party Congress, convened a week earlier in Nuremberg, with a speech outlining the Nazi plan for resolution—by war, if necessary—of the Sudeten German/Czechoslovakian problem. (After annexing Austria in March 1938, Hitler wanted Czechoslovakia as well, where three million people of German origin lived in the Sudeten area.) His speech was defiant but noncommittal; Hitler pledged aid to the Sudetens, but gave no specific plan. On September 15 Britain's Prime Minister Neville Chamberlain flew to Germany to convince Hitler to avert war (see Entry #72 below), and, with the aid of France—but without consultation from the Czechs (Steinbeck rightly suspected a "double cross")—to propose a peaceful solution by directing Prague to hand over to the Third Reich all sections of the country with 50 percent or more German population. The result was the Munich Agreement (September 30, 1938), signed by Germany, Great Britain, France, and Italy, which temporarily avoided war by giving in to Hitler's demands for annexation of Sudetenland (see Entries #80 and #82 below). The agreement proved futile—within a year Hitler took what remained of Czechoslovakia, invaded Poland, and precipitated World War II.

ENTRY #70

Toilet paper scandal. Toilet paper was scarce in the government camps. For this comic scene in Chapter 22 (" 'Hardly put a roll out 'fore it's gone. Come right up in meetin'. One lady says we oughta have a little bell that rings ever' time the roll turns oncet. Then we could count how many ever'body takes' "), Steinbeck borrowed directly from Tom Collins' reports, especially this entry, under "Bits of Migrant Wisdom": "We were discussing with two women how best to cut down on the use of toilet paper in the women's sanitary units. One suggested sprinkling red pepper through the roll. The other suggested a wire be attached to the roll so that every time a sheet was torn off the big bell placed on the outside of the building for the purpose would ring and let every one know who was in the sanitary unit and what she was doing. Note: We have followed neither suggestion thus far." Thomas Collins, Kern Migratory Labor Camp Report for Week Ending May 2, 1936, p. 15. (Facsimile courtesy of Steinbeck Research Center, San Jose State University.)

ENTRY #72

Adamic. Louis Adamic (1899–1951), Yugoslavian-born author, historian, social critic/observer, and liberal journalist, known to Steinbeck for his 1931 narrative of labor violence in America, *Dynamite* (see DeMott, *Steinbeck's Reading*, p. 3). A few months earlier, Adamic had published *My America, 1928–1938* (New York: Harper and Brothers, 1938), an enormous 680-page compendium of narrative, interview, and exposition—part autobiography, part travel book, part history (a section on the rise of the CIO)—about his anxious quest to get "the feel of things" (p. xiii) in Depression America. Like Steinbeck, he distrusted drawing room theory, and rejected ideology for experience; like Steinbeck, he sought a type of radicalism consonant with the American sensibility and democratic traditions.

Time trouble. Planning the termination of Rose of Sharon's pregnancy to coincide with late winter floods.

ENTRY #74

Covarrubias. Miguel Covarrubias (1904–1957), Mexican artist, and caricaturist (especially for *Vanity Fair*). He was also an ethnologist, whose *Island of Bali* had appeared the year before, and an illustrator of a modern edition of Harriet Beecher Stowe's novel *Uncle Tom's Cabin* (1938). He was in San Francisco arranging details for a large mural of the Pacific Islands he had been commissioned to paint for the Golden Gate Exposition, to be held the following year. It is not known whether Steinbeck ever met Covarrubias again, so the following anecdote, recollected by Steinbeck in February 1957, might stem from this visit at the Jacksons' home. When Covarrubias' father was dying ". . . the holy water brought him to and he jumped up and chased the priest out of the house . . . [where] . . . he died in the middle of the street in his long night gown. Now there's a proper death for you! And Miguel said that he winged the priest with brass spitoon as he flew out the door." See Robert DeMott, ed., *Your Only Weapon Is Your Work: A Letter by John Steinbeck to Dennis Murphy* (San Jose: Steinbeck Research Center, 1985), [p. 14].

Noah down . . . river. Steinbeck had to account for Noah Joad's desertion at the Colorado River, when the rest of his family crossed into California from Arizona. Prior to starting on manuscript page 127 (the opening of Chapter 24 in the published version), Steinbeck wrote thirty-three lines (roughly 500 words) explaining Noah's willful action; Steinbeck then inserted the new, but unnumbered, page between manuscript pages 87 and 88 (Chapter 18 of the published version).

ENTRY #79

I AM. The Great I Am movement, an intensely patriotic spiritual cult founded in the early 1930s by Guy W. Ballard (who fancied himself the reincarnation of George Washington). In 1940 two dozen of its leaders were indicted by a Federal Grand Jury in Los Angeles for mail fraud. A sensational and thoroughly biased exposé is available in Gerald B. Bryan, *Psychic Dictatorship in America* (Los Angeles: Truth Research Publications, 1940).

Francis. Francis Whitaker, a blacksmith, metal sculptor, and political radical from Carmel, was a member of the John Reed Club. According to Jackson Benson, in *True Adventures of John Steinbeck* (p. 225), Whitaker "worked hard during the early and mid thirties to convert" the Steinbecks to socialism.

Well reviewed. Annie Laurie Williams' information that "*The Long Valley* is getting a marvelous press" (Annie Laurie Williams/John Steinbeck, letter, September 23, 1938; courtesy of Rare Book and Manuscript Library, Columbia University) proved to be accurate. William Soskin, in the New York *Herald Tribune Review of Books* (September 18, 1938), p. 7, Elmer Davis, in *Saturday Review of Literature*, 18 (September 24, 1938), p. 11, and Stanley Young, New York *Times Book Review* (September 25, 1938), p. 7, all gave *The Long Valley* affirmative reviews. Young predicted Steinbeck ". . . may become a genuinely great American writer."

ENTRY #80

Margolies. Joseph A. Margolies (1890–1982), former sales manager of Covici-Friede, was an executive at the New York City headquarters of Brentano's bookstores.

ENTRY #81

Fadiman's. Clifton Fadiman's review of *The Long Valley* appeared in *The New Yorker*, 14 (September 24, 1938): "On the whole . . . a remarkable collection by a writer who has so far neither repeated himself nor allowed himelf a single careless sentence" (p. 92).

Review in . . . *Chronicle*. In his column, "A Bookman's Notebook," Joseph Henry Jackson singled out the four "Red Pony" stories of *The Long Valley* for special praise. About Jody's grandfather's belief, in "The Leader of the People," that only the process of pioneering mattered, Jackson stated: "Unquestionably it is Steinbeck's knowledge of the new westering, today's machine-economy-driven migratory movement, that leads him to say this. Because it is plain as a pikestaff that though the old kind of westering is done with, there must be a new kind, something to take the place of the old—a westering of ideas perhaps" (p. 14).

ENTRY #83

Parsons. Syndicated Hollywood "gossip" columnist Louella Parsons (1881–1972) divulged that Chaplin liked the Los Gatos/Saratoga area so much he was thinking about buying property there. The cause of Steinbeck's confusion in this entry and in the next one (note the self-confessed "gibbering" below) cannot be precisely identified, beyond its being either somehow connected to his relationship with the impetuous Chaplin, his concern over growing tensions in Europe, or unspecified marital difficulties with Carol; obviously, something deeper than the normal disturbances and interruptions was at work.

ENTRY #84

The party. Steinbeck took Chaplin to Martin Ray's Masson vineyard, where they helped process the newly harvested Chardonnay grapes. Much to Martin Ray's pleasure, Chaplin and Steinbeck exhibited a similarly ceremonial attitude toward the work. Afterward Chaplin took charge of roasting a turkey on the rotisserie spit and entertained the guests with singing and music (Mrs. Eleanor Ray/Robert DeMott, interview, June 4, 1985). The hilarity of the event evidently did nothing to ease Steinbeck's current confusion, though apparently he hid it well from his companions.

ENTRY #85
Criticism.   It is difficult to ascertain whether Steinbeck is taking a cavalier attitude toward what he imagines will be adverse post-publication criticism of the novel, or whether he is reacting to contemporary responses to his manuscript, perhaps Louis Paul's dislike of the title, or the fact that Chaplin might not have been as moved as Steinbeck hoped he would be.

ENTRY #89
Mary and Bill.   The Dekkers, Steinbeck's younger sister (1905–1965), and her husband (d. 1943), a scion of the Bemis Bag Corporation in San Francisco. They were living in Carmel, where William Dekker had an insurance business. Steinbeck's posthumous *The Acts of King Arthur and His Noble Knights*, ed. Chase Horton (New York: Farrar, Straus and Giroux, 1976) is dedicated to Mary, "who for gentle prowess had no peer living."

ENTRY #90
Fill out.   When he reached the top of manuscript page 151, Steinbeck finished the last 22 lines of Chapter 26 (9 lines of manuscript), and, without breaking stride, he filled out the remainder of his ledger page with the complete general Chapter 15 (27 in the published version).

ENTRY #91
Sis.   Sarah "Sis" Reamer was an agricultural union organizer whom Steinbeck had known since 1934, according to Benson, *True Adventures of John Steinbeck* (p. 297).

La Follette people.   From 1936 to 1940 Senator Robert La Follette (R, Wisconsin), chaired the La Follette Civil Liberties Committee, a subcommittee of the Senate Committee on Education and Labor, which was empowered to investigate violations against labor's right to organize and bargain collectively. Although the committee did not actually conduct full hearings on California's embattled agricultural labor situation until a year later (at which time the veracity of *The Grapes of Wrath* was established beyond doubt), during October and November of 1938 ". . . a small contingent of La Follette Committee staff members conducted a limited inquiry [into the Associated Farmers' vigilante activities], which the exhaustion of funds abruptly terminated." See Jerold S. Auerbach, *Labor and Liberty: The La Follette Committee and the New Deal* (Indianapolis: Bobbs Merrill, 1966), p. 178.

ENTRY #92

Carl. Finnish-born Carl Wilhelmson was another of Steinbeck's Stanford classmates and English Club cronies. During the winters of 1926–27 and 1927–28, when Steinbeck was living in the caretaker's cabin at the Brigham estate in Lake Tahoe, Wilhelmson visited briefly, but in such close quarters the two got on each other's nerves. Wilhelmson's "nervousness" created "a like nervousness in me," Steinbeck told Carlton Sheffield (letter, February 25, 1928; courtesy of Stanford University Library). Wilhelmson published one novel, *Midsummernight* (New York: Farrar and Rinehart, 1930), which Steinbeck admired, but had then gone into other ventures in San Francisco. See Benson, *True Adventures of John Steinbeck* (pp. 119–22), and DeMott, *Steinbeck's Reading* (p. 119).

ENTRY #94

Louis. Next day Steinbeck responded: "Many thanks for your letter. I'm glad it holds interest. I don't want to hear criticism now—until I am finished and then I want to hear all of it" (John Steinbeck/Louis Paul, postcard, October 18, 1938; courtesy of University of Virginia Library).

ENTRY #96

Chapter. Covici refused all magazine requests for excerpts of the novel except *The Saturday Review of Literature*, which previewed Chapter 2, "No Riders," in its April 1, 1939 issue (pp. 13-16). Steinbeck himself never allowed magazine serialization or abridgment of *The Grapes of Wrath*.

McWilliams. A man of renaissance capacities, Carey McWilliams (1905–1980) was a Los Angeles lawyer, activist, author, and dedicated humanist whose vigorous, timely, and perceptive articles in the mid-1930s (for *The Nation* and *Pacific Weekly*) on the abuse of foreign and American migrant workers in California's industrialized "farms" made him a respected authority. His research and field investigations culminated in a landmark book, *Factories in the Field: The Story of Migratory Farm Labor in California* (Boston: Little, Brown, 1939), which appeared a few months after *The Grapes of Wrath,* and which (like Steinbeck, with whom he is frequently linked) made him an enemy of large-scale corporate agriculture. Steinbeck held *Factories in the Field* in the highest regard: "It is a complete and documented study of California agriculture past and present. It should be read by those people who are confused by the liars and lobbyists who have covered this situation for years," he told Elizabeth Otis on July 30, 1939 (Quoted in DeMott, *Steinbeck's Reading,* p. 73). Here, McWilliams contacted Steinbeck either in regard to the La Follette staff inquiry (see Entry #91 above), which McWilliams campaigned for, or in regard to activities of the Steinbeck Committee to Aid Agricultural Workers (see Entry #34 above), which McWilliams chaired. Later that year, when Democrat Culbert Olson was elected Governor, he appointed McWilliams California's Commissioner of Immigration and Housing (1938–1942). Ironically, for all the coincident aspects of their careers, McWilliams and Steinbeck never met. See Carey McWilliams, The *Education of Carey McWilliams* (New York: Simon and Schuster, 1979), p. 78.

ENTRY #98
Over sell. Still not convinced about the importance of his book, Steinbeck repeated his concern about Covici's enthusiasm to Elizabeth Otis: ". . . Pat was here. We went to S.F. Friday night and got him and went bowling. Had fun and it was a good rest and I am full of a deep-rooted tiredness so could use the change. I expect to finish my first draft this week and Carol is back at typing. . . . Let me implore you not to let Pat over sell you on this ms. You know how he is. He hits the ceiling easy and the cellar almost as easy. So when he talks, just don't listen." In Shasky and Riggs, eds., *Letters to Elizabeth* (p. 9). After reading Carol's typescript Covici felt it was neat enough to be

the final draft. Steinbeck's cynicism neither dampened Covici's enthusiasm for the novel nor dissuaded The Viking Press from laying out $10,000 on an aggressive prepublication advertising campaign, and printing 50,000 copies of the novel's first edition. See Steinbeck and Wallsten, eds., *Steinbeck: A Life in Letters* (p. 177), and Goldstone, *John Steinbeck: A Bibliographical Catalogue* (p. 44).

NOTES: PART III

ENTRY #101

Enemies. There was nothing fabricated about Steinbeck's fear of reprisal or bodily harm. "The Associated Farmers have begun an hysterical personal attack on me both in the papers and a whispering campaign. I'm a Jew, I'm a pervert, a drunk, a dope fiend," Steinbeck lamented to Elizabeth Otis in late August 1939. See Shasky and Riggs, eds., *Letters to Elizabeth* (p. 19). Saddened, Steinbeck defended his German-Irish background and responded to criticism that *The Grapes of Wrath* was "Jewish propoganda" [sic] in a letter to Reverend L. M. Birkhead, National Director of the Friends of Democracy in 1940 (Steinbeck and Wallsten, eds., *Steinbeck: A Life in Letters*, pp. 203–204). Years later, in 1957, Steinbeck recalled to Chase Horton that after *The Grapes of Wrath* was published, "a lot of people were pretty mad at me. The undersheriff of Santa Clara County was a friend . . . [who warned] . . . 'don't stay in a hotel room alone . . . [because] . . . the boys got a rape case set for you. You get alone in a hotel and a dame will come in, tear off her clothes, scratch her face and scream and you try to talk yourself out of that one. They won't touch your book but there's easier ways.' " Quoted in Steinbeck and Wallsten, eds., *Steinbeck: A Life in Letters*, (p. 187). An excellent summary of the sordid effects of *The Grapes of Wrath*'s success is recorded in Benson, *True Adventures of John Steinbeck* (pp. 418–25).

Snapped up. In late July 1939 Steinbeck complained to his agent: "Let me tell you how bad it has got. Little presses write to ask me for manuscripts and when I write back that I haven't any, they write to ask if they can print the letter saying I haven't any. And I think that is going a little bit too far. I mean it's going beyond my ability to think." In Shasky and Riggs, eds., *Letters to Elizabeth* (p: 18).

John Cage. Already a notable avant-garde musician, then teaching at the Cornish School in Seattle, Cage (b. 1912) was married to Xenia Kashevaroff, Natalya Lovejoy's sister. A month earlier the reconciled Steinbecks had fled Los Gatos and driven to the Northwest, where they visited the Cages and journeyed with them to Vancouver. Like some other projects during this period, the proposed musical theses were never written, probably because—at a moment when Steinbeck wanted to embark on a new direction—they represented, thematically anyway, a return to older work, notably his "Argument of Phalanx," and "Case History," two unpublished pieces from the mid-1930s.

ENTRY #102

Pipe play. "The God in the Pipes" began as a straight dramatic play, which became so unwieldy he threatened to "burn" it: "I feel freed from an incubus in kicking it out." (John Steinbeck/Elizabeth Otis, letter [October 5, 1940]; courtesy of Stanford University Library.) In mid-1941 he was ready to begin rewriting it from the beginning. He conceived it as a "playable novel" of "39,000 words" not intended to be submitted to The Viking Press (John Steinbeck/Elizabeth Otis and Mavis McIntosh, letter [June?], 1941; courtesy of University of Virginia Library); it was to be "another little story in technique" like *Of Mice and Men*, "a small novel that can be played" (John Steinbeck/Elizabeth Otis, letter [August 9, 1941]; courtesy of Stanford University Library.) The manuscript was never finished and has been lost or destroyed.

ENTRY #103

Picture. Earlier in the year Steinbeck hosted screenwriter Eugene Solow in Los Gatos while they made final adjustments on the script of *Of Mice and Men*. "It is amazingly good and doesn't change the story at all. . . . I think the picture will be better than the play" (John Steinbeck/Elizabeth Otis, letter [February 9, 1939]; courtesy of Stanford University Library). Later that summer Solow and producer Lewis Milestone came to Los Gatos for a final conference with Steinbeck. The powerful, poetic film version, starring Burgess Meredith (George) and Lon Chaney, Jr. (Lennie), opened in Hollywood on December 22, 1939.

After seeing a preview on the fifteenth, Steinbeck told Elizabeth Otis, ". . . it is a beautiful job. Here Milestone has done a curious lyrical thing. It hangs together and is underplayed." In Steinbeck and Wallsten, eds., *Steinbeck: A Life in Letters* (p. 195). Benson, *True Adventures of John Steinbeck* (pp. 407–408), records some amusing anecdotes about Steinbeck and Milestone. For a discussion of the film version, consult Millichap, *Steinbeck and Film* (pp. 13–26). See also Entry #110 below.

Joe . . . Ray. The Steinbecks retained both men. Joe Higashi was hired to be a combination grounds keeper, general handyman, security agent, servant, and cook. "Good" Joe had the uncanny ability of screening the Steinbecks' calls and letting through only the ones they wanted. (John Steinbeck/Joseph Henry Jackson, letter [spring 1940]; courtesy of Joseph Henry Jackson Papers, Bancroft Library, University of California, Berkeley). Ray (last name unknown) was "an Okie boy" hired for outdoor work because "he needs the money so dreadfully," Steinbeck told Carlton Sheffield in July 1940. In Steinbeck and Wallsten, eds., *Steinbeck: A Life in Letters* (p. 208).

ENTRY #106

Hand book. Steinbeck was working in Monterey at Ricketts's Pacific Biological Laboratory on the "San Francisco Bay Guidebook." It was designed to reveal the ecological aspects of the Bay littoral (rather than the strictly taxonomic aspects). The book was abandoned in March for the Gulf of California venture. See Joel Hedgpeth, *The Outer Shores: Part 1, Ed Ricketts and John Steinbeck Explore the Pacific Coast* (Eureka, CA: Mad River Press, 1978), pp. 31–41; and Benson, *True Adventures of John Steinbeck* (pp. 427–30).

ENTRY #107

The Fight for Life. Pare Lorentz's first feature-length documentary for the United States Film Service spelled the end of his plans to make *In Dubious Battle*. It was based on Dr. Paul de Kruif's book of the same name (New York: Harcourt, Brace, 1938). The film's subject was infant mortality in the context of social unemployment, city slums, and disease. The idea for a film on health problems had been suggested to Lorentz by President Roosevelt. Carol's information about Roosevelt's reaction was apparently erroneous. Robert L. Snyder, in *Pare Lorentz and the Documentary Film* (Norman: University of Oklahoma Press, 1968), says that the film's private screening at the White House on New Year's Eve 1939, elicited approval from Roosevelt (p. 112), a point confirmed by Lorentz himself (Pare Lorentz/Robert DeMott, telephone interview, March 22, 1988). The film's reviews were uniformly excellent.

Tracy. Film star (he had acted in nearly forty films by this time and had won two Oscars) Spencer Tracy (1900–1967) was "very enthusiastic," Steinbeck told Elizabeth Otis on December 15, 1939, about making a nonprofit film (to be directed by Victor Fleming) of *The Red Pony*, which would benefit local children's hospital wards in cities where the film would be shown. See Steinbeck and Wallsten, eds., *Steinbeck: A Life in Letters* (pp. 195–96). The project fell through, as did Tracy's attempts to get a boat for the upcoming Steinbeck/Ricketts expedition to Sea of Cortez, and a little later—because of legal difficulties with his employer, MGM—his narration for Steinbeck's documentary film, *The Forgotten Village*. (Burgess Meredith eventually spoke the narration.) Tracy did, however, star as Pilon in MGM's production of *Tortilla Flat* (1942).

ENTRY #108

Garden book. Between her recently inaugurated mail-order piano lessons and her sketches of plump nude women (Chaplin framed two sketches by Carol), Carol had also been writing, or compiling, a seed book for gardeners. By the middle of January she had submitted it to The Viking Press (see Entry #110 below), but it was never published. "I do hope something may come of her book. It is a good idea I am sure of that," Steinbeck wrote on February 5, 1940. In Shasky and Riggs, eds., *Letters to Elizabeth* (p. 22).

Boats. Initially, Steinbeck and Ricketts planned to drive from Monterey to Guaymas, Mexico, and there rent a boat, with a Mexican crew, for the journey around Sea of Cortez. Instead, they ended up chartering Captain Tony Berry's 76-foot purse seiner, *Western Flyer*, directly out of Monterey. They sailed on Monday, March 11, 1940 (stopping briefly in San Diego to let off Toby Street), and returned six weeks later. Berry's log of the trip is available in Hedgpeth, *The Outer*

Shores, Part 1 (pp. 152–59). Carol was a member of the crew, but her presence was almost totally expunged in *Sea of Cortez*.

ENTRY #109

Bill Black. Black attended Salinas High School with Steinbeck and also enrolled at Stanford. See Benson, *True Adventures of John Steinbeck* (pp. 24–27, 36, 93).

No . . . sleep. Ten years later Steinbeck expanded this anecdote about Ricketts's Chicago youth in the memorial preface to *The Log from the* Sea of Cortez " 'I don't think there was time to sleep. I tended furnaces in the early morning. Then I went to class. I had lab all afternoon, then tended furnaces in the early evening. I had a job in a little store in the evening and got some studying done then, until midnight. Well, then I was in love with a girl whose husband worked nights, and naturally I didn't sleep much from midnight until morning. Then I got up and tended furnaces and went to class. What a time,' he said, 'what a fine time that was.' " In "About Ed Ricketts" (p. xlviii).

ENTRY #110

Milly. Russian-born Lewis Milestone (1895–1980) was one of Hollywood's most respected directors and a winner of two Oscars (for *Two Arabian Knights* in 1928, and for *All Quiet on the Western Front*, 1930). His best films—he was especially good at adapting novels—were known for their vivid realism, sharp dialogue, and fluid camera technique, all exemplified in his masterful production of *Of Mice and Men*. Steinbeck admired Milestone, who was considered something of a maverick in Hollywood, and interceded with Annie Laurie Williams (something he rarely did) so that Milestone could make *The Red Pony*. Production of the movie (Steinbeck wrote the script), however, was held up for many years and wasn't released until 1949. Except for the buoyant musical score by Aaron Copland, the film was not very successful.

ENTRY #111

Pictures on *Grapes*. Twentieth Century-Fox mounted an enormous publicity campaign for the film version of *The Grapes of Wrath*, not an unusual thing to do considering the whopping price the company paid for the rights ($75,000). Steinbeck had in hand an advance copy of the January 22, 1940, issue of *Life*, with its three-page spread, featuring photographs by Horace Bristol, pointing out the veracity of director Darryl F. Zanuck's film. Steinbeck, who had viewed the film a month earlier, wrote Elizabeth Otis: "Zanuck has more than kept his word. He has a hard, straight picture in which the actors are submerged so completely that it looks and feels like a documentary film and certainly it has a hard, truthful ring. No punches were pulled—in fact, with descriptive matter removed, it is a harsher thing than the book, by far. It seems unbelievable but it is true." In Steinbeck and Wallsten, eds., *Steinbeck: A Life in Letters* (p. 195). The movie was written by Nunnally Johnson and directed by John Ford; Tom Collins was hired as a technical assistant and advisor. Steinbeck was justly proud, for many critics consider it one of the best novel adaptations ever made by Hollywood. See Warren French, *Filmguide to* The Grapes of Wrath (1973), and Millichap, *Steinbeck and Film* (pp. 26–50).

ENTRY #112

Washington.　Steinbeck made two trips to speak with President Roosevelt in the summer of 1940, both in the interest of national security. At the first—Wednesday, June 26—he discussed establishing a "propaganda office" using radio and motion pictures to combat distorted views of America that were circulating abroad. At the second— Thursday, September 12—Steinbeck and his friend, Professor Melvyn Knisely (see Entry #118 below), suggested flooding Germany and its occupied countries with counterfeit German paper money. During the 1944 presidential campaign Steinbeck worked as a speech writer for Roosevelt.

Paragraph my dialogue.　Throughout the 1930s, in an effort to conserve paper, and to maintain a constant sense of intensity, Steinbeck eschewed traditional sentence and paragraph style, preferring instead to run together all of his exposition and dialogue into a compressed block form, using only the ¶ symbol to indicate breaks or shifts.

ENTRY #113

Sandburg.　Carl Sandburg (1878–1967), one of America's most popular writers, was a man of kindred social and democratic tendencies, exemplified by his recent poetry, *The People, Yes* (New York: Harcourt,

Brace, 1936), and his monumental biography of Lincoln, *Abraham Lincoln: The Prairie Years*, two volumes (New York: Harcourt, Brace, 1927), and the Pulitzer Prize-winning *Abraham Lincoln: the War Years*, four volumes (New York: Harcourt, Brace, 1939), both sets of which Steinbeck owned (the latter a Christmas gift from Carol). Steinbeck told his agents, "Carl Sandburg was here at the ranch last week and we had a very nice time and he got the pants beaten off him at horseshoes" (John Steinbeck to Elizabeth Otis and Mavis McIntosh, letter [August 9, 1940]; courtesy of Stanford University Library). During the visit Sandburg inscribed the first volume of the *War Years* set: "John Steinbeck, as between two soldier citizens and fellow strugglers—with affectionate good wishes." See DeMott, *Steinbeck's Reading* (pp. 97–98).

ENTRY #114

Military service. Congress passed The Burke-Wadsworth Selective Service Bill on September 14, 1940. Steinbeck was too old to be conscripted into active duty, and his "radical" past, which had become the subject of an extensive FBI file, repeatedly foiled his request for an Army officer's commission. ("Do you suppose you could ask Edgar's boys to stop stepping on my heels? They think I'm an enemy alien. It's getting tiresome," Steinbeck told United States Attorney General Francis Biddle, who in turn forwarded Steinbeck's note to FBI director J. Edgar Hoover on May 11, 1942.) Eventually Steinbeck worked under the auspices of the Office of War Information, and the Air Force, for which he wrote—and John Swope photographed—*Bombs Away: The Story of a Bomber Team* (New York: The Viking Press, 1942). In 1943 he was accredited as a war correspondent and spent June through October of that year writing dispatches from Europe and North Africa for the New York *Herald Tribune*, which were later collected as *Once There Was a War* (New York: The Viking Press, 1958). Jackson Benson, in *True Adventures of John Steinbeck* (pp. 485–541), is the first to establish the factual order and significance of Steinbeck's World War II activities. At J. Edgar Hoover's direction the FBI kept detailed files on American writers they considered subversive and dangerous. Steinbeck was no exception; the FBI monitored him from 1939, when *The Grapes of Wrath* first appeared, to March 1968, nine months before he died. The chilling story is evident in Jack Sirica, "FBI tracked Steinbeck's travels and friendships for nearly 30 years," *San Jose Mercury News*, June 14, 1984, pp. 1, 12A, and in Herbert Mitgang, *Dangerous Dossiers: Exposing the Secret War Against America's Greatest Authors* (New York: Donald I. Fine, 1988) pp. 71–79.

ENTRY #115

The Woods.   Charles Erskine Scott Wood (1852–1944) was Steinbeck's neighbor in Los Gatos. He was married to the poet and liberal activist Sara Bard Field (1883–1974). Wood had published numerous books, among them the satiric *Heavenly Discourse* (New York: Vanguard Press/The New Masses, 1927), and its sequel, *Earthly Discourse* (New York: Vanguard Press, 1937), both of which were in Ed Ricketts's Pacific Biological Laboratory library. (See DeMott, *Steinbeck's Reading*, p. 120). Probably as a result of this visit with the Woods, Steinbeck heard his eyewitness account of the U. S. Army's defeat of Chief Joseph and the Nez Perce´ Indians in 1877, recollected years later in *Travels with Charley* (New York: The Viking Press, 1962), pp. 143–44. Perhaps at this visit, too, Steinbeck inscribed a first edition of *The Grapes of Wrath* to "Sara and Cal Wood who are associated in their souls with this song." See Morrow, *John Steinbeck: A Collection of Books & Manuscripts Formed by Harry Valentine* (p. 30).

Decent letter.   Steinbeck's "decent" letter to Sheffield, written after this entry and full of exultant information about the Biddle "estate," including news of Carol's swimming pool, appears in Steinbeck and Wallsten, eds., *Steinbeck: A Life in Letters*, (pp. 207–209), but is misdated as July 9, 1940. See Riggs, ed., *A Catalogue of the John Steinbeck Collection* (p. 82).

Roll top Desk.   The psychological symbolism of this purchase is nakedly apparent. "I have bought myself a lovely old roll top desk with sixty pigeonholes. When I file something now, it will never be found." In Shasky and Riggs, eds., *Letters to Elizabeth* (p. 22).

ENTRY #118

Nosler.   Lloyd Nosler was Lorentz's assistant editor on *The Fight for Life*.

Idell and Paul.   The Budds, Carol Steinbeck's sister and brother-in-law, just returned from Japan.

Japanese situation.   Steinbeck was concerned about the growing "hysteria" toward the Japanese in California, and he feared a "witch hunt" conducted through "the formulated and calculated oppression of aliens by men of power, and . . . the generalized hatred of uninstructed people who must have sacrificial victims" (John Steinbeck/Edward G. Robinson, letter, November 7, 1940; courtesy of Steinbeck Research Center, San Jose State University). Following the attack on Pearl Harbor in December 1941, hysteria reigned: internment of the entire alien and nonalien Japanese population of the West Coast began the following April.

ENTRY #119

Now comes.   Plans for filming Steinbeck's short story, "Flight," for which Pare Lorentz had written a treatment, were abandoned (Pare Lorentz/Robert DeMott, telephone interview, March 22, 1988). In 1961, with Steinbeck's blessing, novelist Barnaby Conrad adapted and produced a film version. Steinbeck eventually drew on an introduction to the abandoned "San Francisco Bay Guidebook" for his Foreword to the second edition of Ricketts's and Calvin's *Between Pacific Tides* (Stanford: Stanford University Press, 1948), which reads in part: "This book then says: 'There are good things to see in the tidepools and there are exciting and interesting thoughts to be generated from the seeing. Every new eye applied to the peep hole which looks out at the world may fish in some new beauty and some new pattern, and the world of the human mind must be enriched by such fishing' " (p. vi).

Much magic.   Steinbeck had a pronounced mystical streak and was intrigued by fatalism, magic, superstitions, and totemic items. He returned from his film work in Mexico with presents for Gwyn, including a mummified bird of luck, like the one featured in *The Forgotten Village* (p. 15), and the "little bird in the black coffin," referred to later in Entry #119. Both items seem to have been favorite mystical charms of Steinbeck's: in Poem 6 of his love suite for Gwyn, he wrote, "And the bird of promise lies still in his casket"; and in Poem 9 he beseeched, "Pray for me a little on the bird / As I pray for you on the bird / On

the colored bird who is life and death / And all desire and all fulfillment"
(Halladay, ed., " 'The Closest Witness,' " pp. 43, 306, 309).

ENTRY #120

Quarrels with Herbert.   Herbert Kline's direction of the documentary film, *Lights Out in Europe*, about Hitler's invasion of Poland
in 1939, led to his collaboration with Steinbeck on *The Forgotten Village*. Their quarrels stemmed from Steinbeck's defensiveness—he didn't
want Kline, the director, or Alexander Hackensmid, the photographer,
to tell him how to do his script-writing job. Kline's reminiscence of the
making of *The Forgotten Village*, which won First Prize as the Best
Feature Documentary at the 1947 Brussels World Film Festival, is told
in "On John Steinbeck," *Steinbeck Quarterly*, 4 (Summer 1971), 80–
88. Valuable background on Steinbeck's first meeting with Kline is
recorded in Bosley Crowther's "Steinbeck & Kline, Inc.," New York
Times, April 7, 1940, Section 9, p. 5x.

Esther's house.   Steinbeck's older sister, Esther Steinbeck Rodg-
ers (1892–1986), and her husband, Carrol (d. 1962), lived in Wat-
sonville, but owned a small cabin near the beach in Pacific Grove.
Shortly afterward, during Carol's absence in Hawaii, Steinbeck bought
himself a small house at 425 Eardley Avenue, Pacific Grove. In April
it was the scene of the confrontation between Carol and Gwyn to decide
which woman would claim Steinbeck. Gwyn eventually won out. See
Benson, *True Adventures of John Steinbeck* (pp. 477–479).

ENTRY #121

Toby.   Webster F. Street (1899–1984), World War I veteran, Stanford classmate (an unpublished play by Street provided the basis for
Steinbeck's 1933 novel *To a God Unknown*), boon companion (Steinbeck
was best man at Street's wedding in 1925), and lifelong friend had
become a lawyer (LLB, Stanford, 1928) and moved from Palo Alto to
Monterey in 1935. A prolific writer and specialist in maritime law,
Street helped secure the *Western Flyer* charter, and later he handled
Carol's and John's divorce. His colorful, but self-deprecating, reminiscences are available in Richard Astro and Tetsumaro Hayashi, eds.,
Steinbeck: The Man and His Work (Corvallis: Oregon State University,
1971), pp. 35–41; and in an interview published in *San Jose Studies*,

I (November 1975), 109–27. Steinbeck immortalized "The Webster F. Street Lay-Away Plan—a martini made with chartreuse instead of vermouth," in Chapter 23 of *Sweet Thursday*, and the valorous fighting deeds of "Sir Tobinus Streat de Montroy" in *The Acts of King Arthur and His Noble Knights* (p. 61), the latter called to my attention by John Ditsky.